THE WAR TRAP

The War Trap

Bruce Bueno de Mesquita

New Haven and London, Yale University Press

Published with assistance from the foundation
established in memory of
Calvin Chapin of the Class of 1788, Yale College.

Designed by James J. Johnson and set in Monophoto Times
New Roman type. Printed in the United States of America by
The Alpine Press, Stoughton, Mass.

Library of Congress Cataloging in Publication Data

Bueno de Mesquita, Bruce, 1946–
  The war trap.

  Bibliography: p.
  Includes index.
  1. War — Mathematical models.   2. International
relations — Mathematical models.   I. Title.
U21.2.B83   327.1'17   80–24631
ISBN 0–300–02558–0
     0–300–03091–6 (pbk)

10   9   8   7   6   5   4   3

For my parents, Abraham and Clara Bueno de Mesquita, who have been ensnared by and have suffered from the war trap, and for my children, Erin, Ethan, and Gwen, with the hope that their only experience of war will come from their grandparents.

Contents

Preface

My purpose in writing this book is to present a general theory of war and foreign conflict initiation and escalation, including both the logic of the theory and a broadly based analytic test of the theory's most critical deductions. I have made a conscious and conscientious effort to limit the empirical portions of my study to the investigation of those propositions that are shown to follow as direct deductions from the theoretical framework I construct. Although many plausible propositions not derived from the theory fit the data, I have chosen not to report them. I have made this choice because I wish *The War Trap* to be judged in terms of the logical truthfulness and empirical usefulness of its expected-utility theory. For too long the divorce of explicit, rigorously derived theory from explicit, rigorously derived evidence has hampered the study of international conflict. Because of this separation, we do not know which empirically supported statements are spurious and which are true. Nor do we know how one set of seemingly logical statements about international conflict is linked to others. Both the theory of deterrence and the theory of the arms race seem, for instance, to be plausible explanations of certain types of conflict, and yet these two theories appear to be mutually contradictory. The two propositions that war follows periods of unequal power distributions and that war follows periods of power balance seem plausible to many analysts, with each finding supporters able to marshal evidence in behalf of their chosen view. Yet these two propositions also seem to conflict.

In the past, emphasis has been placed on the examination of

history—whether statistical or case by case—in an effort to reveal patterns of behavior that might be shaped into lawlike statements. Such efforts must be counted as having failed. Nearly twenty-five centuries after Thucydides wrote *The History of the Peloponnesian War*, we continue to debate whether a "balance of power" is good or bad, whether alliances are entangling or liberating, whether great powers behave differently from lesser powers, whether decision-making patterns vary markedly or are essentially the same in different centuries or in different cultures. The expected-utility theory suggested here purports to answer all of these questions while also providing insights into other old issues and some new ones. I have tried to find theoretical explanations—within the framework of a general theory—of commonly observed phenomena and simultaneously to explain cases of conflict that heretofore were considered anomalous. For instance, the expected-utility theory tries to explain why such allies as Prussia and Austria-Hungary in 1866, the Soviet Union and Czechoslovakia in 1968, or El Salvador and Honduras in 1969 could become embroiled in bloody conflicts with each other, and it does so in a manner fully consistent with its explanation of much more conventional wars.

Although much of my theory is developed using mathematical characters, even the least mathematically informed readers should not be discouraged. Little more than ninth-grade algebra is necessary to understand the mathematics, and in any event, I have tried to offer verbal explanations and historical examples for each important observation made from my expected-utility equations. The second half of the book examines extensive statistical tests of the theory. Again, I hope those not inclined toward statistical analysis will not be tempted to ignore the fourth and fifth chapters. Testing of most of the theory's propositions is so straightforward that little more than two-by-two tables is required, and these are generally discussed in the text, along with additional historical examples.

Chapters 1 and 2 present the philosophy-of-science perspective that guided this work and elaborate the theoretical assumptions I make in constructing a theory of necessary, but not sufficient, conditions for conflict. Chapter 3 develops the theory; chapter 4 develops the empirical measures and indicators used to test the theory. Chapter 5 includes all the empirical tests of the theory on historical conflict, while the final chapter sets forth potential applications of the theory to contemporary foreign policy problems.

This book is as much the work of my teachers, colleagues, and students as it is my own. My indebtedness is indeed deep and unrepayable. Nor can I possibly thank here all those who helped shape my thinking about international conflict or even those who helped shape this book. Many of my undergraduate and graduate students at the University of Rochester have served both as critics and as guinea pigs in the development of my ideas. Similarly, my colleagues in the political science department have tolerated innumerable outbursts of excitement or dismay as ideas emerged or collapsed in response to their probing comments and conversations. Still, there are some who have played so critical a role that I must single them out for special recognition and thanks.

Among my present and former graduate students. Michael Altfeld, Douglas Beck, Bruce Berkowitz, Chung Hsiou Huang, James Morrow, and David Newman were particularly helpful in forcing me to clarify and extend the development of the expected-utility theory. Bruce Berkowitz and Chung Hsiou Huang were involved almost from the start, and on a day-to-day basis, giving generously of their time, knowledge, and patience. Without their assistance, I truly could not have completed this project. I hope that they and my other students have derived as much value from the experience of working on this project as I have derived from their help.

A number of colleagues have read all or parts of the manuscript during its gestation period. Among those whose advice has benefited me, even if I did not always follow it, are Profs. Richard Cottam, Jacek Kugler, Alan Lamborn, Richard Niemi, Kenneth Organski, Bruce Russett, J. David Singer, and Dina Zinnes. Ambassador Herman Eilts and Profs. Richard Cottam, Charles Gochman, and J. David Singer generously assisted in providing me with most of the data I used.

During the several years that I actively worked on this book, a number of organizations were generous enough to provide me with the funds necessary to conduct my research and to develop the study free from the daily obligations of the classroom and of committees. I would particularly like to thank the John Simon Guggenheim Memorial Foundation for providing me with a Guggenheim fellowship. During that period I developed the theoretical portions of this study and many of the analytic tests as well. The Scaife Family Charitable Trusts provided me with additional funding that made possible the development of several concrete foreign policy applications of this work, as explained in Chapter 6. Finally, the dean's office of the College of Arts and Science and the Department of Political Science at the University of Rochester provided additional funding for computer programming, computer analysis, and for a leave of absence. I thank all of these agencies for their support and confidence in this project.

I have been the beneficiary of considerable wisdom and insight provided by others. Sometimes, however, I have been stubborn in my refusal to heed their advice. Consequently, I would not wish any of the people mentioned above, nor any others who offered me help, to be held accountable for errors of omission or commission that may be revealed in this work.

1 Introduction

Genesis records two thousand years of history from biblical creation to the time when the kings of Shinar, Ellasar, Elam, and Goiim fought the kings of Sodom, Gomorrah, Admah, Zeboiim, and Bela in the first war. Never again would two thousand years pass—or even two hundred—without war. Today, more than twenty-four centuries since Thucydides created the scientific study of war, international conflict remains the single greatest threat to man's survival since the ark rested upon the mountains of Ararat. Modern weapons place at the command of national leaders the God-like power to elect peace or war, life or death, for those whom they lead. For some, the choice between war and peace is a deadly election encompassing not only their own followers but all of humanity. Fortunately, it is an election that only rarely culminates in war, for although almost no time is without some war, most nations are at peace (or at least not at war) most of the time. Yet wars, like cancers, are ravaging, deadly events; they strike only a very few, but they capture the attention of all. Each of us is intimately linked to some war, even though very few among us can claim personal experiences in any international conflict. Still fewer can claim personal involvement in the decisions and diplomacy that produce wars. Perhaps it is because war is both rare and cataclysmic, remote from our everyday lives yet lurking in every tense exchange between our nation, our friends, and our enemies, that its causes have so fascinated and exasperated philosophers, historians, social scientists, journalists, and laymen.

There is no dearth of hypotheses concerning the causes of war.

No one, whether empirical or metaphysical in bent, whether seeking prescription or prediction, should fail to find propositions that appeal to his taste. But all who search for general explanations of those deadly war elections will be disappointed. Despite the attention of such intellectual giants as Spinoza, Rousseau, Kant, and Clausewitz, we know little more about international conflict today than was known to Thucydides four hundred years before Christ. Indeed, the failure to identify a generally accepted theory of war leads some observers to conclude that scientific explanations of such conflicts are not possible. Certainly the record to date provides no encouragement for those who reject that conclusion. Nevertheless, my objective is to present systematically derived, lawlike statements about war and other serious disputes and to explore the relationship between history and those statements.[1]

So many have studied the causes of war and have produced so little knowledge of those causes that yet another such undertaking seems arrogant. But perhaps by standing on the shoulders of those who have gone before, we may be able to see beyond the confusion and contradictions that characterize the study of conflict. Perhaps the belief that generalizations about the origins of war are possible is not at odds with the empirical record, even if we accept the proposition that there are no general causes of war. While some see the cause of war—and the hope for peace—in man's nature, others find the guarantor of peace in the balance of power or in the end of arms races or in the alleviation of those inequities that foster frustration and aggression or in the establishment of domestic tranquillity and security. The proponents of each of these views seem to make a plausible case for their beliefs. And yet the same men whose nature sometimes leaves them at peace are sometimes at war. As many times of peace (such as the Pax Romana or the period of the Concert of Europe) have been produced by an overwhelmingly preponderant power as by a balance of power. The eruption of global war is sometimes prevented by the deterrent effect of a balance of terror such as that created by the Soviet-American arms race. At other

1. For the sake of presentation I use the terms "war," "dispute," and "conflict" interchangeably throughout the text unless noted otherwise. In Chapter 4, when I operationalize the variables that emerge from my theory, I will distinguish empirically between international threats, interventions, and wars.

times wars follow arms competition. For every instance of war—or peace—that coincides with a causal explanation of war, one can find another example that contradicts the explanation. The very existence of such a vast array of seemingly plausible but mutually contradictory hypotheses about the causes of war, each with its own proponents and detractors, suggests that none of the hypotheses is compelling as a general explanation of the origins of war. If this is true, what reason is there to believe that lawlike statements about the origins of war are possible?

For some, the lesson learned from previous studies is that each war is a unique event with its own idiosyncratic causes and its own idiosyncratic consequences. This position—which utterly rejects the scientific study of war-in-general—is manifested in the many case studies focusing on the detailed analysis of events leading to a particular conflict. Though thought-provoking, these studies offer no hope of providing insights into future wars, for the events of past wars, the personalities of the relevant world leaders, the mood and climate of past international relations, will never again recur. Such studies provide no means of distinguishing between recurrent patterns and important but largely accidental happenings. Between the extremes represented by those looking for the cause of war and those looking for the causes of a particular war are the many positions of those who search for the cause or causes of some wars. Hobson's theory of imperialism and its subsequent Leninist interpretation; Morgenthau's, Gulick's, and others' interpretations of the balance of power; Organski's power transition; studies of bipolarity and multipolarity by Waltz, Deutsch and Singer, Rosecrance, and others; and Galtung's analysis of status inconsistency represent some of the efforts to provide general explanations of the causes of classes, or sets, of wars. This is one of the approaches to war that does offer hope of scientific explanations. To date, however, this approach has not provided many theoretically and empirically compelling results. Few such studies have identified stable empirical relationships that explain many wars. Those few that do seem to provide a useful explanation of some wars, such as Organski's theory of the power transition, do not afford much hope that they can be expanded to include more than a handful of very rare—though deadly—events. Such studies generally examine plausible but ad hoc hypotheses that lend shape to the pieces of the war puzzle but do not join together enough pieces to provide clear guidance for future analysis.

An additional possibility lies between the positions of those looking for the cause of war generally and those searching for the cause of a single war. One may accept the proposition that each war has its own unique causes without accepting the implication that scientific generalizations about the origins of war are not possible. Political assassinations, phony telegrams, military mobilizations, and the like may sometimes trigger wars (and sometimes not), but I will argue that they can do so only in certain contexts. We remember the sinking of the *Maine* on the eve of the Spanish-American War and Bismarck's Ems Telegram and the subsequent Franco-Prussian War, but we have largely forgotten the *Liberty* and the *Pueblo* and the article "Is War in Sight?" that created such a stir in France after it appeared in the Berlin *Post* in 1875. These latter events, unlike the sinking of the *Maine* or the assassination of Archduke Franz Ferdinand in Sarajevo, were not the immediate, or even the remote, causes of any wars.

Wars do not occur so suddenly that they take their initiator completely by surprise, finding the aggressor unprepared or unwilling to fight. The instant of initiation, the specific event triggering the eruption of violence, may be a surprise or even an accident, but it occurs in a context of prior planning and preparation that can leave no doubt that the inauguration of a conflict serious enough to become a war has been carefully calculated. One might not intend to start a war with a particular action, but it is difficult to imagine that the risks inherent in such an action are not considered before it is committed. The pondering of such risks takes place within a framework of circumstances that renders the level of risk sometimes unacceptable and sometimes acceptable. *The framework of circumstances comprises a set of necessary conditions that must be satisfied before a war is initiated.* After the necessary conditions are met, other largely idiosyncratic—or even chance—factors must also fall into place. Put somewhat differently, the set of conditions sufficient for war may be so large that its specification is virtually impossible, but the set of necessary conditions may be small enough to be specified and encompassing enough to prove useful in discriminating between candidates for war and candidates for peace. This proposition is consistent with both the weak empirical support for any causal explanations of war and the correlations found between a host of variables and the onset of war. It is a proposition as consistent with the assertion that no causal explanation of war-in-general is possible as with the assertion that scientific generalizations about war are possible.

The decision to search for necessary, though not sufficient, conditions is not based solely on grounds of convenience, nor does it arise only from consideration of the modest results of those who have pursued causal explanations of war. Most efforts to find the cause or causes of war focus on environmental circumstances that compel policymakers to wage war, but if we attempt to show causal relationships between environments and war, we are forced to ignore the role of national leaders and to act as though nations were no more than automatically reacting mechanisms.

Balance-of-power theorists, for instance, propose that nations must align with one another to wage war against any expansionist state that threatens to upset the balance of power and to become preponderant. Some arms race theorists suggest that the "arms race spiral" must inevitably compel one or another decision maker to initiate a war as the last means of escaping the spiral. Yet the fact that the conditions alleged to compel decision makers to start serious disputes occur far more frequently than do such conflicts suggests that different policymakers react differently to these "compulsions." Indeed, we might reach the encouraging conclusion that decision makers are ultimately responsible for their actions. They are not the victims of outside forces inescapably driving them to war. The selection of war or peace is a choice that is initiated, conducted, and concluded by individual leaders who must accept responsibility for their decisions. They must be as ready to accept vilification and deprecation as they are to seek the glorification and exaltation of their deeds. The choice of war or peace depends on the choices of individuals and not on compulsion by circumstance. Their choices depend on their estimation of costs and benefits and their comprehension of right and wrong. Scientific analysis cannot evade this ultimate accountability and responsibility of the decision maker, though it may identify the conditions under which policymakers are confronted with the need to make such choices. We cannot provide a general framework of moral values that reveals what decision makers believe to be right or wrong, but we may be able to capture some essential characteristics of their assessment of the expected costs and benefits associated with particular war-or-peace situations. It is in those calculations that necessary conditions for war are to be found. Consequently, whenever any of the necessary conditions are not satisfied, a calculation of conditions sufficient for peace is identified.

TOWARD A THEORY OF WAR

Every great conflict from the Peloponnesian War to the Second World War has stimulated studies of war. Unfortunately, the experience of war, and not the contemplation of peace, has provoked almost all of the literature on the subject, most studies having been brought into focus by empirical considerations rather than by theoretical reasoning. Reasoning—the attempt to reach a priori generalizations—is too often secondary to empiricism, so that the task of separating spurious generalizations from true ones is made more difficult. How many times have policymakers been beguiled by empirical generalizations based on their own (or their predecessors') experiences? It has become commonplace to note that the cures for the alleged causes of the latest war tend to become the causes of the next war. Chamberlain's "appeasement" of Hitler is sometimes explained as his way of compensating for the apparent lack of patience by world leaders on the eve of World War I, just as Hitler's impatience reflected his fear of repeating "the mistake of waiting, of hoping for a miracle that would enable us to get by without fighting it out" (Speer 1971, p. 667). The absence of rigid alliance networks in the 1930s—one of the factors that encouraged Hitler to believe Britain would not wage war to protect Poland— indicated a reaction by European leaders to their unhappy experience with rigid alliances in 1914. The rigid alliances of the Cold War, in turn, were a reaction to the experience with weak alliances in 1939. And so the cycle of experiences and counterexperiences continues, inadequately informed by carefully constructed, reasoned arguments or by more than the most recent experiences with war. We would do well to remember Kant's conclusions about experience and reasoning, that "no conditions of judgments of experience are higher than those . . . pure concepts of the understanding, which render the empirical judgment objectively valid. . ." (1950, p. 53). One has only to study the history of war to find vivid examples of the catastrophes that may result when empiricism alone is substituted for reason.

Research on war since the end of World War II has tended to be somewhat atheoretical and largely empirical, typically attempting to evaluate some loosely drawn hypotheses by using sophisticated, powerful analytic tools. The principal controversy among students of war, at least since the 1950s, has concerned the merits of quantification and nonquantification rather than the merits of the hypotheses under examination. The debate centers largely on whether quantification or nonquantification provides greater precision, validity, reproduceability, and generalizability. These are, however, relatively minor issues that are distracting us from fundamental theoretical questions. It is ironic that so much attention is being given to a methodological debate, when so little effort has been spent on the rigorous construction of testable propositions in the first place. Since most studies explore hypotheses that are informed (but not rigorously derived) hunches rather than carefully constructed propositions, it is not clear what one's statistical or nonstatistical criteria are or ought to be. Let me give one rather simplistic and untested hypothesis as an example that highlights the difficulty inherent in constructing tests of loosely drawn propositions.

Suppose we wanted to test A. J. P. Taylor's proposition "If every state followed its own interest, all would be peaceful and secure" (Taylor 1971, p. xx). Now, let us assume that we know what is meant by such terms as "the state's interest"—a concept that I will later show to be almost meaningless—or "peaceful and secure." If 5 cases of states following their own interest were found, 3 of which were peaceful and secure and only 2 at war, would we conclude that there is some truth to Taylor's proposition? What if 10 nations followed their own interest, 8 of them at peace and 2 at war? What about 100 nations, only 2 of them at war—or 1,000, of which only 2 were at war? The standard statistical test would be to see if 3:2, 8:2, 98:2, or

998:2 deviates significantly from the null hypothesis that the pursuit of a state's interest is unrelated to its being peaceful and secure. That is, is the association significantly different from no association? What if it is? Should we conclude that Taylor's hypothesis is supported by the evidence? Perhaps not. After all, Taylor says *all* will be peaceful and secure. Perhaps the test should be to see if 3:2, 8:2, 98:2, or 998:2 is not significantly different from a perfect association in which the ratio of states pursuing their own interest and being peaceful and secure to states doing likewise but being at war is N:0. Of course, even if the first proposed test yielded a significant result, the second might not. (A supportive result in the second test, however, implies a supportive result in the first test as well). Although the second is considerably more stringent than the first, one might still object that it is too weak. After all, Taylor said all—not almost all, but *all*—would be peaceful and secure. If Taylor's condition that all states are pursuing their own interest is met, one might argue that a single case of war is sufficient to falsify his proposition. The point is that without specifying precisely what is meant by "all" (a ratio significantly different from N:N, a ratio not significantly different from N:0, or a ratio precisely equal to N:0?), we cannot readily explore the meaningfulness of the proposition.

Statistical or nonstatistical empirical explorations can only be given the status of tests when the question to be tested has been rigorously derived and properly specified. Yet hypotheses are frequently proclaimed supported or falsified on empirical grounds, even though the precise expectations to be derived from the hypothesis are unknown. And so we may raise an important epistemological question: what constitutes falsification or verification of a hypothesis? Since the remaining chapters of this volume explore both theoretical and empirical questions about international conflict, it is essential that I answer this question.

STANDARDS OF FALSIFICATION AND VERIFICATION

What might be a reasonable set of standards for determining falsification? The question is almost rhetorical. A wide variety of criteria, however, are currently in use by students of international conflict. One element contributing to this variety is the confusion surrounding the concepts of falsification and verification. In a recent article, Waltz wrote: "Theories, though not divorced from the world of experiment and observation, are only indirectly connected with it. Thus the well-known statement that theories can never be proven true" (1975, p. 4). Yet theories must be either logically true or logically false. Theories are no more nor less than a priori reasoning about the relations among variables. The truthfulness of such reasoning depends upon whether it shows logical flaws in arriving at its deductions. If a deduction follows logically from a set of assumptions, then that deduction is necessarily true for all circumstances that comply precisely with the assumptions of the theory. Hence the truthfulness of a deduced relationship among variables in a world that complies with the theory's assumptions is a logical, and not an empirical, question. Consequently empirical relationships have little relevance for the truthfulness or falseness of a theory per se.

To be sure, the discovery of an empirical case that is inconsistent with one's logically derived expectations is reason for reflection. Such a case may be inconsistent for one of two reasons. Either a logical flaw exists, or else the case does not conform precisely with the theory's assumptions. If the logic is flawed, the theory is false and can be rendered true only by eliminating the logical flaw. This may represent a minor change in the theory or a major change leading to radically different empirical expectations. If the cause of the inconsistency is an assumption that excludes the particular empirical case from the purview of the theory, then one must determine whether a theory that excludes such a case is useful. That is, are the assumptions so far-fetched that the events the theory addresses seldom actually occur in the real world? Evaluating a theory's usefulness is a difficult task. Reality rarely complies precisely with theoretical assumptions. Just as Galileo's inclined plane was not free of friction and Newton's apple did not fall without wind resistance, so too wars do not occur under the precise conditions assumed by the theorist. Ultimately the most crucial role of empiricism is to reveal which truthful, logical deductions are useful explanations of reality and which are merely trivial exercises in logic. The issue is not one of inductive versus deductive logic. Because a theory's usefulness can only be judged empirically, while an empirical generalization's truthfulness can only be judged logically, neither inductive nor deductive reasoning by itself is adequate. Inductively derived generalizations that cannot be derived logically must be spurious, just as deductively derived generalizations that do not explain events of interest to the researcher must be trivial. It is immaterial whether one's research strategy is initially deductive or inductive, but it does matter that one eventually provides the deductive, logical framework for any empirical generalizations and the empirical referents for any deduced relationships.

The purpose of theory, of course, is not to replicate reality but rather to provide a coherent, organized understanding of real events. Axioms and assumptions provide a basis for simplifying and organizing reality by delineating the precise conditions about which one is theorizing. Such axioms and assumptions are intended to help the researcher sort out critical phenomena from incidental phenomena, providing a basis for simplifying reality without distorting its essential characteristics. Since assumptions function in this way it is as inappropriate to speak of their truth or falsity as it is to speak of a theory's empirical truthfulness. Assumptions, like the theories derived from them, are either trivial or useful. Assumptions simply delineate the constrained conditions under which subsequent deductions—if logically consistent—are necessarily true. The theorist's task is to make assumptions so "realistic" that subsequent deductions are not, in Sir Isaac Newton's words, "dreams and vain fictions of our own devising."

The empiricist's task is to construct tests that approximate as closely as possible the requirements of a theory, without excluding so many events of interest that the tests or the theory seem trivial. The extent to which the constraining theoretical assumptions are helpful to the empiricist largely depends on the theorist's knowledge and understanding of the reality he is trying to explain. When assumptions are made without sensitivity and knowledge about "real" experiences, the result is likely to be a trivial theory about an unreal world. But if we inductively select assumptions upon which to base our deductions, then we have good prospects for discovering useful explanations for real-world phenomena.

SOME PROBLEMS WITH
COMMON ASSUMPTIONS ABOUT WAR

The single greatest hurdle standing in the way of our understanding of the origins of war is overly restrictive assumptions, whether they are used explicitly or implicitly. Although most research on war is largely inductive, with a strong tendency toward theories built around history, researchers typically accept two erroneous assumptions far too casually. The first is the assumption that a group of people — whether a constituency, a nation, or even the entire international system — is itself a purposive, indivisible actor endowed with goals, motives, and strategies. The group's policies are assumed to be connected to some generally held view of "the group's interest" or "the will of the people." A statement such as "Neither the United States of America nor the world community of nations can tolerate deliberate deception and offensive threats on the part of any nation, large or small" (Kennedy 1969, p. 154) makes fine use of metaphor, but we must be careful to acknowledge that nations do not possess tolerance; nor do they deceive or threaten. People do these things. Sometimes, when they are leaders, they do them in the name of their nation, but still, only individuals can be threatening, tolerating, or deceiving. Once we speak of aggregations of individuals (for example, of "the community of nations") behaving with one voice and one purpose, we violate common sense as well as history and the logic underlying much of social choice theory, to which we will turn our attention momentarily.

The second problematic assumption, closely related to the first, concerns risk-taking behavior. Explicit discussions of risk taking are almost nonexistent in research on war (except in studies of deterrence), but most theorists implicitly assume that all decision makers share the same propensity to take risks. Some seem to suppose that all are fearful of risks, while others assume that all decision makers have a gambler's streak that makes them exceptionally willing to accept risks. Yet common sense and our everyday experiences teach us that some individuals plunge optimistically into risky situations, whereas others approach risky situations with considerable pessimism and foreboding. There are those who like the Irish sweepstakes and those who like savings accounts; there are those who in playing draw poker pursue an inside straight with two cards needed, and there are those who fold with such a hand; there are those who readily capitulate and those who fight as long as there is a slim chance of success. Treating individuals with such diverse attitudes toward risk as if they follow the same rules of decision making so misrepresents reality that logically and historically incorrect generalizations are bound to result.

ARROW'S PARADOX AND THE PURPOSIVENESS OF GROUPS

When Louis XIV proclaimed "L'état c'est moi," he was probably right. So long as we are prepared to think of the "national interest" as being embodied in the welfare of a single individual, we may describe national policies as being responsive to the national interest. If the royal "we" means anything, it means that the good of the state and the good of the ruler—as dictator—are the same. Linking national policies to a purposive national interest is logically meaningful under two other circumstances. When a national policy, program, strategy, or objective derives from unanimous consent, then the interests and purpose of any individual regarding that policy are the same as for all others. Since individual and collective interests are identical in this case, no conceptual problem arises in describing a policy as the national interest. In addition, if we assume that certain orderings of policy preference are socially untenable, it is possible to construct situations in which a genuine consensus emerges from a limited diversity of individual priorities. If such a limitation cannot be assumed, and therefore choices among options are controversial, and if policy depends on more than one "will" or "interest" (as is the case in committees and other pluralist decision-making systems), we cannot speak of a social collectivity—whether it is a handful of individuals or the entire international system—as having a single purpose, goal, or interest. We may identify national policies, but there is no reason to expect those policies to be related to "the will of the people" or to "the public good" when they result from collectively made decisions. Decision-making rules, from unanimity to dictatorship, may permit the advice of any number of people to influence public policy, but once consent is required from more than one and fewer than all, the danger is great that decisions on controversial questions will be unrepresentative of *anyone's* interest. Once decision making is bureaucratized, the quest for acceptable compromises increases the likelihood that there will be little or no congruence between national policies and the individual intentions or purposes in that society, offering even less reason to believe that there is anything resembling the national interest.

When groups make a collective decision, whose interests are most likely to be reflected in the final outcome? The pluralist response is that such decisions, if made democratically, represent the general — perhaps majoritarian — view. But is this true? Might such collectively made decisions represent the desires of a minority, a single individual, or no one at all? One conclusion to be drawn from the work of Kenneth Arrow, a Nobel Prize-winning economist, is that social choices may indeed represent the interests of no one or of anyone. To illustrate, I will present a simple example.

Anyone who has studied the Cuban missile crisis can appreciate the statement that the leaders charged with the responsibility for formulating a response to the Soviet missile buildup were deeply divided. The policy ultimately followed by the United States government emerged after intense debate. Three prominent policy options were a naval blockade, an invasion of Cuba, and surgical air strikes against the missile sites. Let us suppose that the executive committee assigned to consider American options, rather than the president, was collectively responsible for formulating a national policy on this issue. To simplify matters, let us also assume that three factions, each with roughly equal influence, attached different priorities to the three courses of action. I will denote the surgical air strike by the letter s, an invasion by i, and a naval blockade by b. Preference is denoted by the letter P, so that sPb means a surgical air strike is preferred to a naval blockade, whereas bPs means the blockade is preferred to the air strike. In our hypothetical example, the preferences of the three groups are: (a) $sPiPb$, (b) $iPbPs$, and (c) $bPsPi$. The first group prefers the air strike to an invasion or a blockade, the invasion to the blockade, and so forth.

What is the collective decision—the policy of the United States of America—to be? The answer depends in this case on the skills with which the leaders of each group manipulate the agenda and not on any usual notion of the policy closest to the national interest. Indeed, the division among the three groups indicates that there are at least three legitimate opinions about the national interest. To illustrate, let us consider three different agendas.

If the committee members choose between the air strike and the invasion, they will find general agreement that the air strike is more desirable, with only the members of the second group favoring an invasion over an air strike. Having rejected the invasion, they might then consider the merits of an air strike as compared with a naval blockade. In this case, the consensus favors the blockade, with only the members of group 1 still preferring a surgical air strike. It seems reasonable, then, to suppose that the blockade should be the national policy. Yet most of the members of the committee think that an invasion is a better response to the crisis than is a naval blockade, with only those in group 3 favoring a blockade over an invasion.

If the agenda had considered the air strike and the blockade first, the national policy would ultimately have provided for invasion of Cuba; if the invasion and blockade had been considered first, the consensus policy would have appeared to be an air strike. One might hope to resolve this dilemma by considering all three options simultaneously, but then the committee would be hopelessly deadlocked, with no policy emerging at all. Thus by simply altering the sequence in which options are considered, any option could end as the apparent "consensus" position, provided there is sufficient division among the members of the collective decision-making body.

Even if the committee unanimously prefers one option (rather than one platform, or complete ordering of the options) to another, the decision-making process may produce this "second choice" as the apparent consensus. During the Cuban missile crisis, some leaders—most notably Adlai Stevenson—believed that no response beyond diplomatic contacts was required. Let us suppose (remembering that this is a purely hypothetical illustrative example and not an accurate portrayal of decision making during the missile crisis) that the three groups held the following preferences, with d

denoting a diplomatic response only: (a) $sPiPdPb$, (b) $iPdPbPs$, (c) $dPbPsPi$. If the invasion and diplomatic options are considered first, the invasion is found to have more support. As we already know from the earlier example, the air strike enjoys more support than the invasion, and the blockade is generally preferred to an air strike. Hence the blockade could emerge as the national policy, even though in this example *everyone* would rather pursue a diplomatic response than a naval blockade. Surely this suggests that the apparent consensus is more imagined than real. Yet no other choice is any closer to representing a generally held view. After all, the diplomatic response, though unanimously preferred to the blockade, is considered less desirable by a majority than is an invasion, while an invasion generally is held to be less desirable than a surgical air strike. Simply by varying the agenda, any of the four options could readily and fairly be chosen as the consensus position. Indeed, given the pressures of the missile crisis, one can easily imagine a highly skilled advocate of any of the major alternatives carrying the day simply because he could outmaneuver his colleagues.

The above examples are only hypothetical, but they do show that when controversial decisions must be made collectively — as in bureaucratic models of decision making — they are more likely to reflect the manipulative skills of particular leaders than they are any collective, representative sense of the "general will." Numerous historically accurate examples of Arrow's paradox might be cited, but the point is clear. If one assumes that social groupings (such as nations) pursue policies that reflect some collective *purpose*, one cannot assume that decision making is bureaucratic unless one is willing to assert that certain logically possible orderings of options are socially unacceptable. Alternatively, if one is inclined to treat the social grouping's policies as purposive, one may either assume that decision making is controlled by a dominant leader, so that one individual's interest is the same as the national interest, or that it is unanimous, so that any individual's interest is the same as the national interest. If the study of nations as unitary actors in international politics is meaningful, we must be able to justify the particular assumption we make to provide a basis for avoiding the possibility of Arrow's paradox and to legitimize the treatment of the nation as a purposive actor. The criterion for judging our assumption is, in this case, the degree to which the assumption is realistic and robust enough to yield empirically useful generalizations in the context of nations engaged in serious international disputes, including war.

Approaching foreign policy decision making from the bureaucratic perspective is both theoretically and empirically informative, especially when one is studying decisions that do not involve such cataclysmic events as war (Allison and Halperin 1972). But when one does study decisions about war, the bureaucratic decision-making approach seems to be somewhat less helpful. Allison and Halperin — the two principal advocates of the bureaucratic approach — concede, for instance, that "shared attitudes and images" rather than individual differences "provide common answers to such questions as: who are the actual or potential enemies . . . ? What are their intentions and capabilities? Who are our friends? What are their capabilities and intentions? What influences the behavior of other nations?" (1972, p. 56). These are precisely the questions I hope to answer in examining decisions about war and peace. Apparently the internal bargaining and maneuvering that typically precedes most foreign policy decisions is not common to decisions regarding these questions. Of course, we may expect that such bureaucratic processes resume once the major choice, for war or for peace, is made, with different views on the best way to conduct a war, or to negotiate peace, coming to the fore. For those situations in which the bureaucratic model does not seem most suitable, we must be careful to be explicit as to which assumption is providing the basis for treating the nation as a purposive, goal-seeking, unitary actor. As I have noted, three quite different assumptions each provide a theoretically meaningful way of examining national policy as if it represented some goal-seeking, purposive "national interest."[2] Most of the literature on conflict does indeed presuppose

2. Actually a number of conditions besides restriction of preferences make it possible for groups to hold socially transitive preference orderings. Each such condition avoids Arrow's paradox by assuming that one of Arrow's conditions does not hold. Although it is reasonable to believe that many of Arrow's assumptions are violated at any given time in reality, the problem with each such solution is that there is rarely any way to know in advance which conditions will be violated. Hence it is risky to suppose that such assumptions solve Arrow's paradox, especially under such stressful conditions as exist when foreign policy is being made in the face of international conflict.

that national policies reflect the national interest, but this literature rarely makes explicit whether unanimity, decision making by a strong leader, or restrictions on preference orderings are being assumed. Which assumption is adopted has important implications, since each may lead to a different view of policymaking during conflict. When researchers fail to specify the sense in which they mean that national policies are purposive, they make it extremely difficult for anyone to evaluate the logic underlying the derivation of any hypotheses or the appropriateness of any empirical evaluations of those hypotheses.

In the case of some interest groups, unanimity is a reasonable expectation, but unanimity seems unlikely for important national or international policies. As James Madison so persuasively argued in the tenth Federalist paper, "as long as the reason of man continues fallible, and he is at liberty to exercise it, different opinions will be formed," and these differences of opinion will be formed into factions, so that "the public good is disregarded in the conflicts of rival parties." Whether there is unanimity or not, I assume, for reasons explained more fully in the next chapter, that decision making concerning foreign conflict proceeds as if there were a single, dominant decision maker. For now, let me simply note that the other possibilities are theoretically and empirically less likely to aid the search for patterns of conflict-related behavior.

When one focuses on individual decisions rather than on consensus decision making, the danger of falling victim to Arrow's paradox is avoided. That is not to say that international relations must be or should be studied from the perspective of individuals. Although nations, alliances, and systems are not themselves purposive actors, they are entities endowed with attributes that may constrain the possible courses of action open to the individuals responsible for guiding their policy. By understanding how such attributes as the level of industrialization, urbanization, and mobilization of national resources (or the degree of commitment among allies or antipathy between foes) affect the feasibility of various possibilities, we may learn a great deal about the options that particular decision makers in particular places at particular times can or cannot choose. If one ignores these constraints, proceeding directly to an examination of decision makers, the road toward a scientific understanding of the origins of war is bound to be long, strewn with intellectual traps, and hopelessly covered by insurmountable obstacles. By carefully combining theorizing about individuals with theoretical sensitivity to the conditions under which choices are made, we may, I believe, find the most efficient path toward meaningful generalizations about international conflict.

I have delineated a set of standards regarding the construction and evaluation of a theory of international conflict. Among the issues I view as critical are (a) the development of a logical foundation from which propositions about war and peace emerge; (b) establishing that such propositions rely on realistic and parsimonious assumptions about the phenomena being explained; and (c) the specification of the criteria to be used in evaluating evidence about the theory.

In the second chapter, I attempt to satisfy the requirement that all my assumptions be explicit and reasonably realistic, while in the third chapter I attempt to develop the logical foundation for several counterintuitive (as well as intuitive) propositions about international conflict. Chapter 4 provides a full explanation of the procedures used to transform theoretical statements into operational and testable hypotheses about war. Chapter 4 also delineates precise criteria for evaluating the evidence I use to test the theory's empirical usefulness. Chapter 5 parallels chapter 3, this time using empiricism, rather than logic, to evaluate the propositions about war that are derived from my theory. Finally, chapter 6 attempts to evaluate the extent to which the theory I identify and test might serve as a vehicle for engineering conflict toward peace and away from war. In that chapter I will try to show the theory's potential value as an early warning indicator of impending conflict or as a tool for assessing potentially unanticipated consequences of alternative foreign policies.

2 Planning the War Trap: Assumptions of the Theory

War seems to many to be an irrational act of passion. Indeed, only love is a more prevalent theme in poetry and fiction. Poets portray war as heroic or tragic, wise or foolish, righteous or evil, but hardly ever as detached, planned, and calculated. As we look back to antiquity, with days, years, decades, and centuries melding together, leaving us with an amorphous sense of ages, who are the actors starring in our account of history? Certainly some, such as Jesus and Buddha, are remembered for their resistance to violence, but there are so many more remembered for their perfection of violence. Alexander the Great, Genghis Khan, Napoleon—these are men known to every schoolchild for military leadership and cunning, even if their time and place is only faintly suspected. The images we hold of these conquerors are of men in battle, swords raised, horses braying, and armor clashing in a struggle of the noble against the ignoble. We rarely think of the planning and calculating that precedes the battle. Yet for all the emotion of the battlefield, the premeditation of war is a rational process consisting of careful, deliberate calculations. Before war can be waged, armies must be raised and trained, weapons developed and built, civilians mobilized and motivated. Not even the most charismatic leader or fanatical people can hope to use force successfully without preparing and mobilizing the resources necessary for war. One clear indication of the rational planning that precedes war is that only about 10 percent of the wars fought since the defeat of Napoleon at Waterloo have been quickly and decisively lost by the nation that attacked first.[1]

1. By "quickly" I mean within six months of the onset of the war. By "decisively" I mean that the initiator suffered more battle fatalities than did its opponent.

Indeed, nearly three-quarters of all wars fought during that period were won by the side that initiated combat.

Since the planning and preparation of national resources during times of peace is so crucial to the successful waging of war, we should be able to gain insights into the possibility of initiating, conducting, concluding, or averting war in the immediate future by examining current expectations about the availability of the necessary resources. To understand how such insights might be gained, I must clarify my assumptions. The most central assumptions, which are explained in detail below, are: (a) war decision making is dominated by a single, strong leader; (b) leaders are rational expected-utility maximizers; (c) differences in leaders' orientations toward risk taking influence decision making; (d) uncertainty about the likely behavior of other states in the event of war affects decision making; and (e) the power a state can use in a war declines as the site of the war becomes geographically distant from the nation.

ASSUMPTIONS OF THE THEORY

As noted earlier, I am assuming that decision making regarding war is dominated by a single leader who, acting as a gatekeeper, may veto policies intended to start a war. Of course, many individuals play important formal or informal roles in shaping war-and-peace decisions, probably so much so that no decision is precisely determined by one individual. One cannot disregard the importance of advisers, cabinet ministers, constitutional provisions regarding declarations of war, legislative actions, or public opinion. All these (and other) sources of information help encourage or discourage the key leader from pursuing one or another course of action. The positions, the arguments and, most important, the potential others have to withhold or contribute resources may dissuade the leader from taking his preferred course of action, but it is still his decision and not theirs. Thus I assume that ultimate responsibility rests in the hands of a single policymaker charged with the final duty of approving a decision to wage war. All such leaders are dictators in the sense that all war-or-peace decisions must be approved by them. This should be construed to mean, not that these actors may start wars whenever they want to, but rather that they may stop policies leading to war if they want to. In that sense, the approval of the key leader is necessary for war, while his disapproval is sufficient to prevent his nation from starting a war.

At least two objections may be raised to this assumption. First, one may question just how important or necessary it is. Second, one may question how "realistic" it is to view all war-and-peace decisions as being controlled by a single policymaker. The first issue was introduced in the previous chapter but needs to be explained more thoroughly before we turn to the second objection.

If we view war as an unintentional, unpremeditated act, then we could readily assume that war results from any decision-making system, including dictatorship, bureaucratic decision making, majoritarianism, or unanimity. Any of these systems can produce decisions that have unanticipated and unintended consequences. However, if we choose to view the initiation of war as intentional, it makes most sense to assume that decisions allowing nations to go to war are controlled by a key leader. Still, before seeing why this is so, we should examine the preliminary evidence that leads me to believe that wars are, with rare exceptions, intentional actions.

If war is unintentional, we should not expect a systematic relationship between those who start wars and those who win wars. After all, if nations stumble into wars rather than plan them, there is no reason to expect the initiator to have a military advantage. Yet the initiators of most interstate wars during the past 160 years do appear to have enjoyed an advantage.[2] One way of evaluating that advantage is to see if the number of victories by attacking nations is significantly different from the number of wars attackers would be expected to win by chance.

If starting a war without prior planning offers no advantages, we should expect attackers and defenders to win an equal share of wars. Indeed, if we accept the common military wisdom that defense requires less strength than offense, we should expect attackers who did not plan on war to have a decided disadvantage. Fifty-eight

2. The set of wars under investigation is primarily drawn from the list of interstate wars provided by Singer and Small (1972), as are the operational definitions of interstate war and war initiation. I have updated this list (and slightly modified it) through 1974. The precise operational coding rules are discussed at length in Singer and Small (1972) and are reviewed in Chapter 4.

interstate wars have been fought since the Congress of Vienna,[3] and we would expect attacking nations to have won about twenty-nine of those wars at best. In actuality, however, the nations initiating combat won forty-two times. The laws of probability tell us that this difference is significant, since fewer than one time in about two and a half thousand samples of war would this many victories occur by chance.[4] Of course, the fifty-eight wars are not a random sample, so that this is only a heuristic exercise, but the results do suggest that a pattern exists. Either initiators of wars have had a systematic advantage, or they have been extraordinarily lucky. Since it appears more plausible that they had an advantage and made use of it, I am prepared to conclude that the initiation of war is not accidental or unintentional.

We can reasonably believe, then, that wars are purposive rather than unintentional. The consequence of this conclusion is that decisions to wage war can only be based on unanimity or on restrictions on the number and type of socially acceptable preference orderings or on the control of a dominant leader. Other decision-making systems might, from time to time, produce outcomes that are systematically related to the desires of the decision makers, but the likelihood that a group of policymakers would agree on the advantages of starting a war diminishes rapidly as the number of decision makers or choices increases. As the first Cuban missile crisis example in the preceding chapter showed, even with as few as three decision makers and three choices it is possible to produce policies that are responsive more to one manipulator's interests than to the collective interest. In fact, as the second Cuban missile crisis example suggested, it is possible for collectively reached decisions to reflect no one's interest.

Even a cursory reading of history encourages the rejection of unanimity as an alternative to the strong-leader assumption. Although there is much more movement toward consensus during a

3. The set of wars included in the analyses, as well as the other conflicts included in this study, is listed in the appendix.

4. The probability is computed using the equation: $Z = (X - Np) \div (Npq)^{\frac{1}{2}}$, with X being the number of victories by initiators (42), N the total number of wars (58), and p and q being the a priori probabilities that an initiator will win or lose an unintentional war ($p = q = .5$). Thus $Z = [42 - (58)(.5)]/3.81 = 3.41$ and $p < .0025$.

crisis than under normal conditions, unanimity is rarely achieved. Even the bombing of Pearl Harbor failed, for instance, to produce a unanimous declaration of war, as one member of Congress cast a dissenting vote. One can appreciate how much more difficult it must be to build a consensus, let alone unanimous agreement, for a policy of aggression rather than one of self-defense.

Even if I were not skeptical of the notion that unanimity is achieved on critical foreign policy choices, I would reject the unanimity assumption. Suppose unanimity were achieved. In such a case, knowing the preference of any single individual would be *precisely* the same as knowing everyone's preferences, and there would be no difference from the case in which the decision is made by a single strong leader. Now, suppose almost everyone agreed on the most desired solution to a particular issue, with only a small group of senior foreign policy decision makers, or the single strong leader, holding a different position. In this case, no single decision could be predicted without assuming that certain preference orderings are inadmissible or that there is a fixed, known weight given to the preferences of each leader in the decision-making process. Below I show that these assumptions are not helpful. However, the point here is this: when the unanimity assumption is valid, it adds no more information than the assumption of the single strong leader, and yet the unanimity assumption is more heroic. When the unanimity assumption is unwarranted, it is not robust enough to avoid Arrow's paradox without the assistance of other assumptions. In either case, the unanimity assumption does not increase our understanding of the foreign policy decision-making process beyond the insights possible with more realistic and helpful assumptions. We must choose, then, assuming either a strong leader or restrictions on admissible preference orderings.

RESTRICTIONS ON PREFERENCE ORDERINGS

The likelihood of reaching consensus is low when the number of supporters required for consensus is large and all of the logically possible preference orderings are socially acceptable. A consensus is more likely when some of the logically possible preference orderings are ruled out as being flatly unacceptable to everyone even before the decision-making process begins (Sen 1970; Altfeld 1979).

Let us consider, for instance, a group of actors trying to decide whether their nation should remain neutral, join side A, or fight A in an ongoing war. Six logically possible preference orderings (with P denoting preference) face each third-party nation:

1. Defend A P Neutrality P Fight A
2. Neutrality P Fight A P Defend A
3. Fight A P Defend A P Neutrality
4. Defend A P Fight A P Neutrality
5. Fight A P Neutrality P Defend A
6. Neutrality P Defend A P Fight A

If, because of history, culture, or common interests (or for some other reason), neutrality cannot be the least preferred choice, then positions 3 and 4 would be socially unacceptable. A decision maker in our hypothetical society could never say he favored war so much that he would prefer aiding any side rather than staying neutral. An American in 1917, for instance, might have favored Britain or Germany, but he could not legitimately have argued (without being ostracized as a warmonger) that it would be better to fight anyone than to remain out of the war altogether.

If platforms 3 and 4 were illegitimate, a consensus would emerge every time these war entry choices were faced. Indeed, if only positions 3 and 4 were eliminated, and if each remaining ordering of preferences were equally common, neutrality would be chosen every time. Eliminating only choices 3 and 4 produces the unrealistic expectation that virtually all wars are bilateral, since no third-party nation would join. To remedy this situation, either we would have to assume that positions 3 and 4 are socially acceptable, or we would have to eliminate some of the remaining preference orderings. If choices 3 and 4 are considered legitimate, then we are back where we began, with some probability that the policy outcome will reflect the manipulative skills of some individual or minority coalition and with the probability that no consensus position exists. We might assume that all platforms that include the juxtaposition of "fight A" and "defend A" without neutrality intervening are socially un-acceptable. In that case, positions 2, 3, 4, and 6 would be eliminated. With cases 1 and 5 alone remaining, a deadlock could emerge only if the influence of supporters for each position were exactly equal. A "nonsensical" intransitive policy choice would be impossible. But is it reasonable to assume that two-thirds of the possible ways of choosing among the three options cannot be considered? If it is, can we be confident that we know which orderings are inadmissible? Such an assumption may lead us to believe that a consensus exists when in reality no consensus exists.

A second difficulty with restricting the allowable preference orderings is that this assumption implies—though it does not so stipulate—that foreign policy and the national interest are highly stable and rigid, with the opportunity for bold initiatives severely restricted by social norms and customs. The assumption thus suggests that national policies are iron rules and are not negotiable.

Norms and previous commitments do influence foreign policy, and at any one instant many policy options are socially untenable. Yet there are so many important exceptions to such a view of foreign policy that the assumption discussed above is just not acceptable here. Consider, for instance, how reasonable it might appear to assume that no responsible American leader can publicly support a Communist regime in preference to an anti-Communist regime. Nevertheless, Franklin Roosevelt aligned the United States with Soviet Russia against the greater evil of Germany's Adolf Hitler, even though Hitler was a democratically elected, anti-Communist leader. More recently, Jimmy Carter severed diplomatic relations with the anti-Communist government on Taiwan to fulfill one prerequisite for normalizing American relations with the Communist government of the People's Republic of China.

Sudden changes in international or national norms do take place and sometimes alter the prospects for war or peace. Anwar Sadat's journey to Israel in a search for peace seemed impossible for an Arab leader until the very instant he proposed going to Jerusalem. With that one gesture it became possible to believe that peace might come to the Middle East. Yet even an hour before he embarked for Jerusalem—or for Camp David, nearly a year later—one might have comfortably assumed that an Arab leader could not publicly support concessions to Israel when those concessions were opposed by virtually all Arab states. That Sadat was able to do so is another clear example of the serious errors that one may commit by assuming that certain policy preferences are socially or politically untenable.

The most serious limitation of the assumption that preference orderings can be restricted, however, is its utter lack of parsimony, almost to the point where a theory based on this assumption becomes unmanageable. When one assumes that preference orderings can be restricted, one implicitly assumes that foreign policy decisions are made by a group (as indeed they probably are). One must then also identify the particular social norms, or rules, used in the group to sum the preferences of its members and arrive at a group policy preference that is socially transitive. Unfortunately for the researcher, such norms may change frequently, they certainly are not explicit or particularly visible, and yet they may greatly affect the group's decisions. Consider the example below.

Alternative weights of each actor in the group

Decision maker	Rule 1	Rule 2	Rule 3
A	1	1	1
B	1	1	2
C	1	2	3
D	1	2	4
E	1	5.1	5

Under rule 1, any combination of three decision makers is a winning coalition, capable of enforcing its policy preferences. Under rule 2, only a coalition including *E* (and perhaps *E* by himself, if opinions are divided among three options), or including everyone except *E*, can win, making it extremely difficult to defeat *E*'s preferred outcome. This is the classic case of a group with a strong leader (such as that in my strong-leader assumption) reported so often in studies of group dynamics. Under rule 3, a winning coalition *must* include either *D* or *E* (unless the group is divided *ABC, D, E*), placing these two actors in the position of being potential rivals for control of the group.

To implement the assumption of restriction on preferences, or of any other group-centered view, then, one must know each individual's preferences and his weight in the group, information that is generally all but impossible to obtain. Indeed, these factors may vary so much that we should not expect to know them even in principle. If most groups are similar to the one depicted under rule 2, as the literature on group dynamics suggests, then the strong-leader assumption, to which I now turn, though imperfect, is robust and realistic enough to give a good approximation of the group decision-making process. The strong-leader assumption will be helpful if groups are organized in a fashion similar to the conditions stipulated by Rule 2 except on those (presumably few) occasions when the leader E is not part of the winning coalition. If that happens often, the leader almost surely will have extinguished his advantages, with some other actor rising in "power" to become the new dominant leader in the group.

STRONG LEADERSHIP IN FOREIGN POLICY

Remembering that the evidence suggests that nations do not generally stumble into wars without adequate planning, only one assumption remains feasible. Since we have already noted that decisions related to the initiation of war appear to be purposive, we can only conclude that such decisions comply with the strong-leader assumption. This means not that we are assuming every state is ruled by an iron-fisted, coercive dictator but simply that a single individual is the critical gatekeeper who might turn the nation away from initiating a war.

We can logically assume, then, that decisions to make war are dominated by a single individual in each state; but how realistic is this assumption? Does war provoke such an approach to foreign policy decision making? John Stoessinger notes that during wartime, even "most democracies have managed to fashion temporary 'constitutional dictatorships' which quickly balanced the initial advantages of the aggressive dictator" (1973, p. 19). Britain, the world's oldest democracy, suspended elections during the Second World War. Indeed, Blainey observes: "In the last two centuries when Britain was threatened by a powerful enemy it abandoned temporarily many of its democratic procedures. . ." (1973, p. 31). American responses to war have not been very different. The American people reelected Franklin Roosevelt to unprecedented third and fourth terms and have replaced presidents during wartime only when the war was going badly. Foreign policies related to war are almost always associated in our minds with individuals such as Richelieu, Metternich, or Bismarck. It was Teddy Roosevelt, and not the Congress, who carried the "big stick"; it was Johnson and then Nixon, and not the Congress, who designed and implemented American policy in Vietnam; it was Eisenhower, and not the Congress, who "brought the boys home" from Korea and sent troops to Lebanon; it was Kennedy, and not the Congress, who prepared for nuclear war in the face of Soviet missiles in Cuba. It was Nikita Khrushchev, and not the Politburo, who ordered the removal of missiles from Cuba; it was Hitler, and not the Reichstag, who decided to invade Poland; it was Chamberlain, and not the House of Commons, who was given a hero's welcome as the "architect of peace in our time." Of course, no leader can afford to ignore completely the desires and interests of those who follow him. Without some support, even the most coercive dictator cannot hope to muster sufficient resources to wage a successful war. Still, it is ultimately the responsibility of a single leader to decide what to do and how to do it.

When we assume that war decision making is dominated by a strong leader, we merely make a simplifying assumption that provides a convenient basis for organizing and explaining reality. If we are to find scientific generalizations about war, we must make some assumption—such as the strong-leader assumption—that allows us to examine decisions to wage war within a logically meaningful framework. Otherwise we will not be able to distinguish between systematic patterns and incidental occurrences related to war. Yet as with any other theory, we should not expect reality to comply precisely with our assumptions. The ultimate test of an assumption's helpfulness is whether behavior in reality tends to be consistent with the expectations of the theory. Thus if war decision making is purposive, as it indeed appears to be, and if it is consistent with the assumption that such decisions are dominated by a key leader, then my decision-making assumption is helpful. We may call this the "as if" principle, by which I simply mean that reality is *as if* decisions were made by a strong leader. If decisions about war are not consistent with such an assumption, then that assumption will not help us understand much about the world in which we live. We must then say that the theory is empirically trivial and hence not useful.

THE RATIONALITY ASSUMPTION

The strong leader, as I have noted, cannot afford to ignore the interests and desires of those whose support helps keep him in power. Yet neither is he an unthinking tool of their interests. The key leader must make sense of the competing, sometimes inconsistent demands placed on him so that he can formulate a policy that accords with his own interests. When he does so, I assume, the leader is guided by a desire to maximize the net benefits he expects from his foreign policy choices. A policymaker will never choose an action that is expected to produce less value—or utility—than some alternative policy. In other words, the leader is assumed to be a rational utilitarian interested in maximizing his own welfare. His welfare, in turn, is assumed to be intimately tied to the overall costs and benefits imposed on the society by his foreign policy. The key leader would not, therefore, start a war or continue to fight in a war if he perceived the net expected result to be less than that of remaining at peace or surrendering to the adversary. Of course, this does not mean that he must expect his nation always to win its wars. Rather, he must expect it to win or at least not to lose more than the leader believed would be lost without the war.

In other words, the particular form of rationality I am postulating is that of expected-utility maximization. This assumption is intended to convey the notion that choices between war and peace are made *as if* to maximize the strong leader's welfare and, by assumption, the welfare of those at whose pleasure the leader remains in a position of leadership. My particular approach to the maximizing behavior of key leaders is shaped by two associated assumptions. First, I postulate that one nation's utility for another nation is a direct, positive function of the degree to which they share a common policy perspective. Thus, while power may be instrumental to achieving particular ends in international politics, I postulate that *utilities* are determined by the congruence of policy ends between states. Second, I assume that one nation's *probability of success* in a contest with another nation (or coalitions of nations) is a direct, positive function of each relevant nation's power compared to that of each other relevant nation. All other things being equal (and, as I will show shortly, they often are not equal), a state has a higher probability of success against a weaker nation than it does against a stronger nation.

In expected-utility calculations, one must estimate cardinal utilities. In formulating expected-utility decision rules, I assume that utility values are bounded such that the perception of perfect agreement or harmony of interests on the relevant policy dimensions is reflected in a utility score of 1, and the perception of complete disagreement is reflected in a utility score of -1.

The rationality assumption I am making is the cornerstone of most economic theory. Nevertheless, its application in this context requires further elaboration and explanation. A rational actor is one who compares options and orders them according to his preference for each. Options may be ordered to reflect one of three relations between them. Given a choice of a or b, a rational actor prefers a to b or b to a or is indifferent. For simplicity, we can again resort to our shorthand for this relationship. Let a and b represent alternatives, let P represent preference, and let I be indifference. Then aPb or bPa or aIb. A rational actor not only orders options but does so transitively, so that if c is a third option and aPb and bPc, the relation aPc must hold. If it does not, the actor is in a hopeless cycle of preferences, liking a better than b and b better than c but c better than a. Such an actor would be incapable of choosing or identifying what is best (or worst) for him.

The rational actor always chooses the outcome he considers most desirable. If $aPbPc$, and if all other things were equal, the actor would select a. However, since "all other things" are not always, or even usually, equal, a rational actor does not always choose the option that is, by itself, most preferred. Recall the example of the 1962 Cuban crisis, and let a, b, and c be three possible resolutions (for example, a is the removal of the missiles and the fall of Castro's government; b is the removal of the missiles; and c is nuclear war). Outcome a, though considered more desirable than b or c, may have a very low probability of actually occurring. Assume that the probability of achieving outcome a is p, the probability of b is q, the probability of c is r, and $q > p > r$. Depending on the exact values of the probabilities, at some point the difference between p and q will be large enough for some rational actor to pursue a strategy appropriate for achieving outcome b rather than a. I will return to this point when I discuss risk taking, but for now suffice it to say that the rationality assumption does not imply that decision makers always select their first choice.

Several misconceptions about the meaning of rational behavior have resulted in some confusion. Occasionally individuals tend to think of "rational" and "normal" behavior as if they must be the same or similar. To be sure, most normal people are rational, but some rational people are not normal. Typically, confusion over this issue leads to assertions, for examples, that Hitler, or some other despised figure, "must be irrational." In the context in which rationality is treated here, it is entirely conceivable that people like Hitler or Goering are completely rational though aberrant and abhorrent. Indeed, their ruthlessness helped propel and sustain each of them in power, providing each with an opportunity to pursue his own perverse objectives. Being rational simply implies that the decision maker uses a maximizing strategy in calculating how best to achieve his goals. The rationality assumption tells us nothing about how actors form their preferences but rather shows how actors behave, given their preferences.

A second misconception about rationality is that in any given situation there is an objectively best, rational choice that all rational decision makers would choose. This is not true. Different individuals have different tastes or preference orderings, which will lead them to make different decisions, even though each of the decisions is rational. This will be as true of individuals' preference for policy outcomes as for strategy or risks. To assert that there is an objectively best preference ordering for everyone is to impose one's own values onto others. Such an interpersonal comparison of utilities (leading to the inference that one's own utilities are just like everyone else's) is illogical. One may postulate a particular preference ordering, for instance, for outcomes, with the intention of identifying the optimal strategy given those preferences, but one cannot say that those who do not hold that ordering are irrational.

A third misconception is that rational actors must be infallible. The confusion here is between doing what is best and doing what one *believes* is best. Rational actors need not be assumed to have a crystal ball. They are assumed to do what they believe is best, given the information they have. Yet even if they have perfect information, rational actors may make honest errors. In calculating what is in their best interest, they can simply make a mistake. People are not perfect. However, to the extent that individuals are rational, we may expect them to try to minimize such errors so long as the expected cost of an error exceeds the expected cost of trying to avoid the mistake. In the case of leaders who contemplate initiating a war, the cost of an error may be extraordinarily high, so I expect miscalculations to occur infrequently.

Is the rationality assumption realistic? As with the strong-leader assumption about decision making, this is really an empirical question best answered by seeing if the actions of decision makers are consistent with our empirical expectations for a rational actor. If we find that policymakers act as if they are rational expected-utility maximizers, then the assumption is realistic. The remaining chapters of this book will help resolve that issue. Still, many will question the appropriateness of ascribing rational calculations to national leaders. The alternative, however, is to assume that such decision makers are irrational. If they are, then no systematic decision making patterns should emerge. After all, if we know that choice *a* is preferred to choice *b* and that choice *a* is more likely to be successful than *b*, it is difficult to defend the irrational expectation that choice *b* might be selected. If we assume decision makers are irrational, then we are compelled either to study each war as a unique event or to study war from some perspective other than decision making. The former approach, of course, should not be expected to offer insights about likely behavior in future wars. The latter approach might provide some insights, though those insights will necessarily be very limited, since irrationality implies behavior detached from the real world. It would not be possible, for instance, to discover how systemic or national attributes affect decisions to wage war or pursue peace, since reactions to these attributes would not be systematically linked to nations or systems of nations. Once one abandons the notion that decisions reflect transitive preference orderings—the minimal requirement for rational behavior— almost anything is possible, no matter how schizophrenic or irrational. Those who question the rationality assumption might do well to ask themselves whether the alternative is more helpful.

RISK TAKING AND UNCERTAINTY

Not all rational actors respond to the same information in the same way. One reason for different decisions is simply that each individual has his own tastes or preferences. A rational Greek Cypriot may be expected to prefer a government for Cyprus very different from that desired by a rational Turkish Cypriot, just as a Chinese leader would choose a resolution of the Sino-Soviet rift different from that sought by a Soviet leader. Beyond differences in preferred outcomes, individuals may also differ in their willingness to take risks or in their response to uncertainty.

"Risk taking" refers to the probability of success that a decision maker demands before pursuing a course of action. "Uncertainty," on the other hand, refers to the degree to which the probability of success of a course of action is unknown. To make the distinction clear, let us consider this example. Suppose some leader is eager to increase the power of his nation. If he starts a war and wins, he will achieve his goal. However, there is also the possibility that he might lose, in which case his nation would be even less powerful than it was at the outset. His war option, then, has some probability of being successful and some probability of being unsuccessful. Besides the two possible outcomes of initiating a war, the leader must also consider the third possibility of continuing to pursue his current policy.[5]

For argument's sake, let us assume that the current policy of some leader is certain to produce no change in his nation's power.

5. The probability of any event's occurring can range from zero, when the event will not occur, to one, when it is certain to occur. If we speak of an event that can have one of several outcomes, then the sum of the probability that each outcome will occur is one, since some outcome must occur. If two outcomes are possible, for instance, then we may say that the probability of one of them is p and the probability of the other is $1 - p$. War is an example of this relationship, where we can say the probability of A's gaining from a war with B is p and the probability of A's losing is $1 - p$. One way of conceptualizing this principle is that an entire universe of war outcomes, we expect "A gaining" to account for a certain proportion of outcomes and "A losing" logically to account for the rest.

By changing his policy, then, he may obtain an outcome that is better or worse than his current situation. Let us arbitrarily assign the utility value of 1 to winning and − 1 to losing, and let us assume that winning and losing are equally likely ($p = .5$). The *expected utility* of the war strategy is simply *the sum of the utilities of the possible outcomes times their probabilities*, so that in this case the expected value is $.5(1) + .5(− 1) = 0$. If continuing the current policy with its known consequences has a utility of 0, then it has the same expected value as starting a war. In other words, each strategy has an equal expected value. Given this equality, we can define risk acceptance and risk aversion. A risk-acceptant leader is one who values the chance for success so much that he nevertheless goes to war. A risk-averse leader would prefer not going to war in this situation, while a risk-neutral decision maker would be indifferent to going to war or continuing his present policy, since the expected value of the two options is the same.

Ask yourself if you would rather buy a $1 lottery ticket that gives you a one-in-a-million chance to win $1 million or a $1 ticket offering a one-in-a-hundred .chance to win $100. If you chose the chance at $1 million, you were more risk acceptant than if you chose the chance to win $100. Each choice has the same "expected value." If one spent an infinitely large amount of money buying each of these lottery tickets, one would, according to the law of large numbers, break even. Thus 1 million purchases of lottery tickets good toward the $1 million prize would yield a net expectation of winning $1 million once at a cost of $1 million in tickets. If one purchased 1 million tickets good toward the $100 lottery, one would expect to win $100 ten thousand times, for total winnings of $1 million at a cost of $1 million in tickets. Despite the equal expected value of these two lotteries, many of us perceive a difference between them. That difference reflects our willingness to take risks.

In conventional treatments of risk taking, all expected-utility calculations based on lotteries reflect risk. I wish to be slightly unconventional in my usage. When I speak of risk-acceptant or risk-avoidant behavior, whether it takes place under conditions of uncertainty or under conditions of risk (i.e., when the true probabilities in a lottery are known), I have in mind some reflection of how constrained the key leader feels about his willingness to "take a chance." Risk-acceptant leaders, because they attach some added utility to the act of taking a gamble, are less constrained in making war decisions than are risk-averse actors. Risk-averse leaders, because they associate some disutility with lotteries, are constrained to need to satisfy more conditions before they will initiate a war-threatening conflict, even when they are not faced with serious uncertainties.

In the examples above, the decision maker knew what the real probability of success was in the case of each of his choices. Consequently his decision reflected his preferences under conditions of risk. Uncertainty was not a factor in those decisions. Yet how does uncertainty affect the decisions of risk takers and risk averters? Suppose that the decision maker either did not know enough about the likely costs and benefits of his choices to be certain of his utility for the other possibilities or did not know enough about the chance of success with each to affix a probability value with confidence to each of the options. The choices he must make under these circumstances are fraught with uncertainty. While in the earlier example the hypothetical decision maker could readily estimate the expected utility of his options, under conditions of uncertainty he might not know how likely victory or defeat would actually be.

The best that any country can project under conditions of uncertainty is that a family of outcomes associated with attacking another state may be better or worse than continuing the present policy. Earlier, our hypothetical decision maker knew that the probability of an outcome better than continuing his present policy was .5 if he started a war. Since only two outcomes were posited as being possible, our decision maker also knew the probability of an outcome inferior to continuing his present policy was 1 minus the probability of success, or .5. Now, under conditions of uncertainty, he may only know that the probability of a better outcome is $.5 + k$, where k stands for the amount of uncertainty in the calculation. The probability of an inferior outcome is then, $1 - (.5 + k)$, (with k, of course, not larger than .5 or smaller than $-.5$). Taking a very optimistic view, the leader might conclude that $k = .5$, so that the expected value of starting a war is $1(1) + 0(-1) = 1$. Alternatively, he might take a very pessimistic view, in which case the expected utility could be as little as $0(1) + 1(-1) = -1$. Once a decision

maker is faced with uncertainty, he must make additional decisions
before he is able to derive an expected-utility estimate. He must, for
instance, decide which of the family of uncertain probability or
utility estimates that he has he should treat as the true values, and
then he must make his utility calculation. If he was risk averse before
being faced with all this uncertainty, we may assume that he is as risk
averse or more risk averse now. If he was risk acceptant before, he
might be risk averse (or he might have remained risk acceptant)
when faced with so much uncertainty about the information
relevant to his expected-utility calculations. Under conditions of
uncertainty the risk taker's utility for the status quo approaches his
utility for starting and losing a war, equaling that utility in the
limiting case of total uncertainty. Similarly, the risk averter's utility
for continuing his current policy approaches his utility for winning a
war, equaling that utility under conditions of total uncertainty.

RELEVANT SOURCES OF UNCERTAINTY

A national leader contemplating war is assumed to be particularly concerned about:

     1. the marginal advantage or disadvantage in war capabi-
lities of his nation as compared with the potential opponent,
     2. how much he values the policies adopted by his own
country in comparison with those of the potential enemy,
     3. the capabilities of each other nation that might become
involved in the war,
     4. the relative value or utility that these other nations may
contribute to his nation, as compared with the value that they
may contribute to his potential enemy.

The first two points address the initiator's net expected benefit
from a bilateral war. The last two points address the expected behavior
and potential effect of all other relevant states in the event that the
war is initiated. Uncertainty is most important in evaluating point 4.
The first two points simply concern the potential initiator's
motivation for fighting a war and his knowledge about his own and
his adversary's capabilities. National capabilities change rather
slowly, so that it should not be difficult to make a reasonable

estimate of their value. Of course, this is also true for the national capabilities of potential third parties to the war, so there should not be a great deal of uncertainty regarding point 3. Some may contest this, expressing concern about the impact of sudden technological breakthroughs in the development of weapons systems or other advances that seemingly lead to sudden and dramatic shifts in national capabilities. Chlorine gas at the Battle of Verdun or the atom bombs dropped on Hiroshima and Nagasaki, for instance, might be cited as new technologies that greatly altered the war-making capabilities of their possessors. Of course, the Germans lost both the Battle of Verdun and World War I despite their "advantages" (not only in chemical warfare but in U-boats and perhaps aircraft). The German defeat—though not the timing of it was of no great surprise to those who had studied the relative potential of the Dual Alliance and the Triple Entente for increasing war capabilities. Even before the war had begun, Kaiser Wilhelm indicated his expectation that Germany would lose when he wrote, "If we are to be bled to death, England shall at least lose India" (Holsti 1972, p. 16). Similarly, the American defeat of the Japanese did not depend on the completion of the atom bomb, just as the development of the V2 rocket and the V1 jet drone did not enable the Germans to defeat Britain with its superior resources. The atom bomb made Japan's defeat possible without our landing troops "on the beaches," but the Japanese had long recognized—even before Pearl Harbor—that America's advantage in economic resources and raw materials would probably lead to the defeat of Japan in a long war (Wohlstetter 1962; Russett 1972). New technologies may shorten or lengthen wars, but they can alter the expected outcome only if the two sides are so evenly matched that the marginal impact of the new technology can tip any advantage from one side to the other. This rarely occurs.

Unlike national capabilities, however, national interests and commitments may change suddenly if not frequently. Even a brief review of international alliances in this century makes clear their propensity to create sudden and often surprising changes in the international system. Consider, for instance, Bulgaria's alliances with Serbia and Greece in 1912. On the strength of Bulgaria's tie to Serbia and Greece's indirect tie to Serbia through Bulgaria, those three nations fought as allies against Turkey during the First Balkan War. Less than three months after that war ended, Serbia and Turkey were negotiating a mutual defense pact, Greece and Serbia negotiated a bilateral agreement, and Bulgaria waged war against Serbia, Greece, and Turkey. Within two years of that war the Bulgarians and the Turks fought as allies on the side of Germany and Austria-Hungary during the First World War.

Fleeting commitments are just as prevalent among great powers. After World War I and the Bolshevik Revolution, Russian Communism became the target of European hostility. At the forefront of opposition to the spread of Communist revolutions were the Fascist dictatorships of Benito Mussolini and Adolf Hitler. Though Communists were severely persecuted under Hitler, Germany and Russia concluded an alliance in August 1939. Two years later, Stalin found Russia being invaded by his erstwhile ally. The British, Free French, and the Americans became Stalin's chief allies, just as they were to become his chief opponents four years later. Within a few years after the start of the Second World War, new regimes in Italy and Rumania brought those nations — both of which had fought on the side of the Axis powers — into the war on the side of Britain, France, and the United States. Within a few years of the end of the war, Germany, Japan, and Italy had become close allies of the United States, while the Soviet Union had become our principal adversary.

Changes in commitments among nations may increase or decrease uncertainty, depending upon their particular characteristics, but they are almost always likely to affect uncertainty. To see how, let us examine figure 2.1. For the sake of simplicity I have made each of the six nations in this example about equal in power. The lines linking pairs of nations indicate that a mutual defense commitment exists between those nations.

In condition 1, nations are aligned in two coalitions, with the nations in each coalition committed to each other's mutual defense. No overlapping commitments or interests link the nations in the ABC coalition to the nations in the DEF coalition. Condition 2 is the same except that E has no direct commitment to D, with E and D being indirectly aligned through their mutual defense agreements with F. If the system undergoes a change from condition 2 to

FIGURE 2.1.   Changes in National Commitments: Creating or
Alleviating Uncertainty in a Hypothetical System

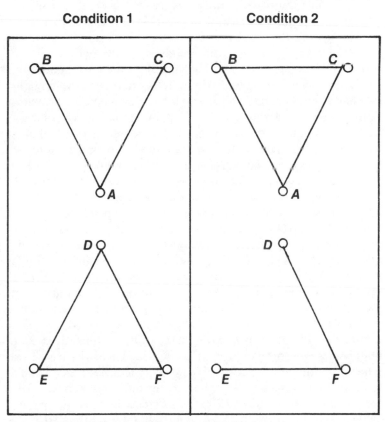

Condition 1   **Condition 2**

Note. A solid line indicates an alliance. Nodes are nations.

condition 1 and if *E* is considering initiating a war against *A*, then *E*
may be more certain about the expected behavior of its allies. *F*,
which had a somewhat different set of interests from *E* (*F* and *E*
shared antipathy toward *A*, *B*, and *C* and friendship toward each
other but differed in their policies toward *D*), now has identical
interests. *D*, which had no direct commitment to *E*, does under
condition 1. Even *A* is less uncertain than it was under condition 2.

Under condition 2, A could not be sure whether or not D, and to a lesser extent F, would aid E. Therefore, A did not know if it had to prepare for a war against E, E and F, or E, F, and D. With the change to condition 1, A "knows the score." If the leader of A is thinking of starting a war against E, he must be prepared to bear the cost of fighting E, F, and D.

If the system changed from condition 1 to condition 2, uncertainty would increase. If the leader of A is thinking of initiating a war against E, he no longer knows whether to expect a war against E, E and F, or E, F, and D. If A is thinking of launching a war against F, the number of A's adversaries is still more uncertain than it was under condition 1. It is true that F has maintained its bilateral commitments to both E and D. But the set of shared interests between F and E and F and D has diminished. While F continues to express an interest in both E and D, D and E are explicitly expressing a loss of interest in each other. Should A infer from this that the difference between D's policy toward E and F's policy toward E is sufficient to keep D (or E) from aiding F? Should A conclude that the bilateral agreements alone are enough to prompt E and D to aid F? Obviously A could reach either conclusion from the information at its disposal. Consequently, A no longer knows the score. Instead, A must make a decision under conditions of uncertainty. It must weigh the cost of arming to fight E, F, and D, recognizing that there is some probability that it will not have to fight all three, against the cost of arming to fight only F or E and F or D and F, this time recognizing that there is some probability it might actually have to fight all three. If all six nations are about equal in power (and if A expects B and C to participate in the war on its behalf), the difference between ABC versus F and ABC versus DEF is the difference between victory and stalemate. If ABC were stronger than DF but weaker than DEF, the evaluation of the expected behavior of D and E—which is so hard to make under conditions of uncertainty—could be the difference between victory and defeat.

DISTANCE AND NATIONAL POWER

The final assumption to be discussed at length concerns the relationship between geographic distances and national power.

Kenneth Boulding (1963) has argued persuasively that the amount of a nation's power that can be brought to bear in any part of the world depends on how much distance lies between the nation moving the power and the nation the power is being moved to. At least four factors lead to a diminution of power when capabilities must be transported over large distances. Combat over a long distance (a) introduces organizational and command problems; (b) threatens military morale; (c) invites domestic dissension; and (d) debilitates soldiers and their equipment.

Soldiers fighting a long way from home are likely to be on unfamiliar terrain, surrounded by people who, though possibly friendly, speak a different and unfamiliar language, prepare foods differently, and interact differently with strangers. If the territory is that of an adversary rather than an ally, it is likely that the adversary enjoys a substantial advantage because of his familiarity with the culture, language, climate, and geography of the area in which the fighting is taking place. Even if the fighting is taking place on the territory of an ally that one is trying to defend, the assisting nation still has the problem of coordinating the efforts of the host government and ally when each has its own command, organizational, and supply structure.

When soldiers must be transported over large distances, one cannot ignore the logistic problems that arise in maintaining supply lines to provide ammunition, spare parts, food, clothing, and a host of other items that may not be readily available near the battlefield, especially if the soldiers are on enemy territory. Russia's inability to transport adequate supplies to the Japanese front, rather than any inherent superiority of the Japanese forces, for instance, was of paramount importance in the Russian failure during the Russo-Japanese War of 1904–1905. Beyond these logistic issues lie problems with morale. Soldiers fighting at home are invigorated by the desire to protect their nation, homes, and families. Soldiers far from home, however, are more likely to be motivated by some less compelling, abstract purpose ("keeping the world safe for democracy") or, though less commonly in recent history, by the expectation of booty. The civilization of armies, which has greatly reduced the legitimacy of pillaging and looting, leaves soldiers far from home with less motivation to risk their lives than is felt by those fighting at home to protect the things that they value.

An even greater lack of motivation may be manifested by the people back home charged with the responsibility of financing a war that is possibly without any immediately apparent relevance to their welfare. Soldiers, at least, are faced with the realization that their lives are in danger. The civilian population is not faced with such a threat, leaving them likely to wonder why they should give up butter for guns. The difficulty of maintaining civilian morale while one's armies are fighting on alien territory far from home plagued the French in Algeria and Indochina and the Americans in Korea and Vietnam. Indeed, much of the severe inflation and the considerable unemployment that wracked the American economy throughout the 1970s was partially the result of Lyndon Johnson's and Richard Nixon's reluctance to ask the American people to make sacrifices to pay for the far-off war in Vietnam. Of course, other factors contributed to French and American losses in Indochina, or to the wave of economic unrest in the post-Vietnam years, but the difficulty of motivating the civilian population to support an army fighting in such remote places as Dienbienphu, Da Nang, or Pleiku should not be overlooked.

Distance increases the likelihood that a nation's military equipment, training, tactics, and leadership are ill prepared or unsuited for the actual conditions of battle. Both the armies of Napoleon and Hitler were not, for instance, adequately trained or equipped to fight in the harsh Russian winter. Similarly, the British in 1776 were unprepared to fight against backwoodsmen who refused to stand in orderly columns and exchange musketry. Coupled with this lack of preparation, especially in the nineteenth century, have been the debilitating consequences of transporting men over vast distances. Long journeys, whether overland or by sea, have generally been accompanied by heavy casualties due to malnutrition, exposure, exhaustion, and a host of other maladies. The Russians in 1904, for instance, finding themselves generally restricted to a single line of track from Russia across Siberia, sent many of their men and much of their materiel by sea to fight the Japanese. By the time the Russian fleet arrived, the men and ships were weakened, thereby greatly reducing Russian strength in the first Russo-Japanese war.

Although the time it takes to move large numbers of men great distances has been greatly shortened and the natural perils of travel have been all but eliminated, each improved means to sustaining a distant war has been accompanied by new obstacles that still make fighting a war far from home more difficult than defending one's own territory. Modern, long-range aircraft, for instance, though capable of transporting men and material quickly and efficiently, are vulnerable to antiaircraft missiles and are limited to use in war zones that possess landing fields capable of accommodating the needs of these aircraft. Similarly, transoceanic travel is quick and comfortable, but since World War I the world's shipping has been vulnerable to submarine and air attack during times of war. Drew Middleton, the *New York Times's* military correspondent, summarized the dangers of fighting over long distances when he wrote: "Reinforcement involves risk. Are transport aircraft available? Can the Navy escort heavy material to Europe, defeat the Soviet submarine threat and keep open sea lanes over which oil and other raw materials pass to the United States?... Other difficulties include the security of air bases in Europe, the slow development of the prepositioning program and political questions. Would a NATO ally agree to the deployment of additional American forces in Europe if this involved transit or landing rights over and on its territory?" (1978). To be sure, the effect of distance has been steadily diminishing, but except for unconventional warfare, some adverse effect still remains.

Apparently, nations are less powerful away from home than they are at home. Yet the exact relationship between distance and capabilities is not this simple. First, the rate at which power declines has diminished due to the general impact of technology. Improved transport systems, medical care, and the like have generally reduced the losses that arise from moving armies great distances. Second, the rate at which power declines is lower for more advanced nations than for less developed nations. While some technologies are so widespread that they benefit all, other technological and organizational developments tend, at any time, to benefit only the wealthier societies that are able to indulge in research or are capable of adapting and adopting new methods that originated elsewhere. We would, for instance, expect the United States to be more capable of fighting effectively in Vietnam than the Vietnamese would be in the United States. Yet even with the most advanced military and organizational technology, there is still some diminution in conventional capabilities across large distances today. The problem of transporting supplies to soldiers in faraway places may be close to solution, but as the Vietnam experience so clearly showed both France and the United States, the problem of maintaining morale — convincing the people at home that the war is important enough for them to supply the money and expertise to mount a war effort and convincing the soldiers fighting far from home, unsure of the purpose for which they are risking their lives, that the war is worth it — is still important in warfare. For these reasons and others, the effect of distance may be so debilitating that even such a great power as the United States may be rendered weaker than such seemingly meek adversaries as Vietnam or Iran. Thus when wars are fought over large distances, the apparently stronger state may be weaker than its adversary if the war is fought on its adversary's territory, while, of course, the adversary would be weaker if the war were fought on the territory of the "stronger" state. If A and B are two distant states and the absolute capabilities of A are greater than those of B, it is possible, depending on the distances involved, for A to be more powerful both at B and A or for A to be more powerful than B at A but weaker than B at B.

   In this chapter I have delineated all of the principal assumptions from which a theory of necessary, but not sufficient, conditions for war is derived. I have assumed that a single senior foreign policy decision maker has final authority for all war-and-peace decisions. That policymaker was assumed to be a rational expected-utility maximizer. Although final authority rests with him, I postulated that his decisions are influenced by the advice and pressures to which he is subjected by a variety of interests. While I am not yet able to incorporate the leader's capacity to mobilize domestic support, or the long-term political costs of his decisions, these are in principle important, but as yet excluded, elements affecting his rational calculations (Rosen 1972; Organski, Lamborn, and Bueno de Mesquita 1973; Organski and Kugler 1980).
   Each leader responsible for choosing between war and peace is,

as I have noted, assumed to be a rational actor. Yet each leader is also assumed to have his own particular orientation toward risk and uncertainty. For this reason, two individuals confronted with precisely the same information, or having the same a priori expectations about the outcome of a war, may rationally choose completely different courses of action. Those who are risk averse require considerably more confidence in their ultimate success than do those who are risk acceptant. Uncertainty is assumed to heighten the difference in choices between those who are risk averse and those who remain risk acceptant even in the face of uncertainty.

Finally, I assume that a nation's power to wage war decays significantly as the location of the war becomes more remote from the nation's territory. I assume that the rate of decay is faster for less powerful countries than it is for more powerful countries and was generally faster in the past than it is at present. I have also indicated that power declines (and hence the probability of success) because great distance from home provides a circumstance making it fairly difficult for even a strong leader to mobilize domestic support for the war effort.

Having stated these assumptions, we may now turn to the development of an expected-utility theory of war that incorporates rational, war-or-peace decision making, dominated by a key leader, with variable orientations toward risk and uncertainty and suitable adjustments for the debilitating influence of geographic distance on usable national capabilities. As we do so, we should bear in mind that many idiosyncratic, and even irrational, elements may enter into war-and-peace decisions. Indeed, even such additional rational calculations as the expected utility of diplomacy or the expected long-term political-strategic rather than policy-based costs of war enter such decisions, although they are not explicitly incorporated in the theory developed in the next chapter. The presumed importance of the theory I will set forth concerns the idea that whatever other factors may encourage leaders away from or toward war, the conditions stipulated in the theory *must* be satisfied for rational leaders to initiate war.

3 The War Trap: The Expected-Utility Theory

The book of Nature is written in mathematical characters.
— Galileo Galilei

Having delineated the assumptions of the theory, we may turn our attention to the theoretical form of the expected-utility model that is hypothesized to discriminate between those who might expect a gain from war and those who would rationally expect to suffer a net loss if they started a war. The size of the expected gains or losses depends on (a) the relative strength of the attacker and the defender; (b) the value the attacker places on changing the defender's policies, relative to the possible changes in policies that the attacker may be forced to accept if it loses; and (c) the relative strength and interests of all other states that might intervene in the war.

EXPECTED UTILITY FROM A BILATERAL WAR

In a bilateral war, success affords one the subsequent opportunity to influence the policies of the adversary, making them more consistent with one's own interests. This opportunity may range from actually manipulating the economic, social, or military policies of the defeated state so that they serve one's own interests to merely preventing the adversary from changing its policies in undesirable ways. Whatever the actual goal or gains, the differences in interests or policies that encourage the war indicates the maximum change an aggressor could expect to achieve. If U_{ii} is the utility some potential conflict initiator i attaches to his most preferred policy platform (so that $U_{ii} = 1$), then the maximum shift in the policies of nation j—i's potential opponent—that can be realized is the difference between the policies that i wants j to hold and j's policy position, or $U_{ii} - U_{ij}$, with U_{ij} (which is less than or equal to U_{ii}) being i's value for j's policy positions before the war. If i loses, then it may expect j to impose changes on it so that i's postwar posture is consistent with the desires of j. Thus the current utility of failure in the war is $U_{ij} - U_{ii}$, or the maximum amount by which i might have to change its world view to satisfy the desires of j.

In addition to i's calculation of current relations with j, it is likely that i also examines, when possible, what it perceives to be the future of its relationship with j. If i believes that relations are improving — that is, that

$$\Delta(U_{ii} - U_{ij})_{t_0 \to t_n} < 0$$

indicating that i believes j will move closer to the policy position i desires for j in the near future—this might mitigate some of any currently existing antagonism. Conversely, if i anticipates a deterioration in relations with j—that is, that

$$\Delta(U_{ii} - U_{ij})_{t_0 \to t_n} > 0$$

indicating that i believes there is something to be gained by preventing j's policies from moving away from those desired by i for j—this may aggravate or even create antagonisms.

I define nation i's expected utility from a *bilateral war* with j $[E(U_i)_b]$ in the following way:

$$E(U_i)_b = [P_i(U_{ii} - U_{ij}) + (1 - P_i)(U_{ij} - U_{ii})]_{t_0}$$
$$+ P_{i_{t_0}} [\Delta (U_{ii} - U_{ij})]_{t_0 \to t_n} + (1 - P_i)_{t_0}$$
$$[\Delta(U_{ij} - U_{ii})]_{t_0 \to t_n} \qquad (1)$$

where

U_{ii} = i's utility for i's preferred view of the world. $U_{ii} = 1$ by definition.

U_{ij} = i's utility for j's policies. U_{ij} can vary between 1 and $- 1$.

$(U_{ii} - U_{ij})_{t_0}$ = i's perception of what might be gained by succeeding in a bilateral conflict with j in which i can then impose new policies on j. This term reflects i's current evaluation of the difference between the policies that i currently desires j to hold and i's perception of j's current policies (hence it is evaluated at time t_0). Thus the greater the perceived similarity between the policies i desires for j and j's current policies (i.e., $U_{ij} \rightarrow U_{ii}$), the less utility i expects to derive from altering j's policies.

$(U_{ij} - U_{ii})_{t_0} = i$'s perception of what might be lost by failing in a bilateral contest with j in which j can then impose new policies on i. This term reflects i's current evaluation of how much j could shift i's policies away from its world view to make them more in line with j's interests as perceived by i. Like the previous term, this term is evaluated based on current policies (at t_0).

$\Delta(U_{ii} - U_{ij})_{t_0 \rightarrow t_n} = i$'s perception of anticipated change in the difference between i's world view and j's policies over the time period t_0 (the present) to some future time (t_n).

$\Delta(U_{ij} - U_{ii})_{t_0 \rightarrow t_n} = i$'s perception of anticipated change in how much j would want to alter i's policy outlook in the future compared to j's current perceived policy differences with i. Thus this term represents i's perception of anticipated future potential policy losses (over the period t_0 to the future period t_n) to j, while the previous term represents i's perception of future potential policy gains to be derived from imposing i's will on j. Both this and the previous term represent i's estimates under the assumption of no war.

$P_i = i$'s current perception of his probability of succeeding against j in a bilateral conflict. And finally,

$1 - P_i = i$'s current perception of his probability of losing against j in a bilateral conflict.

Since $(U_{ii} - U_{ij}) + (U_{ij} - U_{ii}) = 0$, the expectation of a gain or loss in a bilateral war is solely determined by the relative strength of the attacker and its opponent. Of course, while the expectation of a gain or loss is determined by the relative strength of the two sides, the *magnitude* of those gains or losses is strongly influenced by the current and anticipated future values of U_{ii} and U_{ij}. Thus the theory treats bilateral wars as if they are viewed as situations involving pure competition. i believes it can gain as much from a bilateral conflict as i believes j must lose. This is a rather conservative viewpoint, since in reality, j—if it loses—is likely to lose more than i actually gains. Once i must consider the possibility of third parties entering the conflict, however, its viewpoint ceases to be one of pure competition. All other states besides i and j may have mixed motives, with some elements encouraging their outright support for one side or the other, and with other considerations encouraging them to try to mediate the dispute.

EXPECTED UTILITY FROM A
MULTILATERAL WAR

"All other states" may be divided into five categories, so that the leader contemplating the initiation of a war must consider the strength and relative utility of seven types of actors, including the defender and himself. Figure 3.1 depicts a fairly simple system with all seven kinds of nations. The seven types, to which I will repeatedly refer, are:

1. the potential initiator (A in figure 3.1 and i hereafter),

2. the potential defender (D in figure 3.1 and j hereafter),

3. those nations that are friendly toward the initiator but not toward the defender (B and C and called k_1 hereafter),

4. those nations that are friendly toward the defender but not toward the initiator (E, F, and G and called k_2 hereafter),

5. those nations friendly toward both the attacker and the defender (H and called k_3, k_3', or k_3'' hereafter. k_3 prefers i to j, k_3' prefers j to i, and k_3'' is indifferent to i and j. All other notation using a single or double prime follows the same preference pattern),

6. those allied nations not friendly toward either the attacker or the defender (I, J, and K and called k_4, k_4', and k_4'' hereafter), and

7. all nonaligned nations (L and M and called k_5, k_5' and k_5'' hereafter), whose policies reflect no expressed commitment to any nation in the international system.

The last two types are similar in that they are somewhat hostile to both A and D, so that they might be thought of as a single type. However, since a policy of total nonalignment is of particular interest, I will treat nations with foreign policies like those of I, J, and K separately from nonaligned states like L and M. This is done

FIGURE 3.1.   A Hypothetical System Depicting Possible Relations among Nations

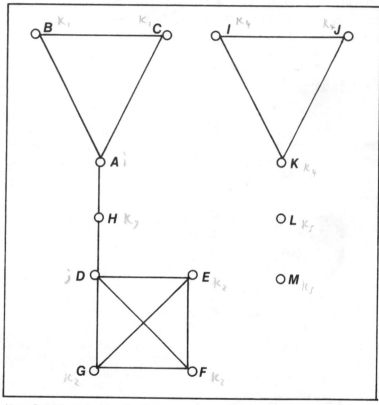

Note. Solid lines depict policy linkages among nations. Nodes are nations.

strictly for convenience and clarity and does not involve any special assumptions about either type of nation.

Let us assume that each bond between nations in figure 3.1 is equally strong and credible, that each nation is equally powerful, and that each nation is the same physical distance from *A* and *D*. Further, let us assume that the leader in each nation, being an expected-utility maximizer, prefers to see his foreign policy interests prevail over hostile interests and, when that is not possible, prefers a less threatening change in the array of interests in the international system to a more threatening change. With these few assumptions, we can infer a great deal about the expected behavior of all the nations represented in figure 3.1.

The similarity of foreign policy interests may be reflected by the similarity of commitments among each of the pairs of nations in figure 3.1, so we can infer the national preferences of each state.[1] As has become the custom, preference will be denoted by P, but to avoid confusion with nation I, indifferences will be denoted by bracketing the states that feel indifference. The postulated preference ordering for each state in figure 3.1 follows:

A: $[BC]$ P H P D P $[LM]$ P $[IJK]$ P $[EFG]$
B: C P A P H P $[IM]$ P $[IJK]$ P $[EFG]$ P D
C: B P A P H P $[LM]$ P $[IJK]$ P $[EFG]$ P D
D: $[EFG]$ P H P A P $[LM]$ P $[BCIJK]$
E: $[FG]$ P D P H P $[LM]$ P $[BCIJK]$ P A
F: $[EG]$ P D P H P $[LM]$ P $[BCIJK]$ P A
G: $[EF]$ P D P H P $[LM]$ P $[BCIJK]$ P A
H: A P D P $[BC]$ P $[EFG]$ P $[LM]$ P $[IJK]$
I: $[JK]$ P $[LM]$ P $[BCH]$ P $[AEFG]$ P D
J: $[IK]$ P $[LM]$ P $[BCH]$ P $[AEFG]$ P D
K: $[IJ]$ P $[LM]$ P $[BCH]$ P $[AEFG]$ P D
L: M P $[BCIJKH]$ P $[AEFG]$ P D
M: L P $[BCIJKH]$ P $[AEFG]$ P D

A, not surprisingly, prefers allies B and C to its other ally, H, both because of the greater set of shared interests between them (B, for instance, shares A's interest in C) and because of the smaller number of unshared interests (B does not share A's interest in H, but then A and H do not share common interests in B, C, or D). A has more in common with D than with the remaining states (though A and D in fact do not have much in common) because, of the remaining states, only D is allied with one with which A is also allied. Starting with D, however, A's preferences result more from the relative scarcity of sources of potential conflicts than from efforts to find shared positive attitudes toward the policies of other states. Of the remaining

---

1. The actual operational method used to estimate the preferences (and cardinal utility) of each hypothetical nation depicted in figure 3.1 is explained in chapter 4 and in Bueno de Mesquita (1975).

nations, L and M, by virtue of their noncommittal stand, are less clearly oriented against A than are either the coalitions of I, J, and K or E, F, and G. I, J, and K are modestly preferred over E, F, and G by A only because coalition IJK does not have coalition EFG's added commitment to D, which, though preferred to any of them, still represents a negative valence for A. The preferences of B, C, D, E, F, and G follow quite straightforwardly from the logic underlying A's preferences, so I will not explain their preference orderings in detail at this juncture. H's preferences are also fairly clear, though I will comment briefly on H's position.

The key leader of nation H is postulated to prefer A's policies to D's despite having a direct commitment to both, because A has fewer diversions (B and C) from the A-H bond than does $D(E, F,$ and $G)$. For the same reason, H prefers B and C to E, F, and G. Finally, the nonaligned posture of both L and M is preferred to the alien alliance of IJK, to which H does not have any link. The position of I, J, and K merits further elaboration. D is postulated to appear more threatening to them than A does because six nations can be expected to back D in a conflict with I, J, or K (A, D, E, F, G, H: $DP[IJK]$), while only five states should be expected to side with $A(A, B, C, D, H$: $AP[IJK])$. Put somewhat differently, D's foreign policy contains fewer similarities to I's (or J's or K's) than does A's. A and I, for instance, share the fact that they are not allied with D, E, F, G, L, and M, while D and I share the fact that they are not allied with A, B, C, L, and M. Finally, we may note that L and M are viewed with indifference by everybody, while L and M prefer nations with few allies to nations with many allies.

By knowing the preferences of the key leader in any state, we can anticipate which side each state will favor in any potential war. We can even determine the total number of supporters on each side. However, though all nations have been assumed to be equal in power and to be equally affected by any loss in strength due to distance from the war, we cannot simply add up the number of nations expected to be on each side to determine which of the initial protagonists has an advantage. Consider, for instance, a war between A and D. Eight nations (B, C, H, I, J, K, L, and M) value A's stand in the international system more than D's, with only E, F, and G preferring a victory by D over A. However, many of A's supporters

($H, I, J, K, L,$ and M) might value A only slightly more than D, while D's allies ($E, F,$ and G) might feel strongly about their preference for D over A. The *utility*, or value, A can *expect* to derive from the assistance of its supporters depends on how much A believes its supporters prefer a victory by A to a victory by D times how much of an impact those supporters can have on the war. If most of A's supporters barely prefer A to D, so that A believes their net utility for

FIGURE 3.2.   Utilities of Third Parties for Nations A and D in a Hypothetical System

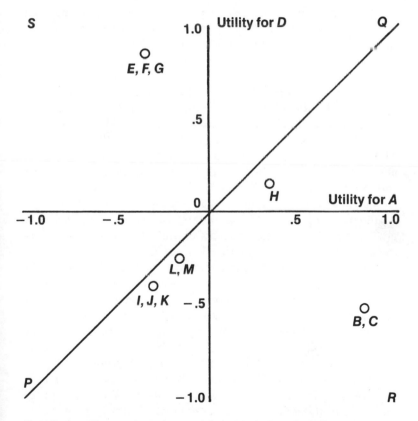

Note. Nodes represent the nations, as labeled, in the hypothetical system.

a victory by A rather than by D is close to zero, then no matter how powerful they are, A must conclude that they will not care to use much of their strength to help A win. If A believes that D's supporters greatly prefer D to A, then the leader in A must calculate that D's allies will make many of their resources available to D, so that D's strength, combined with its handful of allies, could be greater than A's expected strength. If that were the case, then A's expected utility from starting a war against D would be negative, indicating that the war is more likely to lead to a loss than a gain. Under such a circumstance, it would be irrational for A to start a war against D.

As can be seen, the degree to which the other states favor A over D or D over A is a critical issue. Simply knowing the preferences of states may be misleading. Knowing the intensity with which preferences are held is important. Such intensity, which reflects cardinal utility, may mean the difference between A's correctly anticipating D's support or mistakenly believing in A's own superiority. Figure 3.2 depicts the estimated utility values that each state in our example attaches to nations A and D, while figure 3.3 depicts the general case. All the nations in the area PQR prefer A to D, while those in the area PQS prefer D to A, with those on the diagonal line PQ being indifferent in a choice between A and D. A's supporters, except for B and C, hover close to the point of indifference, while D's supporters all feel intensely pro-D. Whether the intensity of E, F, and G is sufficient to overwhelm the preferences of A's supporters depends on a set of multilateral expected-utility calculations to which I now turn my attention.

How can A know whether it should expect to gain or lose? An empirical approach to this question will appear in subsequent chapters, but a theoretical response can be given here. As we have just seen, the leader of A must make a fairly complex calculation to determine his expected utility for war. This calculation considers the probability that his nation can benefit by fighting his potential adversary, as well as the size of any potential benefits.

When a utility-maximizing leader considers attacking a nation, he must consider the likelihood that his nation will benefit and the likelihood that it will lose. The leader must also estimate his utility for the potential benefits and losses. These calculations involve three

FIGURE 3.3.   General Array of Third-Party Utilities for Initiators
and Opponents in International Conflicts

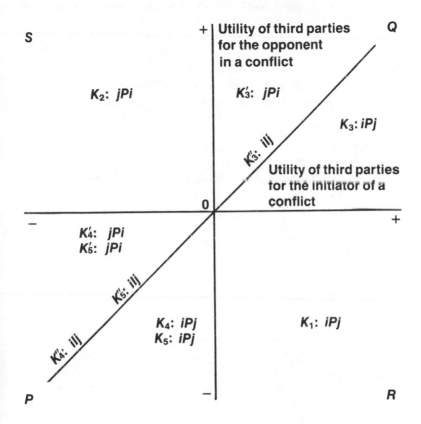

distinct risky situations, or lotteries. First, as we have seen, there is
the probability of success or failure if the war remains bilateral; then
there is the probability of success or failure if other states aid the
attacking nation; and finally there is some chance of succeeding or
failing if other states aid the adversary.

In contrast to the bilateral calculations, once the potential
attacking nation is compelled to consider third-party nations, the
simple test of which side has more strength is inadequate. While the
attacker and the defender are likely to commit as many resources as

possible to their war, third parties, with a more detached perspective, are likely to calculate both which side they favor and how much they favor them. As we saw in the earlier example, some may decide that they are very committed, while others may have only a marginal preference. Some allies may contribute soldiers, equipment, and supplies to a war, while others may offer little more than moral support. The problem for a leader considering the initiation of a war is to estimate how much value, or utility, each other state is expected to contribute to the victory (or defeat) of the initiating or opposing nation. Presumably, those that expect to be significantly affected by the outcome of the war will be inclined to aid their "ally", while those anticipating only minor consequences from the war will be less inclined to become involved. The second and third expected-utility calculations concern i's estimate of the value each third state k is expected to contribute to defending the policies of i or j. Let i's expected utility from the lottery in which each third party k is treated as supporting i equal:

$$E(U_i)_{k_1 1} = (P_{ik} U_{iki} + (1 - P_{ik}) U_{ikj})_{t_0} + P_{ik_{t_0}} (\Delta U_{iki})_{t_0 \to t_n}$$
$$+ (1 - P_{ik})_{t_0} (\Delta U_{ikj})_{t_0 \to t_n} \qquad (2)$$

and let i's expected utility from the lottery in which each third party k is treated as supporting j equal:

$$E(U_i)_{k_1 2} = [(1 - P_{jk}) U_{iki} + P_{jk} U_{ikj}]_{t_0} + (1 - P_{jk})_{t_0} (\Delta U_{iki})_{t_0 \to t_n}$$
$$+ P_{jk_{t_0}} (\Delta U_{ikj})_{t_0 \to t_n} \qquad (3)$$

where

$U_{iki} = i$'s perception of the utility to be derived from each third party actor.

$U_{ikj} = i$'s perception of the utility to be derived by j from each third party actor.

$P_{ik} = i$'s perception of its probability of success against j, given that third party k aids i.

$1 - P_{ik} = i$'s perception of its probability of failing against j, given that third party k aids i.

$P_{jk} = i$'s perception of its probability of failing against j, given that third party k aids j.

$1 - P_{jk} = i$'s perception of its probability of succeeding against j, given that third party k aids j.

$\Delta U_{iki_{t_0 \to t_n}}$ = i's perception of anticipated future changes in the utility i can expect to derive from k (with the change in utility being evaluated as U_{iki} at t_n minus U_{iki} at t_0).

$\Delta U_{ikj_{t_0 \to t_n}}$ = i's perception of anticipated future changes in the utility j can expect to derive from k (with the change in utility being evaluated as U_{ikj} at t_n minus U_{ikj} at t_0).

t_0 = the time at which i is calculating expected utility. Thus any terms with a t_0 subscript are computed based on *current* values.

$t_0 \to t_n$ = the time span over which i estimates expected changes in utility values. This span is assumed to be fairly short, reflecting the fact that policymakers rarely have a long time horizon. t_n then is in the near future. All estimates of change in utility are evaluated as the relevant utility term at t_n minus the relevant utility term at t_0.

$\sum_{l=1}^{5} E(U_i)_{k_l 1}$ — i's overall expected utility from a multilateral conflict with j, given that i treats all third parties k_l (where l includes third parties of types 1 through 5, as defined above) as potentially aiding i.

$\sum_{l=1}^{5} E(U_i)_{k_l 2}$ = i's overall expected utility from a multilateral conflict with j, given that i treats all third parties k_l as potentially aiding j.

Equation 2 represents i's calculation of the utility expected to be contributed by each third party k to i's success or i's failure and the probability of i's winning with k's support, as well as the probability of i's losing with k's support. Equation 3 is i's estimate of the utility k is expected to contribute to j's success or failure, the probability that i will still win even if k sides with j, and the likelihood that i will lose if k joins j. Equation 3 is i's estimate of the value expected if k joins j, and equation 2 is i's estimate of the value expected if k joins i. These are mutually exclusive strategies for each third nation k. Therefore, summing across all k, i's estimate of its *net* expected value from the support decisions of all third parties is:

$$\sum_{l=1}^{5} E(U_i)_{k_l} = \sum_{l=1}^{5} E(U_i)_{k_l 1} - \sum_{l=1}^{5} E(U_i)_{k_l 2} \qquad (4)$$

After substituting, multiplying through, and rearranging terms, we have:

$$\sum_{l=1}^{5} E(U_i)_{k_l} = \sum_{l=1}^{5} \left(P_{ik_{t_0}} \left[U_{iki_{t_0}} - U_{ikj_{t_0}} + \Delta U_{iki_{t_0} \to t_n} - \Delta U_{ikj_{t_0} \to t_n} \right] \right.$$

$$+ P_{jk_{t_0}} \left[U_{iki_{t_0}} - U_{ikj_{t_0}} + \Delta U_{iki_{t_0} \to t_n} - \Delta U_{ikj_{t_0} \to t_n} \right]$$

$$\left. - 1 \left[U_{iki_{t_0}} - U_{ikj_{t_0}} + \Delta U_{iki_{t_0} \to t_n} - \Delta U_{ikj_{t_0} \to t_n} \right] \right)$$

$$= \sum_{l=1}^{5} \left((P_{ik_{t_0}} + P_{jk_{t_0}} - 1) \left[U_{iki_{t_0}} - U_{ikj_{t_0}} + \right. \right.$$

$$\left. \left. \Delta U_{iki_{t_0} \to t_n} - \Delta U_{ikj_{t_0} \to t_n} \right] \right) \tag{5}$$

Note that in equation 5, since $P_{ik} \geq P_i$, and $P_{jk} \geq P_j$ where $P_j = 1 - P_i$, and $P_i + P_j = 1$, it must be true that $P_{ik} + P_{jk} - 1 \geq 0$. In other words, the probability component of the calculation of the net impact of the two multilateral lotteries must be positive, while the overall expected utility from these lotteries can be positive or negative. Consequently, whether i believes a third-party nation k will support i or j is determined, not surprisingly, by i's belief about k's relative utility for i and j. Thus whereas the expectation of gains or losses in a bilateral war depends on the relative capabilities of the attacker and defender, the expectation of support or opposition from third parties depends on utilities. The magnitude of the expected support or opposition, on the other hand, depends both on k's perceived relative utility for i and j and on k's strength across the distance from k to i and from k to j.

When the perceived expected utility of k for i is greater than zero, i believes that k would more likely support i than j. If the expected utility is less than zero, i believes that k will support j. When the expected utility equals zero, k is expected to be indifferent and hence unlikely to favor either the attacker or the defender. How much support k is likely to give, of course, depends on how much i believes that k values i's policy preferences relative to j's. The more $E(U_i)$ for k_l deviates from zero, the more the leader of i is willing to believe that k will commit himself to the war (Starr 1972; Altfeld and Bueno de Mesquita 1979; Altfeld 1979).

When the leader of i sums the expected utility $E(U_i)$ for k_l across all third-party states k, he derives an overall estimate of the expected impact of third states. If the sum of the $E(U_i)$ for k_l is positive, then more support can be expected for i than for j; if it is negative, i believes that more support will go to j. When the sum of $E(U_i)$ for k_l is zero, i believes that, on balance, though some may aid i and some may aid j, the effect of third states is neutralized. Of course, even if this sum is negative and the leader of i believes the effect of the other nations will be against him, this does not mean that i cannot see value in going to war. If $E(U_i)_b$ is greater than $\sum_{l=1}^{5}$ of $E(U_i)$ for k_l, then the overall expected value of the contemplated war is positive, making its consideration rational.[2]

EXPECTED-UTILITY DECISION RULES

The overall utility that i may expect from initiating a war against j [denoted $E(U_i)$], in the absence of uncertainty, is calculated as follows:

$$E(U_i) = E(U_i)_b + \sum_{l=1}^{5} E(U_i)_{k_l} \qquad (6)$$

Equation 6 simply indicates that i is concerned with the overall expected gains or losses from fighting a war with j, where the overall expected value of the war depends on the relative capability advantage i or j has in the bilateral war (as determined by the P_i terms) and on the likely behavior of third parties to the conflict (as determined by the terms involving k). The support of third parties is neither necessary nor sufficient for i to expect to gain from a war with j, just as the value of the P_i terms alone cannot determine i's

2. Note that the computation and summation of the multilateral lotteries is not based on an interpersonal comparison of utilities because each term of $E(U_i)$ for k_l is theoretically equal to i's perception of each k's expected utility contribution. i, then, is simply comparing his estimate of the utility associated with one k to the utility associated with another k.

expectations. Taken together, however, i can know the expected value of the three risky situations that may arise in war: (a) fighting on its own against its adversary; (b) fighting with the aid of some third parties; and (c) fighting in the face of opposition from some third parties. When the three lotteries identified in equations 1, 2, and 3 are combined, as in equation 6, then i knows whether the war is likely to yield gains or losses. In particular, if $E(U_i) > 0$, the war is expected to yield benefits, while if the expected value $E(U_i) < 0$, attacking j is irrational. When $E(U_i) = 0$, i is indifferent, so far as the material calculation is concerned, with respect to attacking or not attacking j. Of course, this calculation only reveals whether minimal, necessary conditions have been satisfied. i must still decide about a number of other considerations, including the "rightness" or "wrongness" of a war with j. War, being a brutalizing and devastating experience, rarely survives as an option once these additional considerations are introduced. For those willing to contemplate attacking another nation, however, *war logically cannot survive as a rational alternative when the value of the expected-utility calculation is less than zero.*

Equation 6 depicts the general expected-utility model. However, it does not reflect responses to conditions of risk or uncertainty nor the additional effects of varying levels of risk acceptance among national leaders. Several different decision rules could be specified to reflect the differences between a risk-acceptant and a risk-averse decision maker. One might, for instance, contend that risk-averse actors take the most pessimistic possible view, in which they assume that their strength must be greater than the combined strength of all other nations before they go to war. With such a "worst possible world" approach, risk-averse decision makers would virtually never start a war. While there may conceivably be some leaders who are this risk averse, it is likely that others, though still risk averse, are less pessimistic. Unfortunately, there is no a priori theoretical way to determine the precise decision rule used by each risk-averse actor, especially since the rule may vary from leader to leader and from time to time. We can, however, select one rule as an assumption that reflects the minimal requirements for risk aversion and, we hope, captures the flavor of most risk-averse decision rules. This criterion is: when risks and utilities are known, risk-acceptant and risk-

neutral actors must simply calculate that the result of equation 6—
the overall expected utility of attacking—is greater than or equal to
zero before they contemplate starting a war. On the other hand, risk-
averse decision makers not confronted with uncertainty (i.e.,
deciding under conditions of risk) must also believe that the result of
equation 6 is positive, but in addition I assume they must believe
that they are capable of defeating (or at least not losing to) their
adversary on their own. With risks and utilities known, then, a risk
averter's calculations must satisfy the following two conditions:

$$E(U_i) \geqslant 0, P_i - (1 - P_i) \geqslant 0$$

With this rule, risk-acceptant and risk-neutral decision makers
should be expected to meet the necessary conditions for war more
often than risk-averse decision makers, thereby satisfying my
requirement that risk averters are more constrained in their
contemplation of conflict than are risk takers.

Before explaining the risk-taking decision rules that I assume
operate under uncertainty, it would be helpful to redefine the five
different types of nations that comprise the set of third states k.
Nations k_1 are i's friends, while nations k_2 are j's friends. k_3, k_3', and
k_3'' are friendly toward both i and j. k_4 through k_4'' have expressed
overt friendship neither toward nation i nor toward nation j, with k_4,
k_4', and k_4'' being aligned states that by definition do have some
friends of their own, and with k_5, k_5', and k_5'' being completely
nonaligned, uncommitted states that by definition have no friends.
k_3, k_4, and k_5 all have in common the fact that $U_{iki} - U_{ikj} > 0$. k_3', k_4',
and k_5' are characterized by the fact that $U_{iki} - U_{ikj} < 0$. For k_3'', k_4'',
and k_5'', $U_{iki} = U_{ikj}$, so that $U_{iki} - U_{ikj} = 0$.

We should remember that the particular kind of uncertainty of
interest here is the uncertainty the strong leader in i has about the
likelihood of gaining support from third-party states. Uncertainty
does not affect the calculation of $E(U_i)_b$. As we have seen, the sign of
$E(U_i)_b$ is solely determined by the relative power of i and j and not by
their affinity for each other. Furthermore, i, being an expected-utility
maximizer with transitive preferences, must have no uncertainty
that his highest utility is toward himself. Let us assign this utility
(U_{ii}) the value 1. Yet what can we say about i's uncertainty of the
other relations in the world? i may have some uncertainty about U_{ij},

but it is likely to be of little consequence if i is willing to consider starting a war against j. We may assume that i will have gone to great lengths to ascertain how it feels about the state most likely to be its adversary. i's uncertainty is most likely to be centered on the value each of the third parties might contribute to i's and/or j's policy goals. Since the sign of $E(U_i)$ for k_l is solely dependent on the difference between U_{iki} and U_{ikj} for each k, i's uncertainty about U_{iki} and U_{ikj} can have a substantial affect on its total expected-utility calculation.

As when the risks of war are known, under conditions of uncertainty several alternative decision rules might be used by risk-averse or risk-acceptant leaders. Again, let us assume that all risk-neutral and risk-acceptant leaders fall within the limits of a single rule, with a separate single rule delineating the behavioral boundaries for all risk avoiders. When the value of $E(U_i)$ for k_l is uncertain, I assume risk-averse leaders take a very pessimistic view in which they discount the likelihood of deriving support from those who appear to prefer them to j. Furthermore, let us also make the assumption that the pessimism of risk-averse leaders causes them to accept at face value all cases where k's utility for them is less than that for their potential opponent ($U_{iki} < U_{ikj}$). In other words, when their uncertain calculation leads to the conclusion that $U_{iki} > U_{ikj}$, risk averters are assumed to believe the true relationship is merely $U_{iki} = U_{ikj}$, but when $U_{iki} < U_{ikj}$, they assume that the likelihood of their opponent receiving support is virtually certain. Thus, I define the expected-utility calculation under uncertainty for a risk-averse leader as:

$$E(U_i) = E(U_i)_b + \sum_{l=2} E(U_i)_{k_l} + \sum_{l=3'} E(U_i)_{k_l}$$

$$+ \sum_{l=4'} E(U_i)_{k_l} + \sum_{l=5'} E(U_i)_{k_l} \tag{7}$$

For nations in category 3', both U_{iki} and U_{ikj} are larger than zero, but U_{ikj} is larger than U_{iki}. Type 4' and 5' nations satisfy two conditions. i's perception of the utility from k for both i and j is less than zero, but j's utility from k is perceived to be greater than i's utility from k. The k_2 nations are those third-party nations contributing negative utility for i and positive utility for j. Of course,

k_2's utility value for j is greater than that for i. A risk averter is treated as if it assumes that all nations appearing to favor i over j are actually indifferent.

Like the risk averter, risk-acceptant leaders when faced with uncertainty make their best possible estimate of each $E(U_i)$ for k_i. Yet unlike risk-averse actors, risk-acceptant or risk-neutral decision makers are not assumed to dismiss the possibility of receiving aid from their allies, while I assume they do believe that nations holding positive utility for either both i and j or neither i nor j will be indifferent and uninvolved in the potential war. Of course, they still

TABLE 3.1. Expected-Utility Decision Rules

Actor's risk orientation	Environmental constraint	
	Risk	*Uncertainty*
Risk acceptant	$E(U_i) = E(U_i)_b + \sum_{l=1}^{5} E(U_i)_{k_l}$	$E(U_i) = E(U_i)_b + \sum_{l=1}^{2} E(U_i)_{k_l}$
	if $E(U_i) \geq 0$, then i can, but need not, initiate a conflict with j.	if $E(U_i) \geq 0$, then i can, but need not, initiate a conflict with j.
	if $E(U_i) < 0$, then i cannot rationally initiate a conflict with j.	if $E(U_i) < 0$, then i cannot rationally initiate a conflict with j.
Risk averse	$E(U_i) = E(U_i)_b + \sum_{l=1}^{5} F(U_i)_{k_l}$	$E(U_i) = E(U_i)_b + \sum E(U_i)_{k_l}$, given that only those third parties for whom $U_{iki} < U_{ikj}$ are entered into the calculation so that, $E(U_i)_{k_l} < 0$ by definition.
	if $E(U_i) \geq 0$ and $E(U_i)_b \geq 0$, then i can, but need not initiate a conflict with j.	if $E(U_i) \geq 0$, then i can, but need not, initiate a conflict with j.
	if $E(U_i) < 0$ or $E(U_i) \geq 0$ but $E(U_i)_b < 0$, i cannot rationally initiate a conflict with j.	if $E(U_i) < 0$, given that it is defined to exclude third parties where $U_{iki} \geq U_{ikj}$, then i cannot rationally initiate a conflict with j.

realize that j may be aided by its allies, and they may be aided by those clearly committed to them. Hence the risk-acceptant leader's calculus under conditions of uncertainty is defined as:

$$E(U_i) = E(U_i)_b + \sum_{l=1}^{2} E(U_i)_{k_l} \qquad (8)$$

Equation 8 indicates that those who are predisposed to be risk acceptant believe that overall the sum of multilateral $E(U_i)$ for k_3 through k_5'' is equal to zero. With equation 8 it is possible for a risk accepter to believe that there are more adversaries against which a gain could be achieved under conditions of uncertainty than there were when the risks and utilities were known. This would be true for all cases where multilateral $E(U_i)$ for k_3, k_4, and k_5 in the absence of uncertainty was less than the sum of multilateral $E(U_i)$ for k_3', k_4', and k_5', with the overall difference large enough to tip the scales in j's favor. Conversely, it is possible for the actor predisposed to be risk acceptant to conclude that uncertainty diminishes his chances for success. If multilateral $E(U_i)$ for k_3, k_4, and k_5 under conditions of risk were sufficiently larger than the multilateral $E(U_i)$ for k_3', k_4', and k_5' to tip $E(U_i)$ in favor of i, then uncertainty would reduce the number of "attackable" nations for those predisposed to accept risk. These two possibilities are consistent with the argument outlined earlier, in which I contended that some who are risk acceptant under risk might become risk averse under uncertainty, while others might remain risk acceptant. Table 3.1 summarizes the expected-utility decision rules I use for risk accepters and risk averters, under conditions of both risk and uncertainty.

SOME OBSERVATIONS ABOUT THE DYNAMIC ELEMENTS OF THE EXPECTED-UTILITY CALCULUS

As the equations indicate, the appropriateness or inappropriateness of war as a possible strategy depends not only on current strength and utility but also on perceptions of what the future holds. If the leader of i believes that j's policies will be more acceptable to i in the future, i will be less encouraged to use war rather than diplomacy against j. If j is believed to become more threatening in the future, then i may be encouraged to launch a preemptive war.

Thus, anticipated changes in i's expected utility for a war against j may affect i's current motivation to consider war as a legitimate strategy. Unfortunately, there are few circumstances where it is possible for i, let alone any observer, to anticipate accurately whether the future holds an increase, a decrease, or a constant value for the expected utility of a war. To know that, i must know not only what changes in its relations with j are in the offing but also what changes are likely to occur both in its relationship with every third party and in every third party's relationship with j. Of course, decision makers do not have crystal balls. Consequently they usually do not have enough information to judge with confidence what policy changes the future holds for j or for third parties k and hence are assumed not to rely generally on such estimates of future utility changes. However, there are circumstances under which, without knowing the particular policy changes that are likely, an actor can have reasonable confidence in his estimates of the direction of future changes in utility values. If we think of changes in utility scores as a random walk in a bounded environment, with steps being of significant magnitude (remembering that I have assumed utility ranges between 1, indicating perfect congruence of interests between actors, and -1, indicating complete disagreement among actors), then it should be clear that as a utility value approaches zero, one is just as likely to anticipate that it will increase as that it will decrease or remain the same, making a reliable estimate of its future value extremely difficult. On the other hand, if we consider utility values that approach either extreme (1 or -1), we can see that as the value gets closer to a boundary, the decision maker is in a better position to estimate the direction that value might take in the near future. Thus when U_{ij} or U_{iki} or U_{ikj} approaches 1, the leader of i can be reasonably confident that the future holds either no change or a movement toward -1, signifying a deterioration in i's relationship with j or k, or a deterioration in i's perception of j's relationship with k. Similarly, if U_{ij}, U_{iki}, or U_{ikj} at t_0 approaches -1, then i has reason to believe the value will not change or else will move toward 1. Clearly, as utility values approach their maximum or minimum values, the prospect of their continuing to increase or decrease respectively declines. Since, as I will show more fully later, there is no systematic basis for i to guess about the future value of U_{iki}, U_{ikj}, or U_{ij}, except when those values are near their extreme boundaries, when these values are not near those boundaries, I treat $\Delta(U_{ii} - U_{ij})$ for t_0 to t_n, ΔU_{iki} for t_0 to t_n and ΔU_{ikj} for t_0 to t_n as if they equal zero.

IMPLICATIONS OF THE THEORY

The four expected-utility decision rules depicted in table 3.1 state conditions that are theoretically necessary before nations can rationally go to war. Whenever any of these decision rules yield an expected-utility value that is less than zero, the relevant type of decision maker is logically prohibited from launching a war.[3] Therefore, by examining these equations closely, we can deduce several interesting circumstances that prohibit war. Furthermore, a number of the existing theories about war can be analyzed within the framework of the expected-utility calculations.

In developing testable propositions from the expected-utility calculus, I will focus my attention on four central issues. These are (a) how do prospective conflict initiators differ from their opponents? (b) who is likely to win an ensuing conflict? (c) when are conflicts likely to be resolved *without* escalating into open warfare? and (d) how does expected utility affect the costs that nations are willing to endure in pursuing their objectives through warfare?

The initial combatants in a war may represent one of three combinations. Wars may be between (a) states that have revealed virtually no preferences with respect to other states (I will call such nations "nonaligned"); (b) states that have revealed preferences

---

3. Some may contend that war is not precluded even if a state's expected utility is less than zero. The argument might be that a greater loss is anticipated from not fighting than from fighting. However, it is hard to imagine that such a circumstance will arise. Since no nation can be forced to make costly concessions to another merely in response to diplomatic pressures, such concessions cannot be expected unless the other party is prepared to seize them through military means. But then it is the "other" who is initiating the conflict. War is so costly that it is difficult to see when diplomacy would involve a larger net loss than would war for an initiator that rationally expects to lose.

regarding the policy positions of other nations (I will call these the "aligned" states); or (c) a nonaligned state and an aligned state. A war between nations L and M in figure 3.1, for instance, would be of the first type, while a war between A and D (or A and B) — or any of the states other than L or M — would be of the second type. A war between either L or M and any other nation would fall in the third category. Consider wars in category (a) first.

Wars between Nonaligned States

Nonaligned states are nations whose leader have chosen not to identify or associate themselves with the interests of any other nation. Of course, in reality no nation exists in such complete isolation. While the empirical investigation of the usefulness of the theory will include specific rules for identifying nonaligned nations, for now we should remember that no theory's assumptions or conditions are perfectly satisfied in reality.

Nations L and M in our example satisfy the condition of complete nonalignment. The relations of nations A through K toward L and M are typical of all nations' relations toward nonaligned states. Although one nation's utility for L and M may be different from another's, each nation's utility for L is equal to its utility for M. That is, every other nation in the world of figure 3.1 is indifferent when forced to choose between L and M. Since neither L nor M has made any visible effort to secure support from other nations (or to offer support to other nations), it is not surprising that others are not differentially attracted to L or M. As a result, if L contemplates attacking M, L must expect that the difference in utilities each other country will have for L and for M will be zero. Whenever both i and j are nonaligned and hence have not revealed their preferences for other states, then i's best guess about the impact of third parties in a conflict between i and j may be assumed to be that $U_{iki} = U_{ikj}$. Substituting U_{iki} for U_{ikj} in equations 2 and 3 reveals that:

$$
\begin{aligned}
E(U_i)_{k_1 1} &= (P_{ik} U_{iki} + (1 - P_{ik}) U_{iki})_{t_0} \\
&\quad + P_{ik_{t_0}} (\Delta U_{iki})_{t_0 \to t_n} + (1 - P_{ik})_{t_0} (\Delta U_{iki})_{t_0 \to t_n} \\
&= U_{iki_{t_0}} + \Delta U_{iki_{t_0 \to t_n}}
\end{aligned}
$$

and

$$E(U_i)_{k_12} = [(1 - P_{jk})U_{iki} + P_{jk}U_{iki}]_{t_0}$$
$$+ (1 - P_{jk})_{t_0}(\Delta U_{iki})_{t_0 \to t_n} + P_{jk_{t_0}}(\Delta U_{iki})_{t_0 \to t_n}$$
$$= U_{iki_{t_0}} + \Delta U_{iki_{t_0 \to t_n}}$$

so that

$$E(U_i)_{k_1} = E(U_i)_{k_11} - E(U_i)_{k_12}$$
$$= (U_{iki_{t_0}} + \Delta U_{iki_{t_0 \to t_n}}) - (U_{iki_{t_0}} + \Delta U_{iki_{t_0 \to t_n}})$$
$$= 0.$$

Since the multilateral calculations reduce to zero, it follows that regardless of risk or uncertainty, all decision rules in conflicts involving a nonaligned initiator and a nonaligned opponent reduce to the value of $E(U_i)_b$ having to be greater than or equal to zero for an actor to satisfy my specified expected utility conditions for the initiation of an international conflict. The expected utility of attacking j—$E(U_i)_b$—as we have seen, is positive only if the probability of gaining is not less than the probability of losing $[P_i \geq (1 - P_i)]$ and is negative only if the probability of gaining is less than the probability of losing $[P_i < (1 - P_i)]$. While some nations in the set k may actually prefer one nonaligned state to another, there is no way for the decision makers in the nonaligned states to anticipate such preferences or to calculate their magnitude. Therefore, no nation in k can affect the expected-utility calculation of a leader of a nonaligned state that is thinking of attacking another nonaligned state, so that the overall utility of attacking depends entirely on the attacking nation's probability of gaining when it is unassisted. This leads to the first proposition derived from the theory.

PROPOSITION 1: *Nonaligned states cannot rationally attack more powerful nonaligned states.*

This proposition has two important empirical implications. A nonaligned state fighting another nonaligned state should expect the war to remain bilateral, since other countries have no expressed interest in the outcome. A nonaligned country also should expect to benefit from the war only if it is stronger than its adversary.

Wars between Aligned and Nonaligned States

What expectations should a nonaligned state have if it is facing an adversary that not only is more powerful but also has revealed its preferences about the interests of other states? Since a nonaligned nation could not expect to benefit against a single, stronger nonaligned state, it seems reasonable to believe that a nonaligned state cannot benefit from attacking a stronger adversary that, in addition, can be expected to derive support from some other states. Surprisingly, this is not necessarily true. When a government reveals its policy preferences, it not only gains support but also alienates the governments of some other nations.

Suppose that some people in nation L (from figure 3.1) are eager to launch a war against nation I. Should L's leader veto such a policy? No nations are especially friendly toward L (that is, there are no k_1 or k_3 nations), and some nations are quite friendly toward I (J and K, in figure 3.1, are k_2 nations aligned with I and not with L). Upon examining the preferences of those nations not friendly toward either L or I (that is, k_4 and k'_4, k_5 and k'_5 nations), however, L's leader discovers that A, B, C, D, E, F, G, H, and M all prefer L to I. L realizes that none of those nations actually attaches positive value to L, but all are less hostile to I's policies than they are to I's. These represent nations whose leaders fit the adage "my enemies' enemy is my friend"[4] L recognizes that such states each have a net positive value for L as opposed to I and might therefore support L in a war against I. The greater the disutility any country has for I in comparison with L, the greater the net "positive" utility that nation has for L. If, when it is summed for all states, this utility lends enough support to L for it to overcome the combined resources of I and its allies, then L can rationally attack I.

We may restate and elaborate the expectation of L versus I as the second empirical proposition of the theory.

PROPOSITION 2: *Under some circumstances, a nonaligned state can rationally attack a more powerful adversary, even though the adversary derives support from states that share its preferences.*

4. "My enemies' enemy is my friend" is equivalent, in terms of my notation, to $U_{iki} < 0$, $U_{ikj} < 0$, and $U_{iki} - U_{ikj} > 0$.

What are the specific circumstances under which a weak nonaligned state can attack a more powerful adversary? As we have just seen, such a capability depends on the expected utility to be derived from those nations that are not overtly friendly toward either the potential attacker or its opponent. When risks and utilities are known, risk-averse leaders do not, according to table 3.1, attack stronger adversaries, even if their overall expected-utility calculation is favorable. Consequently, *risk-averse leaders would not attack stronger aligned adversaries* in the absence of uncertainty. Of course, given uncertainty, risk-averse leaders would also be irrational to launch such a war, since according to equation 7, they treat nations that are not overtly friendly toward them as either indifferent or hostile. Even risk-acceptant actors cannot start a war under conditions of uncertainty if the expectation of benefits depends on the support of type k_4 or k_5 nations, whose net utility for them in comparison with their adversary is positive. This is because under conditions of uncertainty, risk accepters also rule out support from nations that are not overtly friendly. The difference here is that risk-acceptant leaders faced with known probabilities and utilities do consider all potential sources of support, including those not overtly committed to either side. If their calculation (according to equation 6) of expected utility is favorable, risk takers can initiate a war against a stronger, adversary that has revealed its policy preferences and is, therefore, aligned. That is, if

$$\sum_{l=4}^{5} E(U_i)_{k_l} > 0 \text{ and } |\sum_{l=4}^{5} E(U_i)_{k_l}| \geq |E(U_i)_b + \sum_{\substack{2\varepsilon l \\ 4'\varepsilon l \\ 5'\varepsilon l}} E(U_i)_{k_l}|$$

then the nonaligned would-be initiator can rationally initiate a war against the stronger, aligned opponent.

Thus the theory predicts that rational leaders of nonaligned states can never start wars against stronger nonaligned states, but nonaligned states can sometimes start wars against stronger aligned adversaries, even if the adversaries expect additional support. This is truly counterintuitive. Is it historically accurate? We will undertake a thorough empirical examination of proposition 2 in a subsequent chapter, but for now consider an example.

The Crimean War provides a very dramatic example of the second proposition. In the weeks leading up to the war, Russian diplomats attempted to negotiate an agreement with the British over the disposition of the collapsing Ottoman Empire. Although the British had some sympathy for the Russian position, as Russia demanded more concessions, strong anti-Russian sentiments rose in England. Meanwhile, Louis Napoleon had already exacerbated his relations with Russia (which had never been good) by negotiating concessions from Turkey for France. This was the setting in which the Turks declared war on Russia in October 1853. The Ottoman Empire, the "sick man" of Europe, was, of course, much weaker than Russia. Turkey had no commitments from anyone to intercede on its behalf. War with Russia appeared likely to be disastrous. Yet hostile feelings toward Russia stoked the fires of war in France and England. By January 1854, the British and French had sent their fleets to protect the Turks, and two months later Britain and France sealed their preference for a Turkish victory with formal alliances. On March 28, 1854, the British and French declared war on Russia.

Why did Britain and France join forces with Turkey, insuring the defeat of Russia in the Crimean War? The Russians, for their part, went into the war confident of victory, believing that their interests were secured by the treaties and relationships that emerged after the revolutions of 1848. The tsar and his advisers believed that "the new Balance seemed to work exclusively for Russia: the powers of Europe cancelled each other out, and Russia was left with a free hand in the Near East" (Taylor 1971, p. 45). The British, the French, and even the Prussians and Austrians, who presumably "cancelled each other out," all had a common basis for cooperation, or at least acquiescence in the opposition of others to Russian ambitions. As one observer noted, Britain and France "have drawn the sword, not for selfish purposes, but to protect the civilized world against the incursions of a barbarous foe" (Buckle 1873, quoted in Blainey 1973, p. 21). Or as Taylor put it, "The Crimean War was fought . . . against Russia, not in favour of Turkey" (1971, p. 61). All feared that Russia would expand into the Balkans, thus gaining control over the warm water ports that Russia had for so long sought as a matter of policy. Consequently the Austrians and Prussians did nothing to prevent the defeat of Russia, while the British and French actively insured a

Turkish victory, thereby depriving the Russians of those territorial gains that might have threatened British and French interests. Thus Russia's revealed policy preferences, and not support for Turkish claims, brought third parties to Turkey's rescue.

The first two generalizations do more than provide several insights into the circumstances under which nonaligned nations might consider starting wars. Taken together, these propositions demonstrate that a power advantage, by itself, is not essential for a would-be war initiator. This statement directly contradicts the commonly held balance-of-power proposition that war initiators are stronger than their opponents. A rather clear statement of this proposition can, for instance, be found in Kissinger's *White House Years*: "Throughout history the political influence of nations has been roughly correlative to their military power. While states might differ in the moral worth and prestige of their institutions, diplomatic skill could augment but never substitute for military strength. *In the final reckoning weakness has invariably tempted aggression and impotence brings abdication of policy in its train*. . . . The balance of power . . . has in fact been the precondition of peace" (1979, p. 195; italics added). Yet the expected-utility framework suggests that a power advantage is sometimes necessary for a war initiator and sometimes not. Furthermore, these propositions help us understand when such nations cannot rationally initiate wars—and thus suggest strategies that leaders in third states might pursue to prevent a war, as we will see later.

As noted, alignment by itself does not insure an advantage to aligned states. Aligned states can be vulnerable under the rather extreme conditions of proposition 2. Furthermore, aligned states can be vulnerable to nonaligned states if they are weaker than their nonaligned adversaries. This can be true even if the combined power of an aligned state, together with its allies, is greater than the power of the nonaligned foe. For an aligned state to be vulnerable to a stronger nonaligned potential initiator (i), only this condition need hold:

$$E(U_i)_b + \sum_{l=4}^{5} E(U_i)_{k_l} \geq 0 \text{ and } \left| E(U_i)_b + \sum_{l=4}^{5} E(U_i)_{k_l} \right| \geq \left| \sum_{\substack{2\varepsilon l \\ 4'\varepsilon l \\ 5'\varepsilon l}} E(U_i)_{k_l} \right|$$

Of course, since $E(U_i)_b$ for proposition 2 was negative and hence a liability, more states are expected to satisfy the condition just specified than to satisfy the more stringent conditions of proposition 2. Even a risk-averse leader making a decision under conditions of risk rather than uncertainty can satisfy these less stringent conditions.

Despite the situations just described, aligned nations generally are in a strong position to consider waging war against nonaligned states. This is true because aligned nations can usually expect more support than nonaligned countries can. Even under conditions of uncertainty, war is often feasible for aligned states. Nonaligned states can expect no support—though they might ultimately receive some—under conditions of uncertainty. Aligned states with risk-acceptant decision makers can expect support. After all, when confronted by uncertainty they do assess the likely reactions of their supporters and their opponent's allies, as indicated in table 3.1. Since their nonaligned adversary has no allies, by definition, war is feasible if aligned i, together with its allies, can overcome any advantage that its adversary might have in a bilateral war. If the aligned state's leader is risk averse, on the other hand, and uncertainty prevails, aligned i will not depend on the support of its allies, and therefore i can rationally initiate a war against nonaligned j only if i by itself is stronger than j (and, of course, if its overall expected utility is not negative).

Wars between Aligned States

What if i's opponent is a country that, like i, has expressed its preferences and attracted supporters? Then several interesting results can be derived. First, we should recognize that there are three situations in which both i and j may find that there are nations positively disposed toward them (with such nations hereafter referred to as allies):

1. i and j each express distinct preferences so that they have no common international friendships.
2. i and j have the same set of international alignments.
3. i and j have some common and some different friendships.

Turning back to figure 3.1, we can see that B and E in our example are in the first type of situation, B and C are in the second type, and A and D are in the third type. One might expect war to be least likely among allies and most likely among states in different — presumably antagonistic — alliances. Yet this is not logically true. Indeed, in the extremes of very close allies and very hostile states, war is logically possible in at least as many circumstances for the close allies as for the enemies. What is more, nations can have strong incentives for war with their closest allies, under some circumstances even stronger than with their enemies.

Let us assume that i and j are in the first situation, each belonging to separate, exclusive alliances. i can be either stronger or weaker than j. i, together with its allies, can also be either stronger or weaker than j together with its allies. We may speak of the general expectations about category 1 conflicts even without knowing the specific circumstances that exist between i and j, including the physical distance that must be covered between i and j, between j and i's allies, and between i and j's allies, as well as the specific capabilities and utilities of each nation. i's overall expected utility, as noted earlier, depends on i's leader's evaluation of the current value of $E(U_i)_b$ and $\sum_{l=1}^{5} E(U_i)$ for k_l plus his estimate of the likely changes in those values in the near future. As can be seen in figure 3.4, in the limiting case in which i and j have diametrically opposed interests, i probably expects the value of $U_{ii} - U_{ij}$ either to remain at its present level or to improve — it cannot get meaningfully worse.

If i believes there will be no change in relations with j, then the rationality of a war with j depends only on the current value of $E(U_i)_b, \sum_{l=1}^{5} E(U_i)$ for k_l, the presence or absence of uncertainty, and the risk-taking orientation of the leader of i. Future developments are unimportant in the calculation under these circumstances. If the leader of i expects a change in relations with j, however, he probably anticipates an improvement in relations given my assumption of a random walk with bounded utilities. Consequently, $\Delta(U_{ii} - U_{ij})$ over the time t_0 to t_n is negative, indicating a decline in the gains to be expected from an attack against j. After all, i believes j plans some of the policy changes that i desires. When the current value of

FIGURE 3.4. Future Utility Expectations for Friendly, Indifferent, and Hostile States

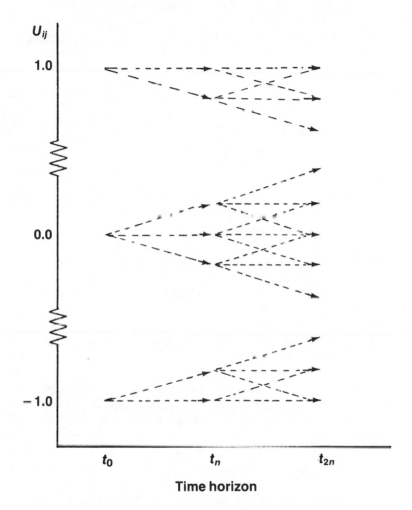

Note. Leaders are assumed to project utility values over the time range t_0 to t_n.

$U_{ii} - U_{ij}$ approaches its maximum (i.e., $U_{ij} = -1$, so that $U_{ii} - U_{ij} = 2$), the opportunity for $\Delta(U_{ii} - U_{ij})$ over the time t_0 to t_n to approach its minimum increases, helping to offset current expected gains. Indeed, anticipated improvements in relations between i and j through such policies as detente, may in the short run be sufficient to countervail current hostilities and preclude conflict.

A variety of circumstances could lead to the expectation that i's utility for j will improve in the near future. The very fact that i's utility for j is about as low as it can get, for instance, might provide i or j with the incentive to use diplomacy in an attempt to resolve some of their differences. Such efforts may or may not be fruitful. If they are not, then i can rationally attack its enemy j only under the circumstances delineated above. If i expects to have more shared interests with j in the future, then i's incentive to start a war with j is reduced. More precisely, as i and j move from being diametrically opposed to being less opposed, i's expected utility from a war with j becomes less positive [with $E(U_i)_b$ moving closer to zero and $E(U_i)$ for k_l moving negatively]. Some of the time, the expected change in utilities resulting from more anticipated common interests between i and j is large enough to change i's positive expected utility into negative expected utility. When i believes relations will improve so much that his expected-utility calculation turns negative, i has no rational basis for attacking j, even though based on their current relationship, i appears to have an incentive for war. Thus unless the leader of i is a warmonger, i would rationally attack his diametric opposite j only if he believed he could realize some additional gains from the war that he could not obtain in the near future through other policies.

Let us assume i and j are allied with each other and are so close that i's utility for j approaches one. What possible incentive might i have for waging a war against j? The answer to this question lies in i's expectations about his future utility for j. *When* $U_{ij} = 1$, i's *potential gains from a conflict with* j *can only be zero or positive, so that conflict cannot be ruled out.* That is, i's relations with j cannot improve, given my assumption of a random walk with bounded utilities, because they are presently "perfect," but they can stay the same or worsen. Indeed, the more U_{ij} approaches one, the less room remains for meaningful improvements in relations between i and j. If i anticipates a change in leadership in j, or some other factor likely to affect j's foreign policy, it is reasonable for the leader of i to believe that such a change will signal deterioration in relations, possibly enough to give an attack against j positive utility. If i can defeat j before such a change occurs, i may be able to prevent an undesirable shift in j's policies either by coercion after the war, by annexing j, or by imposing a puppet regime. Therefore, if present relations are viewed in light of possible future changes, i may have considerable incentive to keep j in line.

Thucydides, speaking through the ambassadors of the Mytilenaeans, put this clearly when he explained their betrayal of the Athenians, with whom they had an alliance:

> We held them not any longer for faithful leaders. For it was not probable when they had subdued those whom together with us they took into league but that, when they should be able, they would do the like also by the rest. . . . Now the reason why they have left us yet free is no other but that they may have a fair colour to lay upon their domination over the rest and because it hath seemed unto them more expedient to take us by policy than by force. . . . So it was more for fear than love that we remained their confederates; and whomsoever security should first embolden, he was first likely by one means or other to break the league. Now if any man think we did unjustly to revolt upon the expectation of evil intended without staying to be certain whether they would do it or not, he weigheth not the matter aright. For if we were as able to contrive evil against them and again to defer it, as they can against us, being thus equal, what needed us to be at their discretion? But seeing it is in their hands to invade at pleasure, it ought to be in ours to anticipate.
>
> ([1959] 3:10–12)

How are other states likely to react to i's intervention against its own ally? If i and j have followed sufficiently similar policies so that $U_{ij} = U_{ii} = 1$, then the two state's policies are indistinguishable. This means that all other states value i and j equally at present. Without some clear indication from j about its future intentions, most states k

have no basis for anticipating that they will prefer i to j or j to i in the future, thus neutralizing them at present, so that $E(U_i)$ for k_l equals zero. This provides the basis for the third major proposition:

PROPOSITION 3: *If* i *and* j *follow essentially identical policies on all issues of relevance to each other or to others, so that* $U_{ij} = U_{ii}$ *and the multilateral lottery* $E(U_i)$ *for* $k_l = 0$, *then* i's *ability to wage a war against its close friend* j *depends only on* $E(U_i)_b$. *Since the sign of* $E(U_i)_b$ *is determined by the magnitude of* P_i *relative to* $1 - P_i$, $E(U_i)$ *must be greater than or equal to zero if* $P_i \geq 1 - P_i$, $E(U_i)$ *will be zero if no change in* U_{ij} *is anticipated and will be positive if any change is anticipated in* U_{ij}.

One might object by contending that while "outsiders" are neutralized in wars among close allies, other states in i's and j's alliance are not neutralized. This might be true. One could argue that they interpret i's actions against j as a betrayal of the mutual trust and cooperation that the alliance is supposed to convey. If that is true, then i must expect each of the nations allied equally with i and j to act as if they are only truly aligned with j. In such a circumstance, i's calculation would depend upon the assumption that all states jointly allied with i and j are equivalent to k_3' or k_2 nations. In the limiting case, with U_{iki} for i's erstwhile allies assumed to be minus one, while U_{ikj} is assumed to be one, i would have to be powerful enough so that his nation is stronger than the combined capabilities of j and all those who are jointly allied with both i and j. This may be restated as proposition 3'.

PROPOSITION 3': *If* i *believes those jointly allied with* i *and* j *will support* j *against* i, *with all other states assumed to be indifferent, then* i's *ability to wage war against its erstwhile ally* j *depends only on* $(P_i) \geq (1 - P_i)$, *and* $|E(U_i)_b| \geq |$ *the multilateral lottery* $E(U_i)$ *for* $k_l|$, *given that all* k *allied both with* i *and* j *support* j, *and given* i's *beliefs about the future.*

Proposition 3' depicts i as having a very pessimistic outlook. It is at least as reasonable for i to assume that all states k equally aligned with i and j will prefer to see the current, friendly policies of i prevail over the unknown but "deviationist" anticipated future policies of j.

In such a case, i might be able to attack ally j even if j is stronger than i. When this is possible is the subject of proposition 3''.

PROPOSITION 3'': *If* i *believes those jointly allied with* i *and* j *will support* i *against* j, *with all other states assumed to be indifferent* (given $U_{ii} = U_{ij}$), *then* i's *ability to wage war against a stronger* j *depends on* k's *estimate of multilateral* $E(U_i)$ *across all relevant* k_l *being greater than or equal to zero and on that estimate of* $|E(U_i)|$ *for* $k_l| \geq |E(U_i)_b|$, *given that all* k *allied with both* i *and* j *support* i, *and* i's *beliefs about the future.*

When two adversaries go to war, the support to be derived from third parties is crucial in estimating the expected consequences of the war. If two close allies fight each other, the role of third parties is greatly reduced. In the limiting case of two allies who share so many interests that their policies are indistinguishable, even to those allied with both of them, the value of $E(U_i)$ for k_l is most reasonably presumed to be zero.[5] Furthermore, in the limiting case where $U_{ii} = U_{ij}$, the current expected utility of a bilateral war $\lfloor E(U_i)_b \rfloor$ must also be zero. Hence, based on current interests, i is indifferent in a choice between war and peace with its close ally j. One might suggest that the very closeness deprives i of any incentive for waging war against j, thus moving i from indifference to peaceful, continued amicable relations with j. Yet this is not so in many instances.

When nations have diametrically opposed policies, their leaders may envision a future world of some improvement in relations. Indeed, detente is based on this principle. Among the bitterest opponents, short-term change implies improvement in relations.[6]

---

5. When $U_{ii} = U_{ij} = 1$, then each third party must have precisely the same utility for i as for j. To see that this renders i and j indistinguishable for third parties k, substitute U_{iki} for U_{ikj} in the expected-utility equations. Note that $E(U_i)$ for k_l is then always equal to zero.

6. Reference to figure 3.4 should help make clear that the anticipation of improved relations between enemies (which is supposed to provide the motivation for pursuing detente) is self-extinguishing. As U_{ij} moves away from -1 toward 0, it becomes increasingly difficult for i to anticipate future values of U_{ij}. This is so because as U_{ij} approaches zero, the range of responses that i can have to new policies by j increases. The increased range, of course, comes from j's expanded opportunities to do new things to which i will react negatively. Indeed, when the core policies of two states are basically at odds with each other, it is unrealistic to believe that

Yet among the closest allies, change must imply at least some deterioration. It is important to note that it does not matter what specific area the policy change affects. If i and j have identical policy portfolios, then *any* unilateral change on the part of j will be disfavored by i.

Yet, unlike the leader of i, who knows that *any* unilateral change in j's policies is undesirable when $U_{ij} = 1$, third parties have no current basis for choosing sides in a war (Altfeld and Bueno de Mesquita 1979). Focusing on the future does not greatly facilitate third-party expected-utility calculations unless $U_{iki} = U_{ikj} \rightarrow 1$ (or -1). Furthermore, the effect of changes in j's policies on third parties can be for the better or worse. If third parties k do not know what the specific changes in j's policies are likely to be, virtually no third parties can know whether a change in j's policies will improve or harm their relations with j. Only those who are diametrically opposed to i can be confident that any change from i's policies by j will mean an improvement in their relationship with j. Similarly, those fully committed to i and expecting to remain so can anticipate that any change by j will bring them closer to i. For others, closer to indifference in a choice between i and j, j's change may make the third parties closer to or farther from i.

The question still remains whether i must wait for j's policies actually to change or whether it is advantageous for i to act on "the expectation of evil intended." Suppose i is stronger than j. On balance, i may anticipate that either (a) the actual changes in j's policies will bring more third-party support to i than to j or (b) the actual changes in j's policies will bring more third-party support to j than to i. In the former case, i can expect support in a future war with j, but i must also expect to share some of the gains with its supporters (Starr 1972). Since i can win the bilateral war with j now without having to share any gains with others, i has one further incentive to fight its ally j now. If i believes that j's shift in policy will gain more support for j than for i, then i may find that a future war with j will be more costly than one at present, thus further motivating i to wage

---

improvements can occur in more than a limited number of areas. Thus, the amount of room left for further improvement in relations through the active pursuit of detente is limited, making the likelihood that detente will reach a limit of effectiveness a virtual certainty.

the bilateral war that it can win now. Indeed not only can i rationally fight his close ally, but he can gain virtually nothing by waiting. Postponing such a war may only increase the risks for i.

Speculation about the logical circumstances under which allies might fight one another is simple enough, but do such conflicts take place in reality? The answer, of course, is yes. In fact, there have been proportionately more conflicts between allies than between apparent foes during the past century and a half. Let us examine some instances that comply with the argument.

In 1968 relations between the Soviet Union and the People's Republic of China were openly hostile. Within a year they would have a series of dangerous border skirmishes bringing them close to the brink of war. American policies in Vietnam continued to exacerbate Soviet-American relations, and the election of Richard Nixon to the presidency must have greatly concerned the leaders in the Kremlin. Civil unrest in France and other west European countries certainly made relations between the Soviets and the NATO nations to their west less predictable. Yet, while Soviet antagonisms were certainly great toward the Chinese and the Americans, as well as our NATO allies, the Soviet Union intervened in the domestic affairs of one of its own allies with a massive invasion of tanks and infantry. Admittedly Alexander Dubcek was a maverick by Soviet standards. The liberalizations during the 'Prague Spring' represented a significant shift away from Soviet interests, for had Dubcek succeeded in giving communism "a human face," other allies of the Soviet Union might have followed suit, weakening the Soviet position in Europe. Undoubtedly, concern over the possibility of such changes in policies prompted the swift, decisive, harsh actions of the Russians in crushing the Dubcek regime and replacing it with leaders more amenable to Soviet interests, exactly as we would expect in light of proposition 3.

More recently, on Christmas Day, 1979, tens of thousands of Soviet troops invaded Afghanistan, overthrowing the regime of Hafizullah Amin. *Pravda,* just two days earlier, had praised Amin, a hard-line Marxist, and had denied reports of any Soviet intention to place troops in Afghanistan. Amin's principal failing was his inability to quell a Muslim rebellion in Afghanistan, a rebellion that, if successful, would have completely eliminated the Soviet Union's hold on that country. Rather than risk such a fate by continuing to support the unpopular and apparently incompetent Amin, the Russians overthrew his government, executed him, and installed Babrak Karmal as the new chief of state. The Russians presumably expected Karmal to be more compliant with Soviet demands, particularly with regard to strategy for dealing with the Muslim rebellion; in other respects, however, there is little reason to believe that Karmal represented a significant change from Amin. It is difficult to imagine that the Russians would have taken such a bold step as to invade Afghanistan before it became a Soviet client state in 1978. Of course, other states in and out of the area might have had a higher probability of being aroused to intervene if the government being overthrown had not already been a puppet of the Soviet Union.

The Soviet invasions of Czechoslovakia and Afghanistan were not isolated incidents in Soviet relations with its allies. In the post-World War II period, Russian intervention has prevented liberalizations in East Germany, Poland, and Hungary. Yet we should not conclude that such interference in the internal policies of one's allies is limited to the Soviet Union. The United States has also followed this course to keep its allies in line. We have only to recall that Lyndon Johnson sent the marines into the Dominican Republic in 1965, thereby preventing Juan Bosch from returning to power in the Dominican Republic. Bosch, who was a socialist, would presumably have followed a more independent foreign policy than had the Dominican Republic to that time. Rather than tolerate such a breach of American interests in Latin America—especially after having "lost" Cuba a few years before—the United States government intervened in the domestic affairs of our ally.

Military interventions against allies are neither an uncommon, nor a particularly recent, phenomenon. The Seven Weeks' War of 1866, fought by Prussia and Italy against Austria-Hungary and the German Confederation of States, represented Bismarck's boldest action to seize control over the Germanic states and, ultimately, to unify them with Prussia into Germany. To be sure, tensions were very high between Austria-Hungary and Prussia. Even in 1864, when they fought alongside one another during the Second Schleswig-Holstein War, each approached the other with considerable suspicion and foreboding. Yet the Prussians and Austrians shared many common interests and maintained a mutual defense pact. Indeed, if it had not been for Bismarck's desire to alter the status quo between Prussia and its ally Austria-Hungary, there would have been no reason for a war between these two nations. Bismarck, however, was not content to let Austria-Hungary dominate the German states. Thus despite their many common enemies and many common interests, Prussian desires to alter the internal affairs of the Germanic Confederation provoked a war among close allies. Thirteen years later, following the establishment of Prussian hegemony over states that included Hesse Electoral, Hesse Grand Ducal, Saxony, and others, Austria-Hungary and Prussia resumed their mutual defense agreement, which ultimately carried them into World War I as allies.

Geographic Proximity and War

Wars most frequently occur between neighboring nations, perhaps suggesting that proximity breeds contempt. Yet friendly international relations also occur frequently among neighbors. The preceding discussion sheds some light on each of these phenomena, at least in the sense that frequent opportunities for interaction help clarify the utility values that seem to play so crucial a role in war-and-peace decisions. Yet alliances, friendships, and animosities also occur across vast distances. While wars are more common among neighbors than among geographically separated countries, there are enough instances of wars involving distant foes for us to conclude that proximity is not necessary for war. How can the theory help explain the few "long-distance" wars while still accounting for the "neighborhood" wars?

I have assumed that the greater the distance between a nation's seat of power and the place where its power must be brought to bear in a war, the smaller the proportion of its total capabilities that it can expect to use. Further, I have assumed that the rate of decline in power is steeper for less powerful nations than for more powerful states. The magnitude of both $E(U_i)_b$ and $E(U_i)$ for k_l depends on the size of the probability terms in the expected-utility equations. Furthermore, the sign of $E(U_i)_b$ is determined by the relationship of

P_i to $(1 - P_i)$. Since P_i diminishes across the distance from i to j, we should expect that even if i at home is stronger than j at home, beyond some distance i at j is weaker than j at home. This means that despite i's apparent power advantage, i cannot expect to win a bilateral war with j. If i's allies are far from j, their capabilities combined with i's may still be less than j's power at home (or j's power combined with that of its allies). Thus unless i (or i together with its allies) is strong enough to expect to gain from attacking j at j, war for i would be irrational. Since weak states lose power at a faster rate than strong states, we may infer the fourth proposition.

> PROPOSITION 4: *The initiator of a long-distance war is likely to be a very powerful nation (at home), in comparison with its adversary (at its home), or is likely to be allied with one or more very powerful nations. The initiators of long-distance wars (or their allies) are likely to be more powerful, on average, than the initiators of neighborhood wars.*

Proposition 4 is not particularly surprising and certainly seems intuitively reasonable. Yet it also represents a departure from "traditional" explanations of neighborhood wars, with their reliance on cultural or historical arguments. According to proposition 4, the motivation for war between neighbors need not differ from that for war between nonneighboring states to account for the frequency with which each type of war takes place. The loss of power across the distance from i to j simply eliminates long-distance wars as rational possibilities for most actors most of the time.

When wars over great distances are possible, who are the likely targets of attack — strong states or weak states? One might suspect that with the loss of power experienced over vast distances, it makes more sense to consider war against a weak state than against a strong state. Yet in at least one circumstance, this is not true. That circumstance is the subject of the fifth proposition.

> PROPOSITION 5: *When* i *contemplates a war against* j_1 *or* j_2, *both of which are allies, it may be irrational to attack the weaker* j_2 *rather than the stronger* j_1.

Suppose j_2 is relatively close to i, while j_1 is far away. Suppose also that i is stronger than j_1 at j_1 and stronger than j_2 at j_2. If i attacks

j_2, i must fight the combined capabilities of j_2 (which are un-diminished, since j_2 is fighting at home) and j_1 (which are diminished to some degree because j_1 loses some power due to the distance between j_1 and j_2). While i is stronger than either opponent, i may be weaker than the combined capabilities of j_1 and j_2. Now suppose i attacks j_1 instead. j_2, the weakest of the three states, suffers, by assumption, the greatest relative loss in power as a result of distance. j_2 is, therefore, much weaker at j_1 than it was at j_2, while i is only somewhat weaker, and j_2 is only somewhat stronger than it was at j_1. Thus it is possible for i to be more powerful than the combined capabilities of j_1 and j_2 at j_1 even though it was weaker against these same nations when fighting closer to home. The weaker j_2 is, and the greater the distance between j_1 and j_2, the more likely i is to find attacking the stronger ally rational. Indeed, in the limiting case, j_2's effective capabilities would be reduced to zero long before i or j_1 lost their effectiveness. In such a circumstance, i's attack against j_1 would lead to i's having only to fight j_1, with j_2 rendered irrelevant. Yet if i had attacked j_2, i would find the war included j_1 and j_2, thus necessitating i's fighting against their combined resources.

Proposition 5 delineates a rather exceptional circumstance. Still, it appears to be close to the conditions surrounding the Japanese attack against Pearl Harbor. By late 1941, Japan's welfare depended on securing control over the southwestern Pacific. The record of events indicates (Russett 1972) that the Japanese leadership believed the United States would not permit those crucial territories to fall into the hands of Japan without a fight. The attack against Pearl Harbor was understood to be a long shot. Admiral Yamamoto, the architect of the attack, warned the Japanese high command: "In the first six months to a year of war against the U.S. and England I will run wild, and I will show you an uninterrupted succession of victories: I must also tell you that, should the war be prolonged for two or three years, I have no confidence in our ultimate victory" (Wohlstetter 1962, p. 350). The attack depended on Japan's belief that it could reduce the probability of a long war by bypassing the main objective for the moment and attacking the more powerful United States. By doing so, the Japanese hoped to concentrate sufficient effort on the attack at Pearl Harbor to destroy our Pacific fleet and to demoralize the American public, so that by the time we recovered, Japan's true objectives would have been a fait accompli, thereby precluding the necessity of our entering the war. Of course, the plan failed, but it did, in all probability, increase Japan's chances for success. As risky as the decision was, the Japanese believed that it was much riskier to attack the weaker link in the Pacific chain before attacking the stronger link.

Japanese hopes were not completely unreasonable. In addition to knowing the potentially demoralizing consequences of the attack on Pearl Harbor and knowing that preparations for war made in the United States had been woefully inadequate, the Japanese could expect our interests and resources to be divided on two fronts. While Japan might threaten American interests in the Pacific, Germany had already defeated France and still represented a serious threat to Britain, a situation the United States was not likely to ignore. It would even have been reasonable, in this context, for the Japanese to believe that they were a stronger Pacific power than the United States, at least in the short run.

Restriction on Rational Escalation with Positive Expected Utility

The initiation of conflict has been viewed to this point as a decision determined solely by the would-be initiator. We have ignored the possibility that the victim can defuse the initiator's war intentions. By allowing the initiator and victim to affect each other's policies during the period of conflict preceding outright war, we can see how a would-be victim can deter an initiator from escalating the conflict, even though the initiator has positive expected utility. The victim can deter the initiator if the initiator appears to anticipate gaining less than the victim anticipates losing. In such a case, the victim concedes to the initiator whatever gains the victim believes will satisfy the initiator's expectations, thus resolving the dispute through diplomacy and averting war. To understand this circumstance, let us briefly consider the potential victim's expected-utility calculation.

Each actor is capable of calculating the expected consequences of war. As we have seen, when that calculation indicates that the war will produce an expected net loss, it is irrational to start a war. Similarly, when a victim perceives the calculation to indicate that one is likely to suffer large losses from the war, it may pay to capitulate to the opponent's demands before armed conflict breaks out.

If the aggressor and the opponent experience different levels of uncertainty or have different orientations toward risk, it is possible for the initiator's estimate of his expected gain to be very different from the victim's estimate of his own expected loss (or the victim's estimate of the initiator's likely gain). When the victim believes he must lose less (or gain more) than the initiator believes the victim must lose, it is unlikely that their conflict will be settled without resort to a mechanism — such as war — that clearly reveals the price each side must pay or the profit that either side is entitled to. But when the intended victim believes that the would-be attacker will derive a larger profit from the war than the aggressor believes will be gained, there is a strong basis for settling the dispute without a war. The victim, expecting to pay a relatively high price by fighting, is in a position to offer the potential initiator all that he expects to gain from a war (and perhaps even more), while still leaving the victim better off than he thinks he would be if he fought. In this situation, depicted in figure 3.5, both the would-be aggressor and the would-be victim are better off negotiating a resolution to their dispute than they believe they would be by fighting. This leads to the sixth proposition, which focuses on one condition when a conflict is not expected to escalate into war.

PROPOSITION 6: *If* i*'s positive expected utility from a war with* j *is less than* j*'s expected loss from a war with* i [*so that* $|E(U_i)| - |E(U_j)| < 0$], *both* i *and* j *are better off negotiating than fighting. Consequently, conflict will not rationally be permitted to escalate into war under these circumstances.*

A second proposition about conditions under which conflicts are not expected to escalate into war can be derived from the theory. Suppose $E(U_i) \geq 0$, making the initiation of a conflict by i against j rational. After i initiates a threat or other action short of war against j, suppose some third party k reveals that it is prepared to commit its resources to deterring i from pursuing its objectives against j, and suppose k has the wherewithal to enforce its threat against i (i.e., k's expected utility against i is positive). For this to happen, i must either

FIGURE 3.5.   Condition under Which Conflicts Do Not Escalate
into Wars and Initiators Win

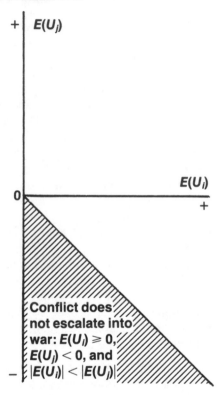

have misperceived the expected contribution of this third party k in
its calculation of $E(U_i)$ for k_i, or this k, consciously or unconsciously,
misrepresented its true preferences, revealing them now only
because of the direct threat to j. In any event, i's rationally initiated
conflict with j has now expanded to include an unacceptable conflict
(for i) with k, creating an incentive for i to back down. This may be
restated as proposition 7.

PROPOSITION 7: i *can be deterred from escalating a conflict
with* j, *even if* $E(U_i) \geq 0$, *provided some third party is willing and
able to threaten* i *with an unacceptable loss in utility. That is,* i *is*

deterred against j *if* $E(U_i) \geq 0$ *against* j, *but* $E(U_i) < 0$ *against the threatening* k *and* $E(U_k) \geq 0$ *against* i.

Proposition 7 describes the conditions of deterrence, including the logic underlying strategic nuclear deterrence. It is interesting to note that the expected-utility theory provides a framework within which we may explain—at least in theory—when deterrence is credible and when it is not, without resorting to the construction of a separate theory of deterrence. Chapter 5 includes a test of the empirical usefulness of this explanation of credible deterrence.

Implications of the Theory Once War Is under Way

Thus far the theory has been discussed in terms of its implications for the initiation or escalation of conflict. Throughout that discussion, emphasis has been placed on the initiator's expectation of gaining as a rational prerequisite for war. By extending this principle of expected gains, it is also possible to derive a few propositions about the outcome and severity of conflicts.

Since both initiators and noninitiators are assumed to be expected-utility calculators, conflicts may rationally begin under any one of three circumstances. The initiator must not expect to suffer a net loss from the conflict. Consequently, his expected utility must be greater than or equal to zero. The victim's expected utility relative to the initiator's might be:

1. negative but less than what the initiator thinks the victim must lose, so that the victim expects the dispute to produce an outcome for his state that is worse than the status quo ante, but not as bad as the outcome demanded by the attacker at the outset;[7]
2. positive but less than that of the initiator;
3. positive and greater than that of the initiator.

7. In his otherwise insightful study of war, Blainey (1973) contends that wars only occur when both sides expect to win. It should be clear that this need not be so. We should expect wars to be fought either because both sides expect to win or because while both sides agree on who the expected winner is, they disagree on the precise nature or cost of an acceptable settlement. Blainey overlooks the latter possibility.

FIGURE 3.6.   Expected-Utility Conditions Affecting the Costliness of War

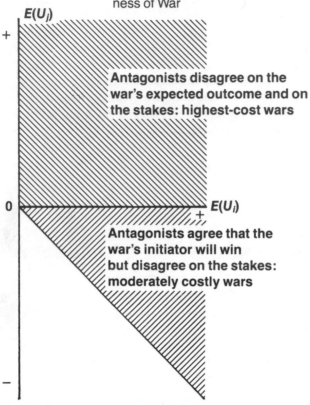

These possibilities are depicted in figure 3.6.

Even in the first circumstance — which is clearly the worst from
the victim's perspective — there must be some benefit to fighting the
adversary. If there were not, the initiator presumably would achieve
its objective through the use of diplomacy, either because it
preferred to or simply because the victim would refuse to fight.
What, then, can a victim who expects to lose gain from fighting?
Presumably such a victim can hope to impose a sufficient cost on the
opponent to reduce the concessions that have to be made at the time
of surrender. It may hope, for instance, to impose enough costs to
prevent the need for a total, unconditional surrender. Yet in fighting

it also imposes a cost on itself. Since the actor is rational, we should expect it to tolerate the cost of fighting only so long as that cost is less than the expected benefits from fighting. Once that point is past it is irrational for a victim whose net expected utility from the war is negative to continue fighting. That is, the principle underlying proposition 6 continues to hold once the war is under way. Combat continues as long as one of the combatants believes it can obtain a better settlement by fighting rather than negotiating.

Wars of the first type—in which the victim expects a decline in utility—differ from the other two types in that both the attacker and the defender agree on who is expected to win. This agreement removes one possible obstacle in the search for a settlement. In these wars the issue is only how much the loser must lose rather than who the loser is to be. As with bargaining in general, it is likely that the greater the difference in perceptions about a fair settlement, the more serious—and hence costly—the dispute will be. Conversely, when the adversaries in a war reach the point where the differences in their expectations about the settlement are small, the conflict should be amenable to resolution at a relatively low cost.

When both sides believe that they will benefit from a war, then differences exist not only as to the amount to be gained or lost but also as to who will win and who will lose. Disagreement about the expected direction of the outcome of the contest may be presumed to increase greatly the cost of the ultimate settlement. When each side believes it will win, the potential for misperceiving setbacks as temporary aberrations is great, hence encouraging intransigence even in the face of losses on the battlefield. Indeed, such setbacks may sometimes be simply aberrations. Surely this was the case for the North Vietnamese during the war in Vietnam, for the North Koreans and Chinese during the Korean War, for the Americans in the Pacific theater of World War II, and for the English, French, and others in the European theater during World Wars I and II.

The preceding discussion suggests two propositions about the course a war takes.

PROPOSITION 8: *When only one side in a war expects to derive positive value from the war, that side will be the initiator and the winner. When both the initiator and its opponent expect to derive positive utility, there will be considerable variation in who wins.*

Generally, the side with the larger positive expected utility—and hence the greater incentive and pool of resources with which to keep on fighting—will win.

PROPOSITION 9: *The greater the difference between what the initiator believes it can gain and what the opponent believes it must lose (including the possibility that the victim believes it can win), the more difficult it is to find a settlement that both sides can accept, and hence the costlier the war.*

The expected-utility model provides a framework from which at least several significant, and several lesser, deductions about the necessary conditions for war have been made. Although the expectations derived from the theory are often counterintuitive, specific historical examples have been suggested to support the propositions. If those examples are found to be consistent with a larger, more systematic body of evidence, then these counterintuitive deductions would appear to provide a useful perspective from which to study conflict-related foreign policy decision making.

In the discussion of general implications, I have directed my attention to those deductions that challenge some commonsense notions about war. Generally, the deductions relate to fairly unusual circumstances. However, we should bear in mind that the theory also produces a number of deductions that are consistent with our intuition about war. For instance, while there are circumstances under which nonaligned states can rationally attack stronger aligned states, the theory also reveals that most of the time nonaligned states cannot attack stronger foes, whether they are aligned or not. The fact that most wars occur under intuitively plausible circumstances and that some do not provides an important basis for evaluating the theory. "Intuitively plausible" wars should be readily explained by the expected-utility theory, but if it is to provide sweeping lawlike generalizations, so should many—if not all—of the "counterintuitive" wars of history. We should expect to find that differences in the expected utility of disputatious dyads should explain which side initiates war-threatening conflicts, which side wins such conflicts, when such rationally initiated conflicts are resolved prior to escalating into open warfare, and at what costs wars are settled.

4 Measuring Expected Utility

To every thing there is a season,
and a time to every purpose under the heaven:
a time to be born, and a time to die;
....
a time to kill, and a time to heal;
a time to break down, and a time to build up;
. . . . .
a time for war, and a time for peace.

—Ecclesiastes

The time for building the logic of war is past. Now I must see if the times for war and the times for peace correspond with the logic that leads some into, and some away from, the war trap. Can the war trap be avoided by the judicious manipulation of its necessary conditions? Is it true that nations "are sunk down in the pit that they made" (Psalms, 9:16), or are they unwittingly ensnared by forces beyond anyone's control? These are no longer questions of logic but rather questions that can be answered only by probing history to see if the expected-utility theory is a vain fiction or a useful portrayal of the election of a policy of war or of peace.

The principal concern in this chapter is to devise some means, albeit imperfect ones, to evaluate the theory's performance. The first problem is to select a set of nations and a period of time that will provide a referent world with which to assess the theory's empirical usefulness. I would most prefer a long time period and a large set of diverse nations, encompassing a history of many wars and other serious conflicts as well as periods of considerable peace. The longer the time span, the more confident we can be that the implications drawn from the analyses are not specifically tied to a particular, or limited, historical context. The more diverse the nations, the greater our confidence can be that whatever implications emerge are not restricted to a particular level of technological development, to a particular form of government, or to a particular linguistic, cultural, or regional portion of the world.

Fortunately, others have compiled sufficient information to make testing the theory possible for an extensive—and rather comprehensive—spatio-temporal domain, including almost all pairs of nations (and therefore virtually every potential interstate war or dispute) in the world for each year from 1816 through 1974. Using such a long time span should help provide confidence in the generality of any results that emerge. However, there is also a cost involved in any effort to analyze events across such a lengthy period of time. Of necessity I will have to restrict myself to broad, general indicators of the concepts embodied in the expected-utility theory. It would be virtually impossible for any individual to develop truly detailed, expert knowledge about the relations between almost every pair of nations for every year of the more than a century and a half that I will investigate. If I could bring to bear the more detailed, specific information that a specialist on a particular case could, the explanations provided by the theory would presumably be more powerful and less error prone than the explanations I will offer. Indeed, in the final chapter I show how more specialized information can be used within the expected-utility framework to forecast and manipulate conflict. Still, I expect that even with the crude indicators and very incomplete knowledge at my disposal, the theory is robust enough to provide provocative insights about war and peace. The reader, however, should be careful to distinguish between the theory and its empirical tests. A test uses only approximations of such concepts as utility, probability, uncertainty, and risk and hence can offer only imprecise approximations of the calculations that might actually be made in reality. The theory, on the other hand, contains precise statements about the process by which a rational, expected-utility-maximizing leader goes about drawing his nation into or away from the war trap.

ONE INTERNATIONAL SYSTEM OR REGIONAL SUBSYSTEMS?

The world may be thought of as comprising one international system, with each nation being potentially the initiator of conflict against each other nation. If such a view is taken, then the "international system" has included more than 560,000 annual nation dyads from 1816 through 1974.[1] That the system was not sufficiently integrated for all pairs to be of interest hardly needs saying. Although on straightforward capability grounds, the Guatemala-Nepal or Nepal-Guatemala dyad is totally uninteresting, it is more significant that with respect to general foreign policy, these nations simply are not particularly attentive to one another. The same may be said for a great many other annual dyads. While the failure of these pairs of nations to wage war with one another or to engage each other in serious disputes is readily explained by the theory, any analysis that heavily emphasizes these uninteresting cases is itself bound to be uninteresting. I have chosen, therefore, to focus my attention initially on a very large—though somewhat smaller—subset of dyads based on a geopolitical division of the world's nations. Instead of examining all nations as if they functioned in a single, integrated, interacting system, I have divided the world into European, Asian, Middle Eastern, all Americas, and African regions. Membership in a region is held by any state physically located in the region and by any state that has taken a sustained and active interest in the affairs of one or more portions of the physical region.[2]

In deciding which nations have taken a sustained and active interest in any given region, I must necessarily make a subjective judgement. Still, I have tried to follow explicit guidelines. In particular, any nation that has controlled or currently controls territory in a region is treated as a part of that region for at least some of the time span I am studying. Spain, Portugal, Britain, France, and Holland, for instance, are treated as members of the all Americas region from 1816 to the present. Of course, their involvement has greatly declined since the nineteenth century. Still, until recently, there were many colonies in Latin America, and currently there are still close ties between each of these states and

1. The coding rules for determining membership in the international system, along with each state's date of entry (or departure), are from Singer and Small (1972). Following their rules, I have brought the data up to date through 1974.
2. I use the regional categorization of Singer and Small (1972) to locate nations in their physical geographic region.

some nations physically located in North, Central, or South America. Russia, too, is viewed as part of the all Americas region in the years since 1945, largely because the Soviet Union's status as a superpower has resulted in its active involvement in the affairs of every portion of the globe. Russia is also viewed as a member of the all Americas region throughout the nineteenth century because of its longstanding ownership of Alaska and other territory.

Outsiders viewed as being in the European region include Turkey, the United States since 1898, Japan from 1895 through 1945, and China since 1950. Turkey, of course, is in many physical respects a European nation as well as a Middle Eastern state. Indeed, long debates were held in Britain's House of Commons during the nineteenth century on the question of Turkish membership in what some balance-of-power theorists have called the European framework (Gulick 1955). American, Japanese, and Chinese interests in the foreign policies of one or more European states are sufficiently obvious not to require further explanation.

I count among the members of the Asian region such outsiders as the colonial powers of Britain, France, Germany, Holland, Spain, and Portugal. Also included are the United States and, of course, Russia/Soviet Union (which is, of course, physically in Asia as well as Europe). Although Austria-Hungary and Italy had some involvement in Asian politics, especially during the Boxer Rebellion, I did not view their concerns as being sufficiently sustained to warrant including them in the Asian region. They were, however, counted as part of the Middle Eastern region (Austria-Hungary until its dissolution in 1918, Italy from 1860 through 1943), as were the British, French, Germans, and Russians throughout the approximately one hundred and sixty years being studied. Also counted in the Middle East are the Spanish from 1816 through 1936, the Americans from 1898 through the present, and the Greeks from the time Greece gained its independence from Turkey to the present. Greece is included because of its sustained extra-European dispute with Turkey, particularly over the Aegean continental shelf and the island of Cyprus.

Included among the members of the African region are the United States (since 1945), Italy (until 1943), Germany (until 1945), Belgium, Portugal, Russia, Britain, France, and China (since 1945).

Although the Netherlands had some interests in Africa, especially in South Africa, they do not appear to have had a sustained, active interest in the international affairs of the region during the period I am studying.

I do not mean to suggest that my categorization of the World into geopolitical regions or my inclusion and exclusion decisions for any region are ideal. Nor do I mean to suggest that other schemes would be less useful or less valid. Indeed, ideally, the expected utility for each dyad should be calculated taking into account the specific circumstances and interests likely to impinge on a potential conflict involving either or both members of the dyad. Such an approach, however, is impractical for a far-ranging study such as this one. If even with the crude indicators and categorizations used here, one finds support for the theory, then more refined tests focused on specific issues or specific nations would be appropriate. For now, I begin with tests on all dyads that fall within the purview of my regional divisions. This includes more than 215,000 annual dyads from 1816 through 1974.

While all the empirical investigations that follow will devolve from the regional division I have just described—with utilities, probabilities, risk orientations, and uncertainty defined within these regions—the analyses will focus on a variety of subsets of the total number of annual nation dyads. Initially I will examine the relative propensity for war or other conflict initiators to come from the subset of dyads with positive expected utility rather than the subset with negative expected utility. However, since many of the more than 215,000 dyads are not especially interesting, I will quickly move to more interesting, and smaller, portions of the dyadic data.[3]

3. Although Britain and France, for instance, are considered members of the European, American, Asian, Middle Eastern, and African regions, I count them (and all other duplicated dyads) only once, generally in the physical region of the state being treated at the moment as the potential opponent in a conflict. Thus Britain versus France (and France versus Britain) is a dyad counted in the European region. Turkey versus Britain, by these rules, is a European dyad, while Britain versus Turkey is a Middle Eastern dyad. If the potential opponent is from a region different from that of the potential initiator, and the initiator is not considered part of the opponent's region, then the dyad is counted in the region of the potential initiator. Britain versus Thailand and Thailand versus Britain, for instance, would both be

98 MEASURING EXPECTED UTILITY

DEPENDENT VARIABLES: WHAT DO I HOPE TO EXPLAIN?

Although hardly a year passes without war or a war-threatening conflict between some nations, when such situations are viewed in terms of the number of dyads in conflict relative to the number that might be, they can be seen to be rather rare events. For instance, interstate wars (as defined by Singer and Small 1972) have included—counting initiators, victims, and other combatants—only a little more than 1,200 annual dyads, or about 5.6 dyads out of every 1,000 regional dyads. If our attention is drawn only to the initiator-victim dyad(s) for each interstate war, then only 79 dyads of more than 215,000 regional dyads are warring pairs. While the proportion of those warring pairs that have positive expected utility to the proportion with negative utility is of concern, it will be more interesting to examine the warring pairs in the context of those dyads that were involved in serious disputes, and such disputes will be of interest in their own right.

Unfortunately, there is not, to my knowledge, a systematic compilation of all serious disputes for the period I am investigating. However, Gochman (1975) has compiled a list of all serious disputes between 1816 and 1970 that involved at least one major power.[4] He categorized such disputes according to whether they involved a threat of military action or an actual military intervention, including interventions that involved fighting, though at a low enough level so that they did not satisfy the Singer and Small (1972) criteria for interstate wars. Gochman considers interventions and fighting to be at the same level of conflict, regarding threats as a lower level of conflict. Wars, of course, are the most intense form of interstate dispute. Gochman defines interstate interventions as "hostilities between armed forces involving at least one member of the interstate

---

considered Asian dyads. Conflicts are treated as taking place in the geopolitical region where they were initiated whenever this is unambiguous.

4. The major powers are Britain and France from 1816 to the present, Russia/USSR from 1816 to 1917 and from 1922 to the present, Prussia/Germany from 1816 to 1918 and from 1925 to 1945, Austria-Hungary from 1816 to 1918, Italy from 1860 to 1943, Japan from 1895 to 1945, the United States from 1898 to the present, and China from 1950 to the present.

system on each side, or hostilities between the armed forces of a member state directed against the territory and people of another member state" (1975, p.A-5). He defines an interstate threat as an "explicit verbal statement by a high official on behalf of a member state's government declaring an intent to use military force against another member state for other than strictly defensive purposes; or, overt mobilization of armed forces by a member state, during periods of dispute or high tension, clearly directed against another member state for other than strictly defensive purposes" (ibid.).

Gochman's compilation, which includes several hundred dyadic interactions, also includes brief summaries of each event (along with sources) that make it possible to designate the initiator — defined to mean the state that took the first overt action (and not necessarily the state that aggressively started the dispute) — and opponent in each dispute. In most instances, it is also possible to identify the winner and loser in the disputes. For interstate wars I use the categorization of winners and losers devised by Singer and Small and also their categorization of initiators and opponents, as determined by the state that first engaged in sustained combat on the opponent's territory (or territory legitimately occupied by the opponent). I utilize this coding scheme for initiator and victim with the understanding that "initiator" should not be equated with "aggressor"; rather, it designates the state that, using the precedence of tort law, had the last reasonable chance to avert the interstate collision represented by combat.[5]

5. I use the coding rules of Singer and Small (1972) to identify initiators and opponents in the vast majority of cases. In a few instances, my reading of history leads me to disagree with their decisions and to recode some cases.

They code no one as the initiator of the 1827 war at Navarino Bay. I consider Britain, France, and Russia the initiators, since they deployed a joint fleet within Turkey's Navarino Bay, thereby using their military might to prevent the Turks from having free entry into their own harbor.

I disagree with the decision of Singer and Small to categorize France as one of the initial opponents in the war of Italian unification. Austria-Hungary attacked Italy on April 29, 1859. France was not part of the war until four days later. Consequently, I view France as a third party, rather than an initial belligerent. Altfeld and I (1979) have proposed and tested an expected-utility model intended to account for the decisions of third parties to remain neutral or to join one side or the other in ongoing wars. That model worked quite well, and I refer to that study readers who are interested in late entrants into wars.

Singer and Small classify Austria-Hungary as the initiator of World War I, with which I agree, and they classify England and allies as the opponents. I label only Serbia/Yugoslavia as the opponent. Austria did not initiate combat against any other states at the outset. Russian troops engaged Austrian troops because of the Russian third-party decision to aid the Serbians. While Germany declared war on Russia, the Russians initiated the first combat between their army and the Germans. France's declaration of war was a response to the Russo-German situation, which itself was a response to the Austro-Serbian conflict. England's entry into the war, in turn, was a response to the already unfolding conflict. Indeed, only Austria and Serbia were at war on July 29, 1914, the first day of fighting. Germany and Russia did not enter the war until August 1, France not until August 3, and Britain not until August 5. These entries are more appropriately viewed as third-party decisions to join an ongoing war. As already noted, I have investigated such decisions elsewhere.

Singer and Small label Germany as the initiator of the Second World War but unfortunately classify England and allies as the opponent. When Hitler's armies invaded Poland on September 1, 1939, no other nation was attacked, nor was any other nation at war with Germany. Indeed, we know that Hitler hoped that the attack on Poland would not prompt Britain (or France) to declare war on Germany. The decision by Britain and France to enter the war on September 3, 1939, as well as the decisions in numerous other capitals, was prompted by the German initiation of war against Poland. Those decisions represent third-party choices, thus making those states not among the initial opponents for my purposes. Even such countries as Belgium and Holland, whose entry into the war was forced by German invasions, were brought in at that time largely as a result of the German strategic reaction to the expansion of conflict that resulted from their invasion of Poland.

Besides the few cases where I disagree with the initiator-opponent decisions of Singer and Small, there are several wars that extend beyond the time period they studied for which initiators and opponents had to be identified. These include the civil war in Yemen from 1962 to 1967, which was an interstate war initiated by the Egyptians against the Royalist Yemenis (whom the Egyptians helped oust from power) and the Saudi Arabians; the Vietnam War, whose interstate war phase began with the American's sustained bombing of North Vietnam, beginning in February 1965. Although North Vietnamese may have participated in the civil war phase in the south from an earlier time, even American statements from that period support the contention that there were not large numbers of North Vietnamese regulars fighting in the south before 1965. Consequently, I code the United States and South Vietnam as the initiators. Israel, of course, initiated the Six-Day War against Egypt, Syria, and Jordan in 1967, El Salvador initiated the Football War of 1969, India initiated the interstate war aspect of the Bangladesh war of 1971. Although the record shows that Pakistani aircraft attacked Indian airfields, it appears that sustained Indian incursions into Pakistani territory preceded those raids. Egypt and Syria were the initiators of the October 1973 war against Israel, while Turkey, of course, initiated the 1974 invasion of Cyprus.

Gochman's list of disputes includes numerous major-power interventions in civil wars. Since I have currently no way to measure the utility terms for insurrectionist groups within a state, I exclude these disputes and all strictly civil war cases in general from my analyses. The theory, of course, should be able to clarify aspects of civil wars as well as interstate wars, and so the reader should not confuse this limitation of data with a weakness inherent in the theory. In the final chapter I give examples of applications of the theory to internal, as well as external, conflicts. After eliminating the civil war–related dyads, Gochman's compilation provides me with 175 serious dyadic disputes short of war for which I have sufficient data to make expected-utility estimates. Using the coding rules of Singer and Small and extending their data through 1974 gives me 79 interstate war initiations, for which I have sufficient data to test my theory on all but 3.[6] The appendix contains a list of the threats, interventions, and wars used in my analyses, along with relevant information about each case. In the analyses that follow, these disputes will be examined in much the same way as the dyadic war data. I will try to determine if there are systematic expected-utility differences between the initiators of such disputes and their victims.

A final data set against which the theory is examined is the list of deterrence situations identified by Russett in "The Calculus of Deterrence" (1963). In examining his seventeen cases in which a major power threatened a lesser state—called a "pawn" by Russett—only to find another major power publicly offering to defend the pawn, I will try to determine whether the expected-utility theory is able to shed light on the tendency for some such crises to end with successful deterrence, while others do not.

THE INDEPENDENT VARIABLES: OPERATIONALIZING EXPECTED UTILITY

Measuring Probability

The expected-utility equations delineated in chapter 3 contain six different probability terms. These are the probability of gaining

---

6. I have insufficient data regarding capabilities for some members of the Asian or American regions to calculate expected-utility scores for the Pacific War of 1879 (Chile versus Bolivia), the Sino-French War of 1884, and the Sino-Japanese War of 1894.

or losing in a bilateral war (i.e., P_i and $1 - P_i$), the probability of gaining or losing with the aid of friendly nations (P_{ik} and $1 - P_{ik}$), and the probability of gaining or losing when opposed by nations friendly toward one's adversary ($1 - P_{jk}$ and P_{jk}). Each of these is operationalized using the composite national capabilities scores developed by the Correlates of War project.

Many measures of national capabilities have been suggested or used in the literature, with most such measures attempting to capture similar attributes of power. These attributes generally include indicators of military capabilities or potential, economic or industrial capacity, and national size or human resources. Those who have attempted to define these aspects of national capabilities include such diverse students of international conflict as Organski (1968), Fucks (1965), Midlarsky (1975), Singer, Bremer, and Stuckey (1972), and many others. Such an approach, of course, focuses on the resources potentially available to a nation and not on such less tangible factors as the willingness of a people to suffer (Rosen 1972), the motivation of a government to keep to its objectives (George, Hall, and Simons 1971), or the capacity of a government to convert potential resources into mobilized, available support for its policies (Organski, Lamborn, and Bueno de Mesquita 1973; Organski and Kugler 1980). While these less tangible factors are important—and any indicator that ignores them is necessarily crude and incomplete—it is all but impossible to obtain reliable estimates of nontangible elements of national power for more than a handful of nations or for more than a small number of years. Consequently I have decided to rely on the national composite capabilities scores developed by the Correlates of War project. Of the many possible indicators, this is the only one that is both readily available for almost every nation across the entire time span encompassed by this study and carefully coded and precisely documented.

These data reflect three theoretically distinct dimensions of national capabilities: military, industrial, and demographic. Each dimension is composed of component resources contributing to national capabilities. The military dimension, which includes the number of military personnel and the military expenditures for each sovereign member of the interstate system, reflects the "war readiness" of a nation. This index is measured as a proportion to reflect each nation's share of the total military capabilities in the interstate system. The industrial dimension, which consists of each nation's share of the interstate system's production of pig iron (pre–1900) or ingot steel (from 1900 on) and its share of the system's industrial fuel consumption, reflects the potential a nation has to increase its power and support its troops. The third dimension, which reflects each nation's share of the system's total population and urban population, indicates the potential each nation has to augment its power by drawing on its civilian population during a potentially protracted war. The three dimensions are combined into a single proportion—the composite-capability index—for each nation. This is done by adding the three dimensions and taking the mean proportion. This indicator of national power, which has been widely used in research on war (Singer, Bremer, Stuckey 1972; Wallace 1972; Bueno de Mesquita 1975; Gochman 1975; Altfeld and Bueno de Mesquita 1979; Ray 1979) is available for every fifth year from 1816 through 1970.[7]

The composite-capabilities index for each nation provides the basic building block from which I construct the probability estimates required for an empirical investigation of the expected-utility theory. Before explaining how these scores are combined to yield estimates of the probable outcome of a war, however, I must digress to explain how the composite capabilities of a nation are adjusted to reflect the impact of distance.

In chapter 2 I explained that an adjustment in national capabilities to reflect the debilitating impact of distance must reflect three considerations. First, a nation's power must decline monotonically with distance. (At least, its conventional power must. Nuclear missiles, if anything, are a more powerful source of power far from home than they are close to home because of the potentially lethal effects of radioactive fallout.) Second, the rate at which that

---

7. There are a few exceptions to the generalization that the composite-capabilities data are observed every five years. Data are not available for 1915, 1940, or 1945, and 1913, 1938, and 1946 data have been substituted for those years. Also, for a few mostly Latin American countries, I do not have complete composite-capabilities data for the nineteenth century. Generally, I did have data on at least one military, one demographic, and one industrial indicator for those countries, and so I estimated their composite capabilities from the information I did have.

decline occurs must be greater, the weaker the nation is at home. Third, the rate of decline must itself decline with major advances in technology. Boulding's suggested indicator of a nation's "loss-of-strength gradient" reflects most of these qualities. He suggests adjusting a nation's power by the number of support personnel required to maintain a combat soldier across varying distances from home (Boulding 1963). While an indicator of that sort would be quite acceptable, the necessary data are unfortunately not available. I have therefore devised an alternative indicator.

When I say that technology (or basic national power) affects the transferability of a nation's power over distance, I do not particularly mean that some people can travel a certain number of miles, while others cannot. Instead, I mean that certain nations can transfer and support some of their power, even though the lines of supply and command are stretched across several days' travel time, while others can support forces fewer days from their "home base." Consequently my indicator depends on the number of days it takes to transport a major military operation. Using estimates derived from conversations with officers in the armed forces of the United States and corroborated in my reading of military history, I have defined the transport range for the years 1816–1918 to be 250 miles per day. From 1919 through 1945 I define the range as 375 miles per day, while after 1945 it is 500 miles per day. Of course, small airlifts to anywhere in the world can be completed within one day, but major operations involving naval transport require about one day for each 500 miles traveled. It is estimated, for instance, that it would take the United States ten days to launch a full-scale operation in the Middle East, about 5,000–6,000 miles away (Kissinger 1979).

Distances between nations were computed from several sources, including *Distances between Ports* (U.S. Navy 1965), the *Official Airline Guide* (1978), and a variety of atlases. In each case, I attempted to derive the shortest distance between the locus of power of the potential attacker and the closest point of its intended victim. Generally, especially for small nations, that was equivalent to their nearest borders. But for distances between the United States and other nations, and between Russia (pre–1917) or the Soviet Union and other nations, that distance is not necessarily border to border. Until the Spanish-American War, I viewed the locus of American power as being on the Atlantic coast, so that the distance, for instance, between the United States base of national capabilities and the Mexican base of such capabilities in 1846 was approximately the distance from Washington, D.C., to the Mexican border. Today that distance would be zero. In the case of Russia/Soviet Union before World War II, the locus of power was in the area from Moscow to its borders with Europe on the west and from Leningrad to Stalingrad in terms of a north-south axis. Today Soviet conventional power is still concentrated in those areas, but its unconventional power, of course, is global.

By my operational procedure, the distance between nation A and nation B is usually, but not always, the same as the distance from B to A. In 1904, for instance, the distance between Japan and Russia was merely the distance from the Japanese coast to Port Arthur (about six hundred miles, or 2.4 days' journey by sea), but the distance from Russia to Japan was the distance from Moscow to the Japanese coast (or nearly five thousand miles by the most direct route). The obvious scene for a Japanese attack against Russia would be in Asia, while a Russian attack on Japan would (and did) require a trip of thousands of miles. Similarly, the distance from Japan to the target at Pearl Harbor in 1941 was about one thousand miles less than the distance from the American West Coast to our eventual targets on the main islands of Japan. Because the distance from some country A and some other country B need not be the same as the distance from B to A, A versus B is one dyad, and B versus A is a separate dyad involving potentially different values in the expected-utility calculations.

Once the distance from each place to each other place was ascertained, national capabilities were computed in the following manner:

Adjusted Capabilities
$$= Composite\ Capabilities^{\log[(miles/miles\,per\,day) + (10 - e)]}$$

with the number of miles per day varying as indicated earlier. The selection of the particular exponent requires further explanation.

By exponentiating the home composite-capability score of a nation (which, it will be recalled, is defined as a proportion of 1.00) by its logarithm, I compel the power of the nation in question to decline monotonically across all the relevant distances.[8] Because the composite-capability scores are a proportion, the mathematical specification of the decline in adjusted capabilities as a function of the logarithm to the base ten would not begin until the target of attack was more than ten days distance from the home base of the attacker. Yet intuitively I expect the decline to begin sooner.

Two solutions to this problem came to mind. One was to use the natural logarithm rather than the logarithm from the base ten. The natural logarithm, as an exponent, would begin to produce a decline in national capabilities once the distance between adversaries exceeded e (that is, 2.71828...) days, with the adjusted capabilities held equal to the unadjusted composite-capability score for distances that required fewer than e days' travel. While such a range for undiminished capabilities seems reasonable to me, the natural logarithm has the disadvantage that it leads to what appears to be a too rapid and sharp decline in national capabilities — so rapid that, for instance, Russia's adjusted capability score against Japan in 1905 would be about .004, when Russia began with a regional unadjusted capability score of .136. I resolved this difficulty by preserving the range of unlost capabilities implied by the natural logarithm while using the less steep decay function produced by the logarithm to the base ten. This was accomplished by shifting the number-of-days computation by adding ten (the minimal distance required before the logarithm is at least 1.00) and subtracting e so that the adjusted score allows e days' worth of distance within which a nation's power is undecayed. Using this function, Russia's power against Japan diminishes from .136 to about .065 in 1905, while Japan's score is about .061. That result much more closely approximates the view one would have of the Russo-Japanese War from the literature of diplomatic history. By using the particular decay function I have chosen, the smaller the base value being exponentiated, the more quickly the adjusted value approaches zero, thus satisfying my requirement that weaker nations decline more rapidly than more powerful nations. Finally, using this loss-of-strength gradient means

8. Because the analyses are regional, all composite-capabilities scores are transformed so that the sum of these scores (before adjusting for distance) in each region each year is 1.00. This is simply done by summing the composite capabilities of each nation active in a region and then dividing each nation's score by that sum.

that I assume a nation's power to be undiminished within a radius of 680 miles throughout the period from 1816 through 1918. By 1919 that radius has increased to 1,020 miles, and by 1945 it has risen to 1,360 miles. This clearly reflects the notion of a "shrinking" world embodied in common wisdom and in my earlier discussion of the impact of changing technology. Table 4.1 depicts the impact of my approach to distance on a sample of at-home national composite-capability scores.

The loss-of-strength gradient I have constructed is ad hoc and admittedly crude. While it does comply with all of the characteristics I required of such a gradient, one should recognize that many other plausible ways of constructing such an indicator might have been used (Altfeld 1979). In the absence of any compelling logic that would dictate the precise form of such a gradient, I have settled on this particular one. Its strengths include the fact that it does comply with the theoretical expectations for such an indicator and it can tolerate considerable amounts of errors in estimating exact mileage across very large distances. Thus once one is contemplating a war several thousand miles from one's home base, an error of even several hundred miles will not appreciably alter the value of log(miles/miles per day). In my judgment, this is a strength because (a) it must be very difficult for anyone to estimate his precise capabilities several thousand miles from home and (b) there is no obvious way to

TABLE 4.1. Adjusted Capabilities by Distance in Days

Unadjusted capabilities	Days						
	2	3	5	8	12	17	25
.01	.01	.009	.007	.004	.003	.002	.001
.03	.03	.029	.022	.016	.011	.008	.005
.05	.05	.048	.038	.029	.021	.016	.011
.10	.10	.097	.081	.065	.052	.041	.031
.15	.15	.147	.127	.106	.087	.072	.057
.20	.20	.196	.173	.149	.126	.108	.088
.25	.25	.246	.221	.194	.168	.147	.123
.30	.30	.296	.269	.240	.213	.189	.163
.35	.35	.346	.319	.288	.259	.234	.205
.40	.40	.396	.369	.338	.308	.281	.251

estimate the most likely route between two points (since that would depend on a variety of factors, including the weather, relations with any intervening states, and so on), but the most direct route can be determined, which neccessarily entails a marginal error. Consequently, I sought an indicator that was sensitive, but not overly sensitive, to distance. My principal concern was simply to capture the general impact of the distance, large or small, without striving for all of the nuances involved in losing power over distance.

Having explained the adjustment for distance, I can now return to the question of how the probability terms of the expected-utility theory are operationalized. Denoting adjusted composite capabilities for nation i at j as cap_{ij}, for i at home as cap_{ii}, for nation j at i as cap_{ji} and j at home as cap_{jj}, P_i and $(1 - P_i)$ are defined as follows:

$$P_i = cap_{ij}/(cap_{ij} + cap_{jj})$$
$$1 - P_i = 1 - [cap_{ij}/(cap_{ij} + cap_{jj})]$$

The terms involving third-party nations require a brief discussion before we turn to their operationalization. While it is apparent that the capabilities of i (or j) in a bilateral contest must simply reflect i's need to transport its power over the distance from i to j, whereas j's power is simply its defensive "home base" composite capabilities, to which area must third parties transport their power? I assume that each third party projects its power to either i or j, depending on where it is stronger. Those supporting i can do so either by joining in the attack against j or by aiding in the replacement and enhancement of resources at i's home base. The particular strategy of support chosen by those k favoring i will presumably depend on where they can have the greatest impact. Similarly, those third parties favoring j over i can aid j either by joining in j's home defense against i (and other third parties) or by carrying the pressures of the war directly to i's territory. Again, the particular strategy that is chosen is assumed to depend on where k believes it is strongest.

P_{ik}, $(1 - P_{ik})$, P_{jk}, and $(1 - P_{jk})$ can now be operationalized as:

$$P_{ik} = [cap_{ij} + (cap_{kj} \text{ or } cap_{ki})] \div [cap_{ij} + (cap_{kj} \text{ or } cap_{ki}) + cap_{jj}]$$
$$1 - P_{ik} = 1 - [cap_{ij} + (cap_{kj} \text{ or } cap_{ki})]$$
$$\div [cap_{ij} + (cap_{kj} \text{ or } cap_{ki}) + cap_{jj}]$$

$$P_{jk} = [cap_{ji} + (cap_{ki} \text{ or } cap_{kj})] \div [cap_{ji} + (cap_{ki} \text{ or } cap_{kj}) + cap_{ii}]$$
$$1 - P_{jk} = 1 - [cap_{ji} + (cap_{ki} \text{ or } cap_{kj})]$$
$$\div [cap_{ji} + (cap_{ki} \text{ or } cap_{kj}) + cap_{ii}]$$

with the choices resolved by using the larger value.

Measurement of Utility Values

The indicator(s) of utility must capture the congruence of interests between nations i and j, i and k, and j and k. The congruence of interests among states may be reflected by the general similarity of their behavior across a variety of dimensions. To assess the utility one state's leader has for the foreign policies of another state's leader, one might focus on (a) the similarities and dissimilarities in the United Nations voting records of each pair of nations (Alker 1964; Alker and Russett 1965); (b) the similarity or dissimilarity in each pair of nations' memberships in intergovernmental organizations (Wallace and Singer 1970); (c) the degree to which pairs of nations interact with each other economically (Lenin 1933; Savage and Deutsch 1960; Alker and Puchala 1968); (d) the similarities and dissimilarities in the alliance commitments of each pair of nations (Singer and Small 1968; Haas 1970; Wallace 1973; Bueno de Mesquita 1975; Altfeld and Bueno de Mesquita 1979); and so on.

The selection of an indicator to reflect the utility one nation has for another will, of course, greatly influence the results of the analyses that follow. It is important, therefore, to be aware of the advantages and disadvantages of each potential dimension. Ideally, the dimension used to indicate national utilities should (a) be sensitive to subtle changes in foreign policies; (b) be responsive to more than the direct one-on-one interactions between pairs of nations; and (c) be closely related to the array of foreign policy interests likely to influence a nation's decisions pertaining to initiating a war or serious dispute or to maintaining peace. Furthermore, the dimension used to indicate national utilities should (d) be comparable across nations and across time; (e) be based on data that are readily available for the full period from 1816 through 1974 (and beyond); and (f) be readily applied to the full set of nations that comprise my spatial domain.

Voting behavior, whether it is in the United Nations, the League of Nations, or any other international body, is inadequate for two reasons. First, most voting in such bodies only occasionally pertains to decisions regarding the initiation of war. More often, votes that do pertain to war or conflict reflect national policies concerning disputes that have already begun. While policies about conflicts that are already under way are important, they are not the primary concern of the expected-utility theory. What is more, no such international voting body has existed long enough to make possible a test with a sufficiently historical perspective to merit serious consideration.

Data on memberships in intergovernmental organizations exist for a large number of nations across a rather lengthy period (Wallace and Singer 1970). Membership in such organizations, however, is not particularly sensitive to subtle shifts in foreign policies, particularly as those policies pertain to impending wars. Instead, many intergovernmental organizations are concerned with highly specialized subjects, such as the protection of endangered species or the cooperative dissemination of scientific information. Only since the end of World War II has the bulk of intergovernmental organizations been concerned with major international economic and military cleavages. Not surprisingly, the military cleavages are represented primarily by military alliances. Such alliances of course comprise one of the dimensions proposed above. Thus intergovernmental organizations do not constitute by themselves a fruitful dimension with which to assess nations' utilities for each other's general foreign policies.

Economic interactions, including trade, investments, and so on, represent an important aspect of any nation's foreign policies. Yet unlike alliance membership, other intergovernmental organization memberships, or even voting behavior in international bodies, economic relations are not the sole domain of governments and certainly are not easily attributable to the decisions of a single foreign policy leader. Instead, economic relations represent a mixture of governmental policy and the policies and interests of actors in the private sector. Since the mix of private and governmental control over international economic relations varies greatly from nation to nation, and even within nations across time, economic relations are not likely to serve as a sufficiently comparable indicator across time and space to be useful here. Furthermore, economic relations are not generally sensitive to subtle shifts in foreign policy, though they are sensitive to major changes in such policies (Holsti, North, and Brody 1968). Such measures of economic interactions as the relative acceptance index (Savage and Deutsch 1960) and indicators of economic dependence or interdependence also suffer from a lack of sensitivity to many subtle characteristics of economic interaction. Examining trade flows, for instance, might lead one to conclude that the members of the Organization of Petroleum Exporting Countries (OPEC) are likely to be hostile rather than friendly to one another. After all, they generally compete with one another over the export of a single commodity — oil — while having only minimal trade with each other. Finally, economic indicators, though potentially informative if used with caution, are readily available only for very few pairs of nations. Dyadic trade data, for instance, are not available prior to World War I, even for many of the major powers.

Military alliances satisfy the requirement that the dimension used for indicating national utilities be sensitive to subtle policy changes, provided that one focuses on more than the simple bilateral relationship between nations. Figure 4.1 depicts four distinct systems. In the first two, nations A and B share a bilateral agreement with each other, while in the latter two, A and B are not directly linked to one another. Despite the fact that A and B are not directly allied to one another in the third system, I think it is reasonable to say that they seem to have more interests in common than do nations A and B in system 1, even though there they do have a bilateral agreement. By focusing only on bilateral agreements rather than on the similarity in the full array of alliance commitments made by pairs of states, one is likely to overlook a variety of subtle signals about shared interests.

Using military alliances as an indicator of national utilities has several merits beyond the potential sensitivity to foreign policy changes. Such alliances are explicit statements about the contingent behavior of one nation toward another in the event of war. As such, they should be particularly reflective of those factors that influence a nation's war-related utility for another nation. Furthermore, with

FIGURE 4.1.   Bilateral Ties and the Harmony of Interests among
               States

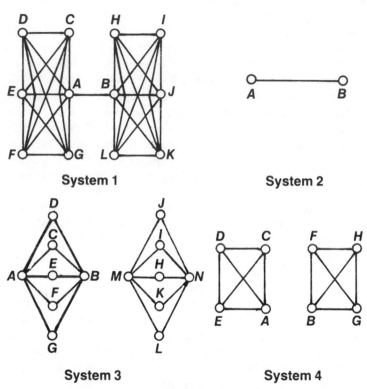

System 1   System 2

System 3   System 4

Note. A solid line indicates an alliance. Nodes are nations.

the application of suitable distinctions between types of alliances,
formal military agreements are both available and fairly comparable for virtually all pairs of nations for the entire time span under
investigation.

The use of formal military agreements as an indicator of national
utilities does suffer from some potential limitations. First, signing an
alliance commitment does not guarantee that one will honor the
agreement under its contingent conditions. However, a surprisingly
large percentage of allied nations have found that their allies do
honor their commitments, even to the extent of declaring war when

the contingent condition arises. In the century and a half after the Napoleonic wars, for instance, 64 percent of the nations that belonged to an alliance and were at war found that at least some of their allies fought alongside them. Only 25 percent of the nonallied nations that were involved in wars were aided by the presence of other combatants on their side. The probability that this difference in percentages occurred by chance is less than one in a thousand. Looking only at those nations that were attacked, thereby excluding war initiators and thus duplicating the principal contingent condition of most alliances, 76 percent of the allied nations received fighting support from some of their allies, while only 17 percent of the nonallied states found anyone fighting alongside them. This relationship would occur by chance less than once in a thousand times, given the number of nations involved. (For the first set of percentages, 137 nations were involved in the analysis; for the second set of percentages, 61 nations were involved.) If the similarity in the overall array of alliance commitments is taken into account, rather than examining the simple bilateral agreements between states, we can account for nearly 99 percent of the decisions to intervene or not intervene in an ongoing war (Altfeld and Bueno de Mesquita 1979), which suggests that military agreements do reflect a great deal about the congruence of interests among states. Alliances, apparently, are not merely pieces of paper torn up at the drop of a hat.

Second, focusing on formal military alliances appears to leave the indicator of national utilities insensitive to important informal links between nations—links forged through common histories, common culture, and so forth. This inadequacy, however, may be more imagined than real. There is no theoretical or empirical assurance that a common culture makes better allies or that different cultures make alliances or mutual interests difficult. To be sure, differences in Hinduism and Islam have been an important source of conflict between India and Pakistan, much as differences between French and English culture or French and Flemish culture are a source of ethnic conflict in Canada and Belgium. Yet the United States and France, the former distinctly not French in culture, have shared a long, almost uninterrupted history of friendly relations, while the United States and Britain, though great friends and close allies today, clashed in 1776 and in 1812 and almost did so during the American Civil War. The Prussians and Austro-Hungarians, though sharing a very similar culture, and with many other similarities as well, have both been close friends and allies (as in World War I) and adversaries (as in the Seven Weeks' War).

Still, many informal links are almost certainly important and yet are not reflected in the signing of a bilateral agreement between states. Yet as the analyses will reveal, almost all such links are reflected in the general similarity of alliance commitments made by states, even when they do not share a direct agreement with one another. Those that are not typify the crudeness that is inevitable in any single indicator of national utilities, but such crudeness is necessitated by my decision to focus on a vast spatio-temporal domain. As with all other indicators in this study, one should not confuse the use of alliances as an indicator symptomatic of utility for the theoretical concept of utility. If one were to focus on a very small number of cases or a very limited time period, as in the final chapter, then additional sensitivity to the subtleties of the actual situation could be achieved.

Because military alliances adequately—but certainly not perfectly—satisfy the requirements I have established for an indicator of national utilities, I use them as the base for the operationalization of all the utility terms in the theory. Following the coding scheme of the Correlates of War project, I distinguish between three types of military alliances. These are (a) defense pacts, in which the signatories agree to come to each other's mutual defense in case any one signatory is attacked; (b) neutrality or nonaggression pacts, in which the signatories agree not to declare war against each other in the event that a third nation declares war against one of them; and (c) ententes, in which the signatories agree to consult each other about possible coordinated action in the event that one of them is attacked by a third party (Singer and Small 1966). Only formal alliances of these types signed at least three months prior to the outbreak of hostilities are included in my analyses. By excluding agreements reached closer to the actual initiation of warfare, I increase the chances that my expected-utility estimates reflect genuine prior planning and not a post hoc recognition of the inevitability of war. Of course, this is a better construction from a theoretical perspective, and it represents a more stringent condition for testing the theory than would using alliances formed in response to the decision to wage war or in response to the recognition that one is about to be attacked.

These three types of alliances, as well as a fourth category indicating no alliance between nations, can be ranked ordinally from the greatest sacrifice of decision-making autonomy to the least sacrifice of such autonomy. I assume that defense pacts represent the most serious loss of autonomy in that they require a declaration of war under the contingent conditions. They deprive their members— at least in principle—of the option of remaining neutral or of choosing the other side. Neutrality or nonaggression pacts require the next greatest sacrifice of autonomy in that they deprive the signatories of the option of joining in the war against the co-signatory while leaving open the question of participating alongside the cosignatory. Ententes require less sacrifice of decision-making autonomy in that they require only consultations between allies while not formally precluding any course of action. The no-alliance condition, of course, requires no loss of autonomy, since there is not even a statement of general support in this case.[9]

The empirical estimation of national utilities from the similarity of alliance commitments requires an additional assumption. I assume that each nation has a defense pact with itself. In behavioral terms this means that each nation is assumed to be prepared to defend itself if it is attacked. In measurement terms this means that a perfect harmony of interests between a pair of nations can occur only if each has the exact same level of commitment with other states as does the other and if they have an agreement to defend one another.

The similarity in the array of commitments that any two nations have with all other nations can be seen by constructing a four-by-four contingency table for each pair of nations each year from 1816 through 1974. The first column depicts all the nations with which the column nation has a defense pact. The second column includes all

9. In future work I hope to obtain greater sensitivity in my utility estimates by including information on diplomatic recognition, on agreements other than formal military alliances, on economic relations and interactions, and on expert estimates of national foreign and domestic policy preference orderings.

TABLE 4.2. Congruence of Interests between the United States
and Soviet Union in Europe, 1956

	USA			
USSR	Defense pact	Non-aggression pact	Entente	No alliances
Defense pact				USR, CZE POL, HUN, RUM, BUL, FIN, ALB, CHN, GDR
Nonaggression pact				
Entente				
No alliances	USA, DEN, UK, FRN, ICE, ITA, LUX, HOL, NOR, POR, GRC, TUR, GFR			SPN, YUG, SWZ, AUS, SWD

Note. $\tau_B = -.694$. ALB = Albania, AUS = Austria, BUL = Bulgaria, CHN = China, CZE = Czechoslovakia, DEN = Denmark, FIN = Finland, FRN = France, GDR = German Democratic Republic, GFR = German Federal Republic, GRC = Greece, HOL = Holland, HUN = Hungary, ICE = Iceland, ITA = Italy, LUX = Luxembourg, NOR = Norway, POL = Poland, POR = Portugal, RUM = Rumania, SPN = Spain, SWD = Sweden, SWZ = Switzerland, TUR = Turkey, UK = United Kingdom, USA = United States, USR = Union of Soviet Socialist Republics, YUG = Yugoslavia.

the states with which the column nation has a neutrality or
nonaggression pact. The third includes only the ententes, while the
fourth column indicates the nations with which the column nation
has no alliance. In the same fashion, the first row indicates all of the
states with which the row nation (that is, the other member of the
dyad) has defense pacts, and so on. Tables 4.2 and 4.3 provide

TABLE 4.3. Congruence of Interests between the United States
and Argentina in the Americas, 1965

Argentina

USA	Defense pact	Non-aggression pact	Entente	No alliances
Defense pact	USA, ARG, BOL, BRA, CHI, COL, COS, DOM, ECU, SAL, GUA, HAI, HON, MEX, NIC, PAN, PAR, PER, URU, VEN			CAN, UK, FRN, HOL, POR
Nonaggression pact				
Entente				
No alliances				CUB, USR, SPN

Note. $\tau_B = .548$. ARG = Argentina, BOL = Bolivia, BRA = Brazil, CAN = Canada, CHI = Chile, COL = Colombia, COS = Costa Rica, CUB = Cuba, DOM = Dominican Republic, ECU = Ecuador, FRN = France, GUA = Guatemala, HAI = Haiti, HOL = Holland, HON = Honduras, MEX = Mexico, NIC = Nicaragua, PAN = Panama, PAR = Paraguay, PER = Peru, POR = Portugal, SAL = El Salvador, SPN = Spain, UK = United Kingdom, URU = Uruguay, USA = United States, USR = Union of Soviet Socialist Republics, VEN = Venezuela.

samples of contingency tables used in the analyses that follow. The commonality of interests—or utilities—indicated by these tables is summarized with Kendall's tau B coefficient. When all of the data fall on the principal diagonal, tau B—or i's utility for j if the row and column nations are i and j, respectively—equals 1.00, and when all the data fall on the opposite diagonal, tau B (and U_{ij}) equals -1.00. All other values in that range, of course, are possible, depending on the distribution of the two nations' alliance commitments. U_{ii} is always 1.00, while U_{ij} is equal to the tau B coefficient for the table that includes i and j. U_{iki} and U_{ikj} are equal to the tau B scores for the table, including i and k and j and k, respectively.

Measuring Uncertainty

The core components of the expected-utility theory — those concerned with probability and utility — have now been operationalized. The particular version of the expected-utility equations that actually is used in computing national expected utilities from war depends on the risk-taking orientation of the relevant leader of the nation in question and on whether or not that leader's decision must be made in the presence of risk or of uncertainty. I turn my attention first to constructing the indicator of uncertainty.

In chapter 2 I noted that the particular type of uncertainty with which I am concerned is uncertainty about the utility one nation has for another. We should recall that the sign of the expected-utility calculation for a bilateral war depends only on the relative magnitude of the probability terms, while the sign of the two calculations concerning the likely behavior of third parties is determined by the relative value of the utility terms U_{iki} and U_{ikj}. The potential initiator of a war or other serious conflict is assumed to be confident about his estimate of his own nation's capabilities and also about the capabilities of his potential adversary. What he may be uncertain about is the likely response of other states to the initiation of a war. It is that uncertainty that I hope to identify and measure.

The dyadic utility scores computed with tau B and described earlier provide a "best estimate" of the congruence of interests between nations as reflected by the similarity of their alliance commitments. Changes in those commitments have the potential to clarify or obscure the level of utility one nation has for another nation's foreign policy. Whether such changes clarify or obscure the expected behavior of potential third parties to wars depends on the context of prior expectations that had been formed. If a set of relations among nations persists unchanged for a long enough time, it should be possible for any decision maker to learn from the actions of states their true level of commitment to one another. If the set of commitments changes in such a way that most relevant relationships are being strengthened by increasing the similarity of relationships, then the leader of i is presumed to become more confident about his ability to estimate the likely behavior of each third party to the war he is contemplating. If commitments are shifting toward a decrease in the harmony of interests, then the decision maker may be more uncertain about the expected behavior of third parties in the event of war. This is especially true when such declines in utility are the result, not of the direct severing of a bilateral agreement between the initiator (or the adversary) and some third party, but rather of changes in the array of interests and commitments of some of the third parties that are not also carried out by the would-be initiator (or his adversary). In such circumstances, the potential initiator is torn between the implications of his (or his adversary's) unaltered bilateral agreement with a third party and the implications of their diverging relations with other states. As suggested in the discussion about figure 2.1 in chapter 2, such divergence is most likely to produce uncertainty by obscuring the precise meaning of the apparent utility shared between i and k or j and k.

Not all changes in relationships seem equally relevant for an indicator of uncertainty. Seemingly most relevant are those relationships for which there was a reasonable prior prospect that the nations in question would act together in the face of an international conflict. The nations most likely to behave in the same — or at least in a similar — fashion are those belonging to the same general international coalition. Decreases in their relationships are likely to alter the fundamental structure of the relevant system of nations (whether that is the entire international system or regional subsystems), creating an international environment fraught with uncertainty. Consequently the measurement of uncertainty requires first that I define a procedure for determining the coalition membership of each nation in the relevant system of nations.

Coalition memberships may be ascertained by referring to the set of pairwise utility calculations that I have already described. A coalition of nations should depict that set of nations — along with suitable indicators of the cohesiveness of the coalition — whose interests are so alike that they represent the primary group to which a member would turn to seek aid against a rival or to acquire security against the possibility of outside aggression. In other words, a coalition consists of that set of nations for whom there is maximal discrimination between their within-group utility scores and their utility scores with all nations outside the group. The coalitions are identified by placing all of the dyadic utility scores in a square matrix representing all possible dyads in the system (or subsystem) for each year. The square matrix is then used to identify the coalition membership of each nation by clustering the dyadic utility scores. Several clustering techniques, including factor analysis (Russett 1968, 1971), typal analysis (McQuitty 1957; Smoker 1968; Bueno de Mesquita 1975, 1978), smallest space analysis (Wallace 1973), and others, might be adopted. I use typal analysis because (a) it keeps between-cluster discriminations as large as possible (that is, it minimizes the congruence of interests among nations in different coalitions); and (b) it is easy and inexpensive to compute. As McQuitty (1957), Smoker (1968), and Lankford (1974) have shown, typal analysis yields results quite similar to those of factor analysis.

The actual computation of the typal analysis is quite simple. The highest utility score (or in other words, the highest Kendall's tau B) in each column of the square matrix is circled, with the highest circled score indicating the dyad that comprises the first two members of the first coalition. The utility scores in the rows for these nations are then examined to see if any other circled utility scores occur with these states. If they do, then the nations represented by those scores are added to the coalition. If, in turn, any of these new members have circled utility scores within their rows, then the nations represented by those additional utility scores are added to the coalition. This procedure continues until all the members of the coalition have been examined and no additional circled utility score falls in any of their rows. Then the highest unclustered but circled utility score is located in the matrix, and the dyad it represents forms the beginning of a new coalition. The earlier procedure is followed until this coalition is completed. The entire procedure is repeated until all the nations in the matrix (and hence all the circled utility scores) have been either associated with a coalition or identified as nonaligned states. Nonalignment is defined operationally by the fact that the nation in question has as its highest utility score a value that is less than or equal to .10. When the circled utility score is .10 or less, the nation is assumed to be unassociated

with any coalition except the coalition of itself. Using these
procedures, joint membership in more than one coalition could
occur only in the unlikely event that a nation has its highest score
with two states each of which has its highest score with a nation in a
different coalition. This is so unlikely that in my analysis of several
hundred thousand annual nation dyads from 1816 through 1974, it
did not occur even once.

Having defined the general coalition structure of the system of
nations under consideration, it is now possible to determine how
changes in that structure signal the presence or absence of uncertainty about the utility that i and j attach to third parties. The
harmony of interests among coalition members may be defined as
the mean dyadic utility score among the coalition members.
Similarly, the overall cohesiveness of the system's coalitions may be
defined as the mean within-coalition utility score, weighted by the
number of within-coalition dyads for each grouping. The formula
below depicts the computation of this overall cohesiveness score,
which I refer to as systemic tightness, or T:

$$T = \frac{\sum\limits_{i=1}^{x} \left(\sum\limits_{a,b \varepsilon i} W_{ab} \right)}{\sum\limits_{i=1}^{x} \left(\frac{(n_i)(n_i - 1)}{2} \right)}$$

with n equal to the number of nations in coalition i, x equal to the
number of coalitions in the system, and W the utility score for each
dyad ab where $a,b \varepsilon i$. As T approaches 1.00, the tightness of the
system's coalitions approaches its maximal value.

As I noted earlier, when the set of common interests remains
unchanged or increases, it is easier for i to discern the likely
behavior of other nations. When the set of common interests in the
regional subsystem decreases, on the other hand, it is harder for i to
anticipate the true set of utilities that each state has for others, and
hence it is more difficult to anticipate the probable behavior of third
parties in the event that i attacks j. This uncertainty may now be
operationalized as the change in the tightness of the system's
coalitions during a two-year period ending in the year when i is
considering attacking j. A two-year interval is chosen because it

seems long enough for meaningful changes to occur, and yet it is short enough so that the leader in i is not likely to have discerned fully all of the implications and meaning of the changed relationships in the system.

When the system's tightness—or the cohesiveness of coalitions—increases or remains unchanged, uncertainty is assumed to be absent, so that decisions are made under conditions of risk, but when the system's tightness declines during a two-year period, culminating in the year in which the expected-utility calculation is being made, then the key leader calculating his nation's utility is alerted to the difficulty inherent in estimating accurately the probable behavior of other states in the event that he chooses to initiate a war against nation j. Having been alerted, the leader's concern may be mitigated or militated by a closer examination of the clarity of commitments among those nations most likely to intervene in the war. These nations, of course, are those in either i's coalition or j's. If i's coalition or j's coalition has declined in cohesiveness (that is, in the average level of commonality of interests) during the preceding two years, then i must be uncertain about the true value of $E(U_i)$ for k_l, and hence calculates i's expected utility against j using the appropriate uncertainty-based expected-utility equation. If neither i's nor j's coalition has declined in tightness, then the general decline in the clarity of commitments in the system is likely to have only a very small effect on i's calculations. Consequently I assume that such situations are treated as if there were no uncertainty.

Measuring Risk Taking

Of all the concepts affecting the expected-utility theory, risk-taking orientations are by far the most difficult to measure. Such concepts as power and uncertainty have attracted so much attention among students of international conflict that a number of indicators have been developed, tested, criticized, modified, retested, and so on. Although these concepts are still measured inadequately, at least we have some notion of the specific shortcomings and merits of each such indicator. The measurement of risk taking in international politics, however, is virtually uncharted territory. Some events-data analysts have tried to incorporate aspects of risk into their indicators of international hostility or tension, but virtually no one has tried to measure the risk-taking orientation of foreign policy decision makers for more than a handful of usually experimental situations. An actor's orientation toward risk is a psychological trait best evaluated through an in-depth examination of the decision maker's personality and environment. Such an analysis, unfortunately, is impossible here. Consequently I must search for clues that are consistent with the symptomatic behavior of a risk averter or a risk accepter. My indicator of risk taking will therefore be several stages removed from a direct measure and so will be crude and error prone. Once again I ask the reader to bear in mind the distinction between the theory and my simplistic operationalization of its components. If it were being applied to a very small number of events, it would be possible to apply more precise means of estimating risk taking.

Since my principal concern is with international conflict it seems that the best place to look for traces of risk-taking orientations is in term of the security or jeopardy implied by a nation's foreign policy. One implication of the general structure of the expected-utility theory is that weak nations, through the judicious formation of alliances, may be able to achieve as much security against foreign aggression as some great powers do. Conversely, some powerful states, despite their inherent strength, may follow foreign policies that leave them vulnerable to attack, perhaps even by nations much weaker than they are. Thus the combination of a nation's own power and the additional power to which it may gain access through direct and indirect alliance commitments sometimes enhances and sometimes reduces its security against outside aggression. If we assume that no leader wants his nation to be vulnerable to attack, we may design an indicator of risk that is tied to the traces left by each nation's policies of alignment and nonalignment.

In principle, any nation may form an alliance with any other nation. Presumably, the only barrier to alignment is that each potential member of an alliance must believe that the pact offers some benefit that would not be obtained without the alliance. For weak states with little power to offer their potential allies, the formation of an alliance with a powerful protector may depend on the weak state's willingness to cooperate in the pursuit of policy objectives of the stronger potential ally. If a weak state is not willing to compromise in ways that can benefit its stronger would-be ally, there is little reason for its leader to believe that the strong state will compromise some of its own interests and risk entanglement in the affairs of the weak state by forming an alliance with it. The success of the German princely states in avoiding acts of agression by nations outside the Germanic Confederacy in the period from 1816 through the unification of Germany in 1870, for instance, is probably due to their protection by the umbrella of the two Germanic major powers, Prussia and Austria-Hungary. Other weak states in nineteenth-century Europe, such as the Papal States, Greece, and The Two Sicilies, were less successful at avoiding outside aggression, at least in part because they failed to place themselves in the protective care of allies. In each state's case, its degree of jeopardy or security can be assessed directly from the results of the expected-utility calculations. I define a state's orientation as being risk acceptant if the state expects to derive positive utility (based on equation 6 from chapter 3) against fewer states than expect to derive positive utility from attacking it. In other words, those nations with foreign policies that leave them vulnerable to more attacks than the number of nations against whom they have achieved a credible level of security are risk acceptant. Conversely, those who have constructed their foreign policy so that fewer nations can credibly threaten to attack them than they can threaten to attack have achieved a fairly high degree of security. Such a posture is what one would expect of a nation following a risk-averse foreign policy. Depending, then, on whether more nations can expect to gain from attacking A than A can expect to gain against, or vice versa, A's risk orientation is assumed to be risk acceptant or risk averse. For states defined as risk averse, the additional computations specified in chapter 3 are then applied to the initial expected-utility calculations, leading to the modified calculations stipulated earlier.

   The risk indicator is especially problematic when applied to the major powers. Many great powers, such as the United States throughout most of this century and Britain throughout most of the nineteenth century, are so powerful that even without any allies they are likely to be secure against outside aggression from most other nations in the regions in which they play an active role.

Consequently, major powers are disproportionately likely to appear to be risk averse with my indicator. Some credible arguments can be made to support this trend. Chung Hsiou Huang (1979), for instance, and others have argued that those with the most to lose tend to behave most cautiously, while those with somewhat less to lose are more willing to take extreme risks. Organski and Kugler (1980) make this argument in the specific context of the initiation of war. Their evidence, however, does not bear out this position. Even a cursory examination of major-power politics suggests that the leadership in these nations, as in all other nations, manifests considerable variation in risk-taking orientations. The American isolationist period can certainly be described as a period of risk aversion when American leaders were not willing to jeopardize our position—buffered, as it was, by the security provided by the Atlantic and Pacific oceans—to enhance the interests of one or another European power. Yet the decades immediately following World War II revealed a United States prepared, even eager, to intervene in conflicts in such faraway places as Asia and the Middle East, as well as in traditional stomping grounds in Latin America. Because the indicator is not sensitive enough when applied to major powers, I am forced to treat all major powers as risk neutral or risk acceptant, applying the decision rules delineated in table 3.1 to all of my estimates of their expected utility.

Nations do not follow a single foreign policy strategy all around the globe. Similarly, they are not likely to manifest the same precise risk orientation within different political contexts, whether those contexts change across time or across space. Of course, the risk indicator can readily vary from year to year for any nation. It can also vary for any one nation across geographic-political regions. Consequently I assume that the senior leader in any country listens to different advisers when making decisions about different areas. Since the information presented to the leader by these advisers is likely to reflect the adviser's own orientation toward risk, and since the leader presumably trusts his advisers, his policies may manifest different risk orientations in the different geopolitical contexts I discussed earlier.

I have now developed indicators of each of the theoretical concepts delineated earlier. These indicators are combined in precisely the same manner as their parent concepts were in the theoretical expected-utility equations. A nation is presumed to expect to gain from initiating a conflict if the estimated expected-utility score resulting from the application of the indicators discussed above is greater than or equal to zero. When a nation's expected-utility score is positive or zero but the nation is risk averse and weaker than its intended opponent, then its expected-utility score is presumed to be negative, as required by the decision rules delineated for risk averters in chapter 3.

With the operational procedures in mind, we may turn our attention briefly to the criteria I will use to evaluate the empirical usefulness of the theory. In chapter 1 I noted that my purpose is to develop a theory of necessary, but not sufficient, conditions for states to initiate serious international disputes, including wars. Because my operational indicators of the theoretical concepts in the expected-utility equations are imprecise, I recognize that it is unlikely that there will be no exceptions to the expectations of the theory. Still, I expect that all tests of the theory will yield results so strong that there can be no question of their substantive significance. As a minimal requirement, each deduction from the theory must be supported by evidence falling in the direction predicted by the theory and (when appropriate) must be statistically significant at least at the .025 level.[10] Furthermore, I expect measures of one-way association (that reflect necessary, but not sufficient, conditions) to be as strong as .70 or more. Results weaker than that, though still potentially of interest, cast doubts on the general explanatory power of the theory.

10. I use significance tests whenever I wish to compare means across two samples created by separating the data according to some theoretically derived treatment effect. I also use significance tests to compare observed distributions to theoretically expected distributions. Finally, I use significance tests as a heuristic device that facilitates comparing results.

5 War and Expected Utility: Analyzing Conflict

I have presented a set of equations—and operational procedures for testing implications derived from those equations—for a theory that purports to make lawlike general statements about the initiation, costliness, and outcome of serious international disputes, including interstate wars. That theory is predicated on the belief that national leaders behave as if they are rational expected-utility maximizers. The broadest—and seemingly obvious— generalization that emerges from the theory is the expectation that wars (or other conflicts) will be initiated only when the initiator believes the war will yield positive expected utility. This simple generalization, based on the notion that people do what they believe is in their best interest, provided the means to deduce several counterintuitive propositions about war. Now I am prepared to turn to the record of history in search of evidence that reveals whether the theory is empirically useful or is merely a trivial exercise in irrelevant logic.

I have and will continue to suggest anecdotal evidence for aspects of the theory, but my central concern now is with a systematic evaluation of the theory in light of all wars fought between 1816 and 1974. While anecdotes and individual case histories often help clarify a difficult point or enliven discussion, they are suspect as evidence because they are specifically selected to make the researcher's point. The same cannot be said fairly of an exploration of all wars, especially when they are all evaluated in precisely the same way, using the same variables and the same operational procedures. Furthermore, no information that could not have been known to the relevant leaders at the time has been used in the analysis of any case. I have made judgments about the rationality or irrationality of any case based not on the subsequent outcome but rather only on information that is relevant to the theory and that was known—or at least knowable—to the principals involved. Moreover, my expected-utility estimates are much cruder and more subject to random error than those that would have been made by national leaders with the much more thorough information they would have had at their disposal.

Unlike national leaders, I possessed information about power derived only from indicators of tangible national capabilities, while they surely knew about such intangibles as the willingness of their people to support a war effort, the quality of their general staffs, the exigencies of climate and terrain, and so on. Such information as might be embodied in secret agreements that they had with other states or that were incorporated in their informal relations with other nations would surely have influenced their calculations about the likely behavior of third parties, yet my indicators of utility rely exclusively on formal, public agreements. The additional information that national leaders must surely have had, if used wisely, could only serve to improve their expected-utility estimates, eliminating much of the "noise" that must be prevalent in my data. Consequently the assessment of the theory's strengths and weaknesses should be made in terms of how well history fits with the deductions delineated earlier, with the caveat that some—but, we hope, not too much—measurement error will inevitably lead to some incorrect judgments of whether a state should have expected to gain or lose in a war.

EXPECTED UTILITY AND CONFLICT INITIATION

I begin my analysis with broad brush strokes, outlining the general tendency for initiators of wars (or serious disputes) to expect to derive positive utility from their actions. Combining Gochman's data on interstate threats and interstate interventions with interstate war data from Singer and Small (which I have updated, using their coding rules, through 1974), I have data on 251 conflict initiators. Of these, 193 by my calculations possessed positive expected utility. Their opponents, on the other hand, had positive expected utility only 39 times. How meaningful is this difference? To answer that question, we must know what the general frequency of positive expected-utility scores is in the population of annual dyads.

Only 14 percent of all dyads have positive expected-utility scores, with that number going up to 38 percent if only the higher risk, regional dyads are counted. Given 251 victims, we should expect about 35 to have positive expected utility based on the worldwide average. Focusing only on regional dyads leads us to expect that about 93 victims will have positive expected utility. Of course, if national leaders do not behave as if they are expected-utility maximizers, we should expect the same frequency of positive expected utility among initiators as in the population of dyads in general. The results cited above clearly bear out the inference that positive expected-utility scores among victims are distributed as one would expect, given the frequency of such scores in the universe of dyads between 1816 and 1974 ($z = .6$, not significant), but the frequency for conflict initiators is radically different. Initiators have positive expected utility far more often than one would expect by chance ($z = 28.6$, $p < .001$).

The results just reported strongly support the proposition that positive expected utility is necessary — though not sufficient — for a leader to initiate a serious international dispute, including a war. This is all the more striking when we examine the initiators and their victims directly, rather than as a proportion of the universe of dyads. Table 5.1 shows the frequency of positive and negative expected-utility scores among war initiators and their opponents, while tables

TABLE 5.1. Interstate War Initiation and
Expected Utility

Expected-utility score	Initiator	Opponent
Greater than[a] or equal to zero	65	11
Less than zero	11	65

Note. Yule's $Q = .94$. $\lambda_A = .71$.

[a]Risk-averse states that are weaker than their adversaries are, of course, treated as having negative expected utility.

TABLE 5.2. Interstate Interventions and Expected Utility

Expected-utility score	Initiator	Opponent
Greater than[a] or equal to zero	78	14
Less than zero	24	88

Note. Yule's $Q = .91$. $\lambda_A = .63$.

[a]Risk-averse states that are weaker than their adversaries are, of course, treated as having negative expected utility.

5.2 and 5.3 present the same analysis for interstate interventions and interstate threats, respectively. In looking over these three tables we should have two expectations. First, positive expected utility should be — within the bounds of measurement error — necessary but not sufficient for states to initiate conflicts. Second, the strength of the relationship should decline as we move from conflictual strategies that involve warfare to those involving lesser levels of conflict and mere threats. After all, threatening action is not the same as taking action. More cases involving threats are likely to be bluffs than are cases involving actual combat. It is relatively easy to back down from a threat without too much loss, but it is very difficult to back down without suffering a serious loss once one has launched a military operation against another state. Consequently, leaders are probably less likely to put themselves in a combat situation from which they might have to back down than they are to elect a situation that only involves verbal assaults.

Since the theory stipulates necessary — but not sufficient — conditions for initiating war (or other serious disputes), a measure of one-way association is appropriate for ascertaining how well the data fit the theory. Yule's Q (also known as gamma) is such a

TABLE 5.3. Interstate Threats and Expected Utility

Expected-utility score	Initiator	Opponent
Greater than[a] or equal to zero	50	13
Less than zero	23	60

Note. Yule's $Q = .82$. $\lambda_A = .51$.

[a]Risk-averse states that are weaker than their adversaries are, of course, treated as having negative expected utility.

measure. Q for table 5.1 is .94. It is .91 for table 5.2, and for interstate threats, Q is .82. Another way of viewing these results is to ascertain how different the distribution of initiator expected-utility scores is from the distribution of positive expected-utility scores in the population of annual dyads. Using chi-square to measure that difference in the distribution of expected-utility scores between the set of interstate war initiators and the total set of dyads reveals that positive expected utility for the war initiators is so much more prevalent than expected by chance that chi-square exceeds 334, indicating an almost infinitesimal likelihood that this difference has occurred by chance. Similarly, for interstate interventions and interstate threats, the chi-square statistics are 331 and 171, respectively. By contrast, the respective chi-square statistics for the distribution of positive expected utility scores among the victims in wars, interventions, and threats relative to the distribution of this attribute in the population of dyads, equals .01, .04, and .88. These results indicate that positive expected utility scores among victims occur about as often as one would expect by chance. In each case the data comply with the expectations derived from the theory. The results for interstate wars and interventions are in fact almost perfect.

Two substantive charges are frequently levied against the notion that a general, lawlike theory of international conflict is possible. The first is that historical movements or developments alter international politics to such an extent that patterns or regularities found during some periods are not found in others. The second charge follows the same logic as the first, but instead of focusing on temporal changes, it focuses on variations in such factors as culture, national character, and the like. I will address each in turn, elaborating the charge before examining the evidence.

HISTORICAL CHANGE

With the end of World War 1, dynastic, monarchical rule seems to have ended in Europe. Many viewed this change as a fundamental break with the past. War was no longer a contest among noblemen but rather a ghastly contest between proletarians and the technicians of war. Whereas before, soldiers largely had confronted each other face-to-face, now such weapons as Krupp's Big Bertha and other long-range artillery, aircraft, and submarines depersonalized war while increasing almost unbelievably the firepower of armies. The political and technological changes forged in the furnaces of World War I and the Russian Revolution seemed to many to have altered the fundamental nature of world politics, much as the French Revolution, the era of Napoleon, and the industrial revolution seemed to an earlier generation to have changed the rules of international politics one hundred years before.

The beginning of the twentieth century brought with it an apparent end to the balance of power—a balance that in reality probably never existed—and the rise of revolutionary forces unparalleled in the nearly three-quarters of a century between the revolutions of 1848 and the success of the Bolsheviks in 1917. The new century also brought into focus the rise of such new great powers as the United States and Japan, each remote from the issues and terrain that had spawned so many earlier conflicts. At about the same time that these new powers were emerging, the Austro-Hungarian empire was on the eve of its demise, while Britain was about to enter its decades of decline. France, of course, had already begun its decline in 1870. Is it possible that with all these, and other, changes in the international system, the process by which nations chose between war and peace remained unaltered? Certainly very few thought so and not without good reason. Some research on international politics suggests that such a view was warranted by the facts. A fundamental finding among recent studies of war, for instance, is that the patterns that fit the history of nineteenth-century conflict oppose those that are consistent with twentieth-century conflicts. Singer, Bremer, and Stuckey (1972), for instance, in a widely cited study, suggest that the balance-of-power notion of peace through power parity fits well with nineteenth-century wars, while the notion of peace through power preponderance is strongly associated with twentieth-century war. Singer and Small (1968) also found opposite relationships between the polarity of the international system and several indicators of war for the two centuries. Many others, including myself (1978), have reported that the correlations between our explanatory variables and the factors we were trying to explain showed a reversal in the direction of association between the nineteenth and twentieth centuries. Still others (Blainey 1973) have reported finding quite substantial differences in their studies of pre-nineteenth-century wars and post-eighteenth-century wars.

More recently, it has been popular to claim that any generalizations about international politics based on analyses of conflicts before 1945 are now useless. The central theme to this argument is that politics in the nuclear age necessarily differ from pre-nuclear politics. Even a cursory examination of history would reveal other ages that were declared to be totally different from earlier times. The logic underlying these assertions is almost always the same. Each time some new discovery or development has led people to believe that they were living at the dawn of a new—and not necessarily better—age. Such arguments are frequently supported by anec-dotes, by the conviction that the position is self-evident or, as in the examples I noted earlier, by rigorous empirical investigations that are not, unfortunately, preceded by rigorous logic. That is not to say that they are wrong, but rather that if they are right, a logical basis for the changes in behavior must be identified. Of course, if temporal changes do alter the process by which leaders choose between war and peace, then my theory is almost certainly useless. However true its logic may be, if the logic is temporally bounded, then the theory cannot provide a vechicle for dealing with future events. Without that capability, the theory is an interesting exercise but not a useful tool.

Tables 5.4 and 5.5 present the relationship between expected utility and war initiation for the nineteenth and twentieth centuries. Tables 5.6 and 5.7 do the same for interstate interventions, while tables 5.8 and 5.9 examine the association for interstate threats. In each instance, the initiators of conflicts are much more likely to have

TABLE 5.4. Interstate War Initiation and Expected Utility:
Nineteenth Century

Expected-utility score	Initiator	Opponent
Greater than or equal to zero	30	4
Less than zero	3	29

Note. Yule's $Q = .97$. $\lambda_A = .79$.

TABLE 5.5. Interstate War Initiation and Expected Utility:
Twentieth Century

Expected-utility score	Initiator	Opponent
Greater than or equal to zero	35	7
Less than zero	8	36

Note. Yule's $Q = .91$. $\lambda_A = .65$.

TABLE 5.6. Interstate Interventions and Expected Utility:
Nineteenth Century

Expected-utility score	Initiator	Opponent
Greater than or equal to zero	27	0
Less than zero	2	29

Note. Yule's $Q = 1.00$. $\lambda_A = .93$.

TABLE 5.7. Interstate Interventions and Expected Utility:
Twentieth Century

Expected-utility score	Initiator	Opponent
Greater than or equal to zero	51	14
Less than zero	22	59

Note. Yule's $Q = .81$. $\lambda_A = .51$.

TABLE 5.8. Interstate Threats and Expected Utility:
Nineteenth Century

Expected-utility score	Initiator	Opponent
Greater than or equal to zero	24	4
Less than zero	13	33

Note. Yule's $Q = .88$. $\lambda_A = .54$.

TABLE 5.9. Interstate Threats and Expected Utility:
Twentieth Century

Expected-utility score	Initiator	Opponent
Greater than or equal to zero	26	9
Less than zero	10	27

Note. Yule's $Q = .77$ $\lambda_A = .47$.

positive expected utility than are their opponents or than one would expect from the distribution of expected-utility scores in the universe of dyads. Q for interstate wars in the nineteenth century is .97, while in the current century the association is .91. The results for interstate interventions are Qs of 1.00 and .81, respectively. As expected, the association between expected utility and interstate threats—though still strong—is somewhat weaker; the respective associations are equal to .88 and .77. In each case, the association is very strong and positive, exactly as it was for the entire 159 years under analysis. Unlike earlier, less explicitly theoretical studies, including my own, a significant difference is not found here between the two centuries. All the coefficients in tables 5.4–5.9 satisfy the .70 threshold requirement I established for judging a result as substantively significant when based on measures of one-way association. Strong results in support of the theory also follow from an examination of conflict in the nuclear era, despite claims by some that nuclear technology has altered foreign policy in fundamental ways. Q for the three conflict types combined equals .81, while the theory provides a proportionate reduction in error of 51 percent in the nuclear period. For war in the nuclear period, Q is a nearly perfect .99.

The evidence in tables 5.4 through 5.9 and for the nuclear age suggests that while many factors are known to have a different relationship to war at different times, the relationship between expected utility and conflict initiation is strong, in the direction predicted by the theory, stable, and seemingly lawlike.

Before turning to an evaluation of the theory's robustness across regional contexts, let me digress somewhat by offering some anecdotal evidence that reinforces the statistical results just reported. Those who doubt that leaders undertake calculations resembling the complex expected-utility estimates outlined in chapter 3 might do well to pause and examine the Book of Joshua in the Old Testament. Joshua's invasion of Jericho is perhaps the earliest account of the political and military preparations preceding a war. It might seem as far removed from modern warfare as the spear or club does from nuclear holocaust or as different as a laser is from a beam of light glancing off the rocks of Jericho's walls on the morning Joshua led his army across the Jordan River and into

Jericho. Yet Joshua's search for information about his prospects for victory and his likely allies and adversaries does not seem to have differed from the calculations I have argued are undertaken each time a leader contemplates war. Indeed, the story of Joshua is all the more startling because the Bible reveals the great effort he made to estimate his expected utility, despite a guarantee of victory from God.

As he prepared for battle, Joshua spoke to his allies, the Reubenites, the Gadites, and to half the tribe of Manasseh, saying, "'Remember the word which Moses the servant of the Lord commanded you, saying: the Lord your God giveth you rest, and will give you this land.'... And they answered Joshua, saying, 'All that thou hast commanded us we will do, and whithersoever thou sendest us we will go'" (Joshua 1:13–16). With these assurances, Joshua knew he could rely on his allies to aid him. Despite God's promise to be with Joshua in battle, and the assurance of support from his allies, Joshua still was not ready to attack. Only part of the information needed to calculate his expected utility had been gathered. And so, having instructed his followers to prepare for battle three days hence, Joshua then "sent out of Shittim two men to spy secretly, saying, 'Go view the land, even Jericho'" (Joshua 2:1). Once the spies returned, they reported to Joshua their estimate of the prospects for victory. God's promise that Joshua would be victorious was supported, with the spies claiming, "Truly the Lord hath delivered into our hands all the land; for even all the inhabitants of the country do faint because of us" (Joshua 2:24). So Joshua knew who his allies were, and he knew he was stronger than the enemy in Jericho, but was he likely to find himself opposed by additional adversaries?

> Hereby ye shall know that the living God is among you, and that he will without fail drive out from before you the Canaanites, and the Hittites, and the Hivites, and the Perizzites, and the Girgashites, and the Amorites, and the Jebusites.... And it came to pass...that the waters [of the Jordan] which came down from above stood and rose up upon a heap very far from the city of Adam, that is beside Zaretan; and those that came down toward the sea of the plain, even the salt sea, failed, and were cut

off: and the people passed over right against Jericho.

(Joshua 3:10–17)

Thus Joshua knew that he might face additional adversaries, and he had reason to believe he could defeat them. After all, God assured Joshua, the enemy would be stopped by the Jordan, while the Israelites would be delivered safely across the waters. Only a generation earlier, the God of the Israelites had made other waters part, delivering the Jews safely across and drowning the Egyptian enemy.

The story of Joshua and the Battle of Jericho as told in the Old Testament, written thousands of years ago, reveals a concern for estimating factors exactly the same as those delineated in the expected-utility theory. The very factors that figured in Joshua's decision to attack have distinguished war initiators from their victims at least since the Congress of Vienna.

THE CULTURAL OBJECTION

Studies of comparative politics are often—though certainly not always—conducted in the context of national or regional analyses. One commonly finds book series, for instance, with titles like *Politics in* ... or ... *Political System*, with the blank filled in with the name of a country or region (for instance, *Politics in Israel*, *India's Political System*, *Asian Politics*, *Politics USA/USSR*). These studies frequently—though again, not always—are predicated on the notion that the factors governing political behavior in some parts of the world are different from those governing behavior in other parts of the world. This same notion is an integral part of the process by which foreign policy is made. The Department of State in the United States, for instance, is largely organized around regional and national concerns. Hence we find a country desk officer for virtually every nation and assistant secretaries of state for such problem areas as the Middle East.

The belief that politics in one place differs in idiosyncratic ways from the politics in other areas is widely held. Such Hollywood images as the "inscrutable Oriental" or the "lazy Latin taking a siesta" also reinforce the belief that cultural, social, or

TABLE 5.10. War Initiation and Expected Utility:
Europe

Expected-utility score	Initiator	Opponent
Greater than or equal to zero	23	6
Less than zero	3	20

Note. Yule's $Q = .92$. $\lambda_A = .65$.

TABLE 5.11. War Initiation and Expected Utility:
Middle East

Expected-utility score	Initiator	Opponent
Greater than or equal to zero	21	1
Less than zero	3	23

Note. Yule's $Q = .99$. $\lambda_A = .83$.

TABLE 5.12. War Initiation and Expected Utility:
Americas

Expected-utility score	Initiator	Opponent
Greater than or equal to zero	10	3
Less than zero	3	10

Note. Yule's $Q = .83$. $\lambda_A = .54$.

other differences fundamentally alter the decision-making processes
in different places. Such a view, of course, is diametrically opposed to
the concept of conflict decision making that I have suggested. That is
not to say I believe there are no differences in politics, or in other
spheres, as one travels from culture to culture. I do believe, however,
that those differences are manifested as variations in the values of
different societies on the variables included in an expected-utility
calculation and not as differences in the rules governing decision
making. Whether conflict decisions are made as if by expected-
utility maximizers is, of course, an empirical question. I believe
tables 5.10 through 5.13 shed some light on the issue.

Whether one examines war initiators and their opponents in
Europe, Asia, the Americas, or the Middle East, positive expected
utility characterizes the initiators and negative expected utility

TABLE 5.13. War Initiation and Expected Utility:
Asia

Expected-utility score	Initiator	Opponent
Greater than or equal to zero	10	1
Less than zero	2	11

Note. Yule's $Q = .96$. $\lambda_A = .75$.

characterizes the opponents.[1] Yule's Q varies from a high of .99 for the Middle East to .83 for the Americas. The "inscrutable" Orient, with Q equal to .96, appears to adhere to the same rules of war decision making as does the rest of the world.[2]

One might rightly object that many of the wars fought outside Europe were initiated by, or at least included, European actors. However, if we examine only those warring pairs in which neither the initiator nor the opponent was a European state or a state (such as the United States in Vietnam) fighting outside its own region, then the theory is still overwhelmingly supported. Twenty-eight of the thirty-two initiators satisfying these regional conditions had positive expected utility against their foes, while only five of the thirty-two opponents had positive expected utility. Yule's Q for the non-European states at war with each other in their own region is .95. These analyses, like the ones focused on the temporal objection to general theories of international conflict, support the broad proposition that conflict initiators act in ways that are consistent with the notions of the expected-utility theory. They may find the structure of their particular environment more or less conducive to war than do others, but given the necessary conditions, they are

1. I have not included a table for war initiation in Africa because only one interstate war took place in that region during the period I am studying. The Italo-Ethiopian War of 1935, initiated by Italy, is consistent with the theory, with Italy's expected utility being positive, as anticipated, and Ethiopia's expected utility negative.

2. I have not included regional tables for interstate interventions and interstate threats because the fact that all the conflicts involve at least one major power tends to make these data somewhat distorted. Yule's Q by region for interventions and threats combined is equal to .83 for Europe, .86 for the Middle East, .92 for Asia, and .99 for the Americas. These results are essentially the same from region to region and are like those for war.

prepared to fall into the war trap. To be sure, foreign policies in some regions—notably the Middle East—have yielded considerably more opportunities for war or serious conflicts than have foreign policies in other regions (by containing a higher proportion of dyads with positive expected utility). Still, the propensity to require the same conditions has not varied meaningfully from region to region or from time to time.

EXPLORING ANOTHER POSSIBLE EXPLANATION

Before we leave the wide-ranging portion of the analyses, let me pause to raise a question about the value of the theory's broadest generalization. Does the statement that conflict initiators act as if they are expected-utility maximizers add any information that we might not already have from such theories as the balance of power? When all the complexity is cut away, is anything more left than the simple statement that those who are stronger tend to initiate wars, while those who are weaker tend to be the victims? This is a view largely consistent with the balance-of-power theory (Kissinger, 1979; Organski and Kugler 1980), though in a rather simplified form (Bueno de Mesquita 1980). Analyses associated with that theory focus on power politics rather than utilitarian politics. To be sure, the two views of politics have much in common. It will be recalled that my theory stipulates that the initiation of a conflict by a nonaligned state against another nonaligned state depends on the initiator's power alone. Similarly, when a risk-averse ally initiates a war against an ally with a foreign policy posture that is essentially indistinguishable from that of the initiator, the expected-utility equation's outcome is determined primarily by the relative strength of the potential antagonists. In all other circumstances, however, the expected-utility equations can produce a positive outcome for an initiator who is weaker than, equal to, or stronger than his intended opponent. The outcome then depends on the expected-utility contribution of third parties.

   Unlike balance-of-power and other *Realpolitik* theories, my theory incorporates elements of both power politics and ideological, policy-based politics. Thus, while the sign of the bilateral lottery in

TABLE 5.14. Power and Interstate War Initiation:
1816–1974

Power	Initiator	Opponent
Stronger (or equal)	59	20
Weaker nation	17	56

Note. Yule's $Q = .81$. $\lambda_A = .51$.

my theory is determined by power considerations, the signs of the
multilateral lotteries (reflecting, as they do, a policy orientation
toward the formation of alliances), are determined by policy-based
utilities and not power. It is in this latter regard that the expected-
utility approach diverges fundamentally from classical balance-of-
power viewpoints.

Balance-of-power theorists focus on alliance activities as well as
on estimating national capabilities. For many of them, however,
alliances represent a means by which nations augment their power
and not a potential irritant that can increase a nation's chances of
becoming the target of international aggression. In my theory,
alliances may enhance security, diminish security, or have no impact
on security, depending on the context within which alliances are
formed or ended. In my theory, alliances are not formed solely for
purposes of power. Later I will explore the relationship between
alliance membership and conflict initiation, but for now I focus only
on the role of national capabilities. I will try to show that having a
power advantage over one's intended foe—though important and
informative—is less important and less informative than having
positive expected utility.

Tables 5.14 through 5.16 depict the relationship between the
composite capabilities—or power—of each war initiator and its
opponent for each interstate war from 1816 through 1974, with the

TABLE 5.15. Power and Interstate War Initiation:
Nineteenth Century

Power	Initiator	Opponent
Stronger (or equal) nation	30	3
Weaker nation	3	30

Note. Yule's $Q = .98$. $\lambda_A = .82$.

TABLE 5.16. Power and Interstate War Initiation:
Twentieth Century

Power	Initiator	Opponent
Stronger (or equal) nation	29	17
Weaker nation	14	26

Note. Yule's $Q = .52$. $\lambda_A = .28$.

latter two tables decomposing the relationship according to century. Overall Q equals .81, which, though strong, is the weakest association with war that I have reported thus far. The more interesting results are found in comparing tables 5.15 and 5.16. For the nineteenth century, Q equals a near-perfect .98, but in the current century, Q is a fairly modest .52. These coefficients compare with scores of .97 and .91 for expected utility and nineteenth and twentieth-century wars. How different are these results? One useful way to answer this question is to ascertain how much additional information the expected-utility theory provides over the balance-of-power notion that states initiate wars against weaker adversaries. Lambda A (λ_a) measures the proportionate reduction in error achieved when trying to predict an outcome if each case's score on the independent variable is known. With power as the known variable, we are able to eliminate a hefty 82 percent of errors in predicting initiators and opponents in nineteenth-century wars but only a meager 28 percent of errors for twentieth-century wars. With expected utility as the known variable, we are able to eliminate 79 percent of the errors for nineteenth-century wars and 65 percent for twentieth-century wars. Across the entire time span, power yields only a 51 percent reduction in error, while expected utility produces a 71 percent reduction in error. Another way we can compare the results based on power with those based on expected utility involves the criteria delineated in chapter 4 for evaluating the evidence. Recall that I stipulated that measures of one-way association would be considered substantively significant only if they were at least equal to .70. While the associations based on expected utility exceed that level in both the nineteenth and the twentieth centuries, the twentieth-century association between power and war initiation ($Q = .52$) does not.

TABLE 5.17. Power and Interstate War Initiation for Cases
Where Power Could Differ from Expected Utility: 1816–1974

Power	Initiator	Opponent
Stronger (or equal) nation	25	12
Weaker nation	12	25

Note. Yule's $Q = .63$. $\lambda_A = .35$.

TABLE 5.18. Expected Utility and Interstate War Initiation for
Cases Where Power Could Differ from Expected Utility:
1816–1974

Expected-Utility score	Initiator	Opponent
Greater than or equal to zero	31	3
Less than zero	6	34

Note. Yule's $Q = .97$. $\lambda_A = .76$.

TABLE 5.19. Power and Interstate War Initiation for Cases
Where Power Could Differ from Expected Utility:
Nineteenth Century

Power	Initiator	Opponent
Stronger (or equal) nation	10	2
Weaker nation	2	10

Note. Yule's $Q = .92$. $\lambda_A = .67$.

The examination of power and expected utility supports the
contention that actors are more concerned with their expected
utility than with comparing their power to that of their intended foe.
In actuality, however, tables 5.14 through 5.16 inadequately compare
the two theories. Those tables include all the cases where the
expected-utility theory's predictions depend only on power, as well
as the cases where the power hypothesis and the expected-utility
hypothesis can — though they need not — diverge. Tables 5.17 and
5.18, 5.19 and 5.20, and 5.21 and 5.22 compare predictions about
initiators and opponents only for those interstate wars where the
predicted outcomes could be different. That is, in these analyses, I
exclude all wars in which the initial belligerents were either

TABLE 5.20. Expected Utility and Interstate War Initiation for
Cases Where Power Could Differ from Expected Utility:
Nineteenth Century

Expected-utility score	Initiator	Opponent
Greater than or equal to zero	10	2
Less than zero	2	10

Note. Yule's $Q = .92$. $\lambda_A = .67$.

TABLE 5.21. Power and Interstate War Initiation for Cases
Where Power Could Differ from Expected Utility:
Twentieth Century

Power	Initiator	Opponent
Stronger (or equal) nation	15	10
Weaker nation	10	15

Note. Yule's $Q = .38$. $\lambda_A = .20$.

TABLE 5.22. Expected Utility and Interstate War Initiation for
Cases Where Power Could Differ from Expected Utility:
Twentieth Century

Expected-utility score	Initiator	Opponent
Greater than or equal to zero	21	1
Less than zero	4	24

Note. Yule's $Q = .98$. $\lambda_A = .80$.

nonaligned or so closely aligned with one another that U_{ij} (the
initiator's utility for the opponent's current foreign policy posture)
equals 1.00 (with the initiator being risk averse). For the entire time
span, Yule's Q based on expected utility is .97, while Q based on the
relative power of the initiator and the opponent is .63. With expected
utility there is a 76 percent reduction in error, while with power there
is only a 35 percent reduction in error. The two hypotheses produce
exactly the same results for nineteenth-century wars, λ_a and Q being
67 percent and .92, respectively. In the twentieth century, however,
the two propositions produce very different results. The expected-

utility theory yields about the same results as it did for nineteenth-century wars; Q and λ_a are equal to .98 and 80 percent, respectively. The power hypothesis, on the other hand, leads to a meager 20 percent reduction in error and a Yule's Q of only .38. As with the earlier comparison of power and expected utility, all Yule's Q involving expected utility surpass the .70 threshold I established earlier, but Yule's Q for twentieth-century power and war initiation does not. Furthermore, Yule's Q between power and war initiation for the entire time span also fails to satisfy the .70 threshold of substantive significance.

These results are interesting in several respects. First, of course, they support the contention that war initiators approach their decisions from a utilitarian perspective rather than from a simpler power-politics perspective. Second, the expected-utility theory fits the thirty-seven cases of war initiation where the expected-utility calculation was not determined by power as well as it does the thirty-nine cases where the power of the initial belligerents determines the sign of the expected-utility calculation. Third, the expected-utility results remain stable across time (and across regions, too), while the power-based perspective does not. The evidence suggests that knowing the relative power of potential adversaries was equivalent to knowing their expected utility in the nineteenth century but not in the twentieth century. And insofar as the power perspective and the expected-utility perspective diverged in the present century, the importance of relative power in conflict initiation declined. Perhaps the declining importance of power is due to the increased frequency of alliances, or to the changing tendency for nations to form alliances with states that are not comparable to one another in power (Midlarsky 1979) or to the increasing tendency toward ideological alliances. Whatever the reasons, expected utility, and not power, has proven to be the stronger and more stable predictor of the predilection to initiate conflict. It appears that all the cases of war initiation explained by a pure *Realpolitik* perspective are also explained by my theory, while a great many cases unexplained by a power-determinist viewpoint are explained by the expected-utility theory. If there is a significant "balance" in international politics, it is more likely to involve values in an expected-utility calculation than power.

PLANNING CONFLICT: CAN MICE ROAR?

Conflict may, according to the theory, arise in any of four distinct situations, including (a) a nonaligned initiator versus a nonaligned opponent; (b) a nonaligned initiator versus an aligned opponent; (c) an aligned initiator versus a nonaligned opponent; and (d) an aligned initiator versus an aligned opponent. While the first situation precludes the expectation that the weaker party can win, the three other situations can arise under circumstances where either the weaker or the stronger belligerent may expect to win. Earlier I noted that the Turkish success during the Crimean War is historically consistent with the contention that a weaker, nonaligned state may defeat a stronger nation that has allies.[3] Now I would like to explore an example of a very strong, aligned state — Prussia — that was compelled to give in to one of Europe's weakest, and avowedly nonaligned nations — Switzerland. Both the theory and the data support the decision of King Frederick William IV to threaten Switzerland with war in 1856 and also provide an insight into how, despite the rationality of the Prussian threat, the Swiss could emerge victorious from the Neuchâtel affair.

Neuchâtel was nominally under the suzerainty of the Prussian king when republican revolutionaries seized control, declared Prussia's claim to Neuchâtel ended, and made Neuchâtel part of the Swiss Confederation. With the great powers reaffirming Frederick William's claim to the territory, he encouraged royalists in Neuchâtel to stage a counterrevolution. Their efforts were successful

---

3. Although the outcome of the Crimean War and the history of the diplomacy leading up to it are consistent with the theory, my estimates of expected utility are not consistent with the Turkish decision to initiate the war. By my estimates, Turkey's expected utility against Russia was − .756, while Russia's expected utility was 1.347. Two explanations for these results seem reasonable. One is that this is a good example of measurement error, for although the data show that Britain and France (and Italy), all of whom joined the war on Turkey's side, favored Turkey over Russia, they do not show a sufficiently strong preference to turn Turkey's expected-utility score positive. Another possible explanation is that this is one of the few wars in my data set for which there is a lively debate about who should be labeled as the initiator. While Turkish troops clearly engaged the Russians first — the principal requirement of the rule I used to distinguish initiators from opponents — they did so on Turkish territory that had earlier been occupied by the Russians.

briefly, but then the republicans again overthrew the royalists, capturing more than 500 of them. Frederick William demanded the release of his supporters and refused to relinquish his claim to Neuchâtel. The newly formed Swiss confederation refused to capitulate to his demands, even though he threatened to launch a war against Switzerland if they did not concede by January 2, 1857—not even one month away. What factors encouraged Swiss intransigence in the face of clearly superior force?

To understand the outcome of the Neuchâtel affair, one must examine the array of interests among the great powers directly affected by the prospect of a war in Switzerland. But first, we should not discount the patriotic fervor the Swiss people felt for their fledgling nation. As one observer noted, "In Switzerland itself the entire population with unanimous enthusiasm . . . awaited the war with heroic composure and an almost religious calm" (Dändliker, 1899). Still, heroism would not have been enough for the Swiss army to defeat the powerful forces of Prussia. It took the intervention of Britain, France, and Austria-Hungary to convince King Frederick William IV to give up his claim to Neuchâtel. Why were these states willing to intervene on behalf of Switzerland? According to my evidence, none of them felt especially friendly toward the neutral Swiss, although even with my crude indicators, Britain and France, on balance, preferred protecting Swiss interests to seeing Prussian interests promoted (Britain's utilities for Switzerland and Prussia were, respectively, $-.037$ and $-.143$, yielding a net utility of .106 favoring Switzerland; France's respective utility scores were the same as Britain's). The historians who have written about this conflict provide a clear insight into the factors motivating British and French behavior.

Bonjour, Offler, and Potter note that "the attitude of Britain had been from the first benevolent to Switzerland. The British government was not prepared to support the Prussian reactionaries for the material reason, among others, that the economy of England required peace on the continent: a continental war might easily spread and entail serious economic disadvantages. Further, Britain was anxious to prevent a rapprochement between France and Prussia to which the Neuchâtel conflict might lead" (1952, p. 278). In other words, Britain was motivated primarily by its own economic and political self-interest. War would have disrupted the British economy and in the long run might have jeopardized British security by strengthening the hands of Prussia and France.

The British might have had less to fear if they had been privy to the private conversations held between Emperor Napoleon III of France and a Dr. Kern, sent to Paris as a representative of the Swiss government. Oechsli reports that "Napoleon's confidential communications to Kern at length enabled the [Swiss] Bundesrat to feel assured that Switzerland would gain all she desired by liberating the prisoners" (1922, p. 404). Indeed, Napoleon III's communications must have been reassuring. Hug and Stead, quoting from Kern's memoirs, note that the French emperor told Kern, "I shall act in the matter as if I were the Swiss Government" (1902, p. 400). But why should Napoleon III have taken such a keen interest in protecting Switzerland against Prussia, especially when we realize that Napoleon had earlier signed an agreement reaffirming Frederick William's claim to Neuchâtel? One convincing explanation is that the French feared having a Prussian army on their south-east flank (Bonjour, Offler, and Potter 1952)—fear of Prussia, rather than friendship for Switzerland, was the key factor. This interpretation is reinforced by the fact that a conflict arose between Switzerland and France almost as soon as the Neuchâtel affair was settled. French and Swiss interests in Savoy were at the root of this new conflict, which was settled in favor of France. At almost the same time, the French and Swiss also disputed the French occupation of the Dappental, in direct violation of agreements reached at the Congress of Vienna. Unlike the conflict over Savoy, this issue was settled in favor of Switzerland.

The potential support available to Switzerland from France and England was critical—though probably not decisive—in encouraging Swiss resistance to Prussia's demands. To be sure, Stampfli—the federal councillor of Switzerland—realized that in several European capitals there was fear that an attack against Switzerland would lead to other uprisings against monarchical rule, and he "used these invisible allies of Switzerland as a threat" (Bonjour, Offler, and Potter 1952, p. 278), but such threats were not enough to assure Switzerland's success against a state as powerful as Prussia. The key lay surprisingly in the hands of Prussia's Austro-

Hungarian allies. While the southern German states gave Prussia's army the right of passage through their territory, the Austrians "kept Prussia at bay, and threw all sorts of obstacles in the way" (Dändliker 1899, p. 278). The Prussians found themselves greatly restricted in their ability to transport troops to Switzerland. This difficulty, coupled with the stiff pressure from Britain and France, was sufficient for Frederick William to agree to relinquish his claim to Neuchâtel in exchange for the release of the prisoners and a general amnesty for the royalists.

Could the Swiss, despite their weakness and their explicit position as a neutral, nonaligned state, have anticipated Prussia's decision to give up its claim to Neuchâtel? According to the evidence that follows from my theory, the answer must be yes. The expected-utility score for Prussia against Switzerland in 1856 was 1.495, indicating that the initial threat was made under circumstances that satisfied the theory's requirements. Yet once the conflict was under way, it became apparent that Prussia was facing a potentially threatening situation from France and England. Pursuing the matter further would only have been sensible if, in the face of these efforts to deter Prussia, the British and French postures were not credible. British expected utility against Prussia, as estimated by the procedures I explained earlier, was .56, while France's expected utility against Prussia's was .15. Prussia's expected utility against each of these states was negative. Thus once Frederick William IV was engaged in the conflict with Switzerland, he found himself confronting two nations each of which had a credible threat of taking some action against him, while he lacked a credible response. Furthermore, he found that his efforts against Switzerland were stymied by the resistance of the Austro-Hungarians. Facing a situation that was turning against him, he rationally backed down, cutting his losses and preventing an expansion of the affair beyond his original intentions. If the Swiss were in a position to judge the likelihood of support from Britain and France, which the data suggest they were, then their willingness to resist the demands of Prussia seem quite sensible, even though Prussia was many times stronger than Switzerland.

The lesson of Neuchâtel is important and should be clear. Neither the possession of considerable power nor the existence of alliances assures nations of success, even when they are engaged in a conflict against a very weak, nonaligned foe. In terms of the expected-utility theory, the important implication is that all forms of conflict, regardless of the circumstances, are governed by calculations about the three lotteries delineated in chapter 3. Now it remains to be seen whether these calculations work equally well in general or are equally useful for explaining the outbreak of conflict, regardless of the alliance status of the initiator or its opponent.

CONFLICT AND THE ALIGNMENT OF BELLIGERENTS

When George Washington bade his countrymen farewell, he left them with the message that their new nation should avoid "entangling alliances." Many others, both before and since, have suggested that alliances ensnare nations in a web of commitments that are likely to increase their risk of being victimized by aggression. Yet others have argued precisely the opposite. Virtually all balance-of-power theorists, for instance, view alliances as the principal means by which nations enhance their own power and therefore their ability to repulse aggressive threats. In this view, alliances are a source of security. Although some systematic evidence can be found to support — or contradict — each of these points of view, the underlying logical foundation for each generally has not been explored. The logic from which my theory follows, however, does directly address the question of whether (or when) alliances enhance or diminish national security.

Viewing alliances as a principal source of utility, the expected-utility approach suggests that the addition or substraction of such a military agreement between a pair of nations *neither necessarily increases nor necessarily decreases* the security of either. Alliance bonds are a source of information, both to the signatories and to other countries. They reveal the degree to which a pair of nations are prepared to make an explicit statement about their strategic intentions under certain contingent conditions. Defense agreements, for instance, are statements that reveal that one nation claims to be prepared to defend another in the event of an attack. The credibility of that declaration, however, is influenced substantially by the array of potentially distracting commitments the signatories may have with other states. Taken in the context of the full array of commitments, bilateral alliances both reveal any added support that a state may have, and the amount of support that a potential belligerent may need, given the expected support available to its adversary (Altfeld and Bueno de Mesquita 1979). The reduction of uncertainty brought about by such information may be all that is needed to facilitate an aggressor's desire to attack another state, or it may be enough to expose the would-be aggressor's plans as impractical.

Beyond providing information about the strategic intentions of states and the availability of auxiliary power that such intentions may suggest, alliances also carry with them information about the foreign policy preferences or interests of states. Such information may thwart an aggressor, it may alienate countries that were formerly neutral or even sympathetic to the now-aligned state, or it may have no bearing on the orientations of other states to the aligned pair. Which implication it has depends on the particular circumstances under which a new alliance comes into existence (or in which an old alliance dissolves). Without knowing the specific circumstances, one simply cannot know whether the new alignment yields a net increase or decrease in expected support. Thus on balance, the fact that a nation is or is not aligned should not reveal much about the likelihood of its being the initiator or victim of an act of international aggression. Instead, its expected-utility score— which is affected differently by alignment patterns, depending on the specific circumstances—should be the factor that reveals its vulnerability or security from an attack.

According to the theory, though alliances play a role in shaping each nation's expected-utility calculation, they should not by themselves provide a means by which we can discriminate between initiators and opponents. Whether they do is easily ascertained. If I am correct, then aligned states should be about as likely to be initiators as they are to be opponents. The same should be true for nonaligned states. Consequently, the a priori expectation derived from the theory is that knowing whether an initial belligerent is aligned or not tells us essentially nothing about whether it is likely to be the initiator or the opponent in a serious conflict. Using λ_a, the measure of proportionate reduction in error explained earlier, reveals that we obtain only an 18 percent reduction in error by knowing whether a belligerent is aligned or not, with an insignificantly larger proportion of war initiators being aligned than of their opponents. The same pattern holds when our attention is focused on interstate threats, with a 14 percent reduction in error, and again with an insignificantly larger proportion of aligned states being initiators and nonaligned states being opponents. The results are somewhat different for interstate interventions short of war. For these cases, knowing whether an initial belligerent was aligned or not reduces by 32 percent the error in guessing whether it was the initiator or the opponent. Though this is still a modest reduction in error, for these cases aligned states are significantly more often the initiator, while nonaligned states are significantly more often opponents. On balance, these results, though somewhat mixed, support the contention that alliance membership by itself is not a significant factor either enhancing or jeopardizing a nation's security.

The role of alliances independent of any expected-utility calculation can be further clarified by looking at the propensity of initiators to win their conflicts as a function of their alliance status and as a function of whether they had positive or negative expected utility when they went into the conflict. Rather than examine each type of conflict separately, I present the analysis for all conflicts combined. The pattern is essentially the same for wars, interventions, and threats.

The appropriate test for the analysis that follows is to ascertain whether an initiator's alliance status (or expected-utility status) is significantly related to the relative frequency with which it wins or loses the conflicts it initiates. The comparison of relative frequencies

TABLE 5.23. Relationship between Alliance Membership and Winning or Losing in All Conflicts

Initiator's Membership	Initiator won	Initiator lost
Alliance	129	35
No alliance	50	19

Note. $\chi^2(1) = 1.048$, not significant.

is done by means of an analysis of variance, with chi-square used to measure significance. Table 5.23 depicts the distribution of victories and defeats for all conflicts as a function of whether the initiator was aligned or not. Of the aligned initiators, 79 percent were victorious, while 71 percent of the nonaligned initiators enjoyed the same outcome. These results are not significantly different, with chi-square equal to 1.048. By contrast, table 5.24 depicts the distribution of victories and defeats as a function of the expected-utility score of the initiators. Of the initiators with positive expected utility, 83 percent won the disputes they initiated, while 57 percent of the initiators with negative expected utility managed to emerge victorious. This time, the difference is significant, with chi-square equal to 17.350 ($p < .001$). What is more, these results understate the goodness of fit achieved with the expected-utility theory.

As noted in chapter 3, there are circumstances when the theory leads us to expect that an initiator with positive expected utility will lose. For instance, initiators are expected to back down when a third party makes a credible threat (based on the third party's positive expected utility against the original conflict initiator) that undermines the initiator's original expectation of success. Sixteen of the thirty-one losses by an initiator with positive expected utility against the original foe involve some subsequent third-party threat. Twelve of these threats were made by third parties with positive expected utility against the initiator. As in the Neuchâtel affair, such threats frequently led to the initiator's failure to pursue its objectives successfully —so frequently that of the 179 initiators with positive expected utility for whom I have complete data, all but 19 emerged from their conflicts with an outcome anticipated by the theory.

As suggested, having positive expected utility not only makes a

TABLE 5.24. Relationship between Expected Utility and Winning or Losing in All Conflicts

Initiator's expected-utility Score	Initiator won	Initiator lost
Greater than or equal to zero	148	31
Less than zero	31	23

Note. $\chi^2(1) = 17.350, P < .001$.

state more likely to initiate a conflict, but once it has taken the initial action, such a state is substantially more likely to achieve its objective than is an initiator with negative expected utility, and is almost certain of success if third parties with credible threats do not intervene. Joining an alliance (or severing an alliance), on the other hand, does not — without calculating the impact of such an action on one's expected-utility score — by itself influence the likelihood that one will initiate a conflict or that one will win such conflicts once they are initiated. Alliances, like power, appear to be somewhat related to national decisions to initiate conflicts — and to the ultimate attainment of victory — but they are not nearly as consequential as is an examination of expected utilities.

THE PROPOSITIONS

The evidence presented thus far establishes that conflict initiators tend to have positive expected utility, while their opponents tend not to. The evidence is consistent with the broadest generalization of the theory. Now I wish to examine the specific types of war — or conflict — addressed by the propositions presented in chapter 3. Here the object is to ascertain whether the details of the theory, as well as its broad implications, are consistent with history.

NONALIGNED STATES IN CONFLICT WITH EACH OTHER

The first proposition stated that conflicts among nonaligned states are initiated by the stronger adversary. The reason for this expectation was that the initial belligerents in such conflicts would have no reason to expect third parties to intervene, thus leading to the implication that the conflict's outcome would be determined solely by the relative power of the combatants.

Tables 5.25 through 5.27 explore the relationship between the alignment status and relative power of initiators of interstate wars, interventions, and threats, respectively. What expectations should we have about these tables as a result of the first proposition? First,

TABLE 5.25. Does Alignment Influence Whether Interstate War Initiators Are Stronger than Their Opponents?

Initiator-opponent alignment status	Initiator's adjusted capabilities in relation to the opponent's	
	Stronger	Weaker
Nonaligned vs. nonaligned	19	4
Nonaligned vs. aligned	5	3
Aligned vs. nonaligned	16	6
Aligned vs. aligned	21	2

TABLE 5.26. Does Alignment Influence Whether Initiators of Interstate Interventions Challenge Weaker Opponents?

Initiator-opponent alignment status	Initiator's adjusted capabilities in relation to the opponent's	
	Stronger	Weaker
Nonaligned vs. nonaligned	17	0
Nonaligned vs. aligned	4	3
Aligned vs. nonaligned	32	6
Aligned vs. aligned	27	13

TABLE 5.27. Does Alignment Influence Whether Initiators of Interstate Threats Challenge Weaker Opponents?

Initiator-opponent alignment status	Initiator's adjusted capabilities in relation to the opponent's	
	Stronger	Weaker
Nonaligned vs. nonaligned	7	1
Nonaligned vs. aligned	9	2
Aligned vs. nonaligned	20	1
Aligned vs. aligned	23	10

of course, we should expect that when nonaligned initiators challenge nonaligned opponents, the initiators should be stronger than their foes. This is true in forty-three of the forty-eight dyadic conflicts between nonaligned states, or in just under 90 percent of such conflicts. Second, we should expect that nonaligned initiators (involved in disputes with nonaligned adversaries) should be stronger at least as often, and probably more often, than the initiators of other types of conflicts. This expectation arises because in many other types of conflict, weaker would-be initiators can, under appropriate circumstances, expect to gain, even though they are weaker than their intended opponents, an expectation that cannot arise in conflicts between nonaligned adversaries. Once again, the proposition is supported by the evidence. Only 77 percent of all other initiator-opponent pairs find the initiator with more power than the opponent. Using chi-square reveals that the incidence of power superiority among nonaligned initiators against nonaligned foes is so much larger than for other alignment combinations that the distribution would occur in fewer than one sample out of a thousand by chance alone.

There are still other ways that one might approach the proposition. One such way is to ask whether the distribution of power among nonaligned belligerents differs significantly from some a priori expectation about that distribution. This approach focuses attention on the fact that a priori, there is a .5 probability of any one member of a pair of nations being stronger than the other member. The appropriate test here is the normal approximation to a Bernoulli distribution, where a "success" occurs whenever the nonaligned initiator is stronger than his opponent and a "failure" occurs whenever the opposite is true. In the case of interstate wars, the distribution of power among nonaligned combatants significantly favors the initiators ($z = 3.13$, $p < .002$), as it does for interstate interventions ($z = 4.12$, $p < .001$), and for interstate threats ($z = 2.12$, $p < .02$). As we have come to expect, the consistency between the data and the theory—though still strong—is least marked when threats are involved and most marked for those conflicts involving actual military action.

SHOULD MICE ROAR? ANALYZING PROPOSITION 2

The calculation of expected utility for nonaligned adversaries is simple, straightforward, and not very different from the examination of their relative power. The expected-utility calculation is most complex for nonaligned states' leaders contemplating the initiation of a conflict with an adversary that has allies. Yet such conflicts do arise and can come about under circumstances that favor the nonaligned state. Indeed, as noted earlier, such situations may favor the welfare of the nonaligned antagonist even when it is weaker than its adversary. Both the Neuchâtel affair and the Crimean War demonstrate that mice can roar. These two examples also suggest that, under suitable circumstances, weak nations *should* roar. The conditions that make it possible for nonaligned states to succeed against aligned adversaries, however, are complex. Support must be derived from third parties that have no direct commitment with the nonaligned state and may even feel antagonistic toward it. Reliance on such states is problematic at best. Certainly, the failure to have an actual agreement means that the leader of the nonaligned state is basing his calculations on a rather tenuous source of cooperation — his belief that some third parties dislike his adversary more than they dislike his own state. This means that potential initiators who behave as if they are expected-utility maximizers under these circumstances rely on a rather fine-tuned implementation of the expected-utility calculus. More than any other set of circumstances, conflict initiations by nonaligned states against stronger aligned adversaries challenge the claim that conflict decision making is utilitarian.

We already know that nonaligned states do initiate conflicts against aligned states, though such conflicts occur less often than between any other combination of alignment statuses. One indication that the decisions leading up to these conflicts are made in

TABLE 5.28. Association between the Alignment Status of Initiators and Opponents and the Outcome of Their Conflicts: Cases Where the Initiator's Expected Utility Was Greater than or Equal to Zero

Initiator-opponent alignment status	Initiator won	Initiator lost
Nonaligned vs. nonaligned	33	5
Nonaligned vs. aligned	7	1
Aligned vs. nonaligned	59	10
Aligned vs. aligned	49	15

Note. $\chi^2(3) = 2.647$, not significant.

the same way as the decisions leading up to the initiation of other conflicts comes from examination of the propensity of initiators to win or lose, controlling for expected utility. We have already seen that positive expected utility is generally indicative of subsequent victory, but is this true regardless of the alignment status of the initiator and its opponent? Table 5.28 addresses this question for initiators with positive expected utility, while table 5.29 addresses it for initiators with negative expected utility. Chi-squares for tables 5.28 and 5.29 are 2.647 and 2.535, respectively. Neither of these chi-squares is significant, as we should expect. These results indicate that, regardless of whether an initiator is aligned or not, and regardless of whether the opponent is aligned or not, the proportion of victories to defeats, controlling for expected utility, is unchanged, suggesting that all such conflicts are about equally consistent with the expectations of the theory.

One way in which the various types of conflict differ is in the propensity of the initiator to have positive expected utility. In particular, using my estimates for expected utility, nonaligned states challenging aligned nations tend to have negative expected utility more often than any other group, with only one-third of my estimates of their expected utility being positive. That my estimates are not too far off the mark, however, is reinforced by the fact that when I did not control for expected utility, such initiators lost nearly half the time, while all other initiators lost only about one-fifth of the time. These results imply that as the expected-utility calculation becomes more complex and hence more difficult, national leaders

TABLE 5.29. Association between the Alignment Status of Initiators and Opponents and the Outcome of Their Conflicts: Cases Where the Initiator's Expected Utility Was Less than Zero

Initiator-opponent alignment status	Initiator won	Initiator lost
Nonaligned vs. nonaligned	4	3
Nonaligned vs. aligned	6	10
Aligned vs. nonaligned	4	2
Aligned vs. aligned	17	8

Note. $\chi^2(3) = 2.535$, not significant.

either behave less like utility maximizers or, as seems more likely in the context of all the evidence, are more prone to miscalculate. That they would have been better off by calculating more carefully is also reinforced by the evidence. After all, we have seen that those who initiated conflicts when their expected utility was negative failed to achieve their objectives far more often than those who had positive expected utility. Later I will examine the victories and defeats—at least for interstate wars—in greater detail to see whether there are also systematic differences in the costliness of success or failure. For now, let it suffice to observe that the data, like the theory, indicate that when leaders initiate conflicts without positive expected utility, their roar tends to be much bigger than their bite. Perhaps that is why a disproportionately large percentage of the conflicts between nonaligned initiators and aligned adversaries involved mere threats. Of all conflicts initiated by nonaligned states against aligned adversaries, 43 percent involved only a threat, while only 21 percent of all other initiator-opponent combinations involved threats. Thus it appears that nonaligned states taking on aligned opponents recognized their difficult situation sufficiently to use the conflict strategy that involves the least risk of severe loss and the greatest incentive for bluffing.

BEWARE OF FRIENDS BEARING ALLIANCES

As already noted, some students of alliances believe that such agreements enhance security, while others believe that they bring the risk that nations will become embroiled in conflicts that might otherwise have been avoided. Virtually no one, however, suggests that alliances may, even while possibly reducing the risk of external aggression, increase a nation's chances of being threatened or attacked by its friends. Yet the expected-utility theory—and almost any police blotter—suggests that close, intimate interaction among friends often leads to violence. Nations allied to one another are very much like husbands and wives, roommates, or best friends. Each has a separate identity, at least some separate interests, and intense interaction with the other. When a difference arises between such closely associated actors there is a reservoir of goodwill to help overcome many difficulties, but there is also the recognition that the dispute is essentially a private affair, unlikely to elicit a serious response by outsiders. When disputes arise within families, neighbors, friends, and the police are very wary of intervening. When allies fight, their friends and neighbors also are wary of intervening since they find choosing sides difficult. This would seem to be an important factor leading to the fact that lovers quarrels are far more common than most other types of conflict. I have suggested that the same is true for nations, and now I am prepared to put that proposition to the test.

Of the seventy-six interstate war initiations between 1816 and 1974, twenty-three were between two nations each of which had at least one ally. Of these twenty-three, fifteen were nations with a formal military agreement between them. Included among these conflicts are the Prussian attack against Austria-Hungary and seven lesser German states. All of these states shared defense pacts with each other at the outbreak of the Seven Weeks' War, also known among Germans as the Bruderkrieg, or "brothers' war." The Russo-Hungarian War of 1956 is another such instance, as is the minor Football War, between El Salvador and Honduras in 1969. In both of these cases, as also in the Egyptain struggle against the Yemenis and the Saudi Arabians to restore an Egyptain-backed government to Yemen, the warring parties all shared defense pacts with one another. The Second Balkan War, initiated by Bulgaria against Yugoslavia and Greece, was also between states with mutual defense pacts, though those agreements were in the process of being severed. Still, even in this case, these nations had fought side by side as allies in the First Balkan War only a few months before the outbreak of the second war.[4]

The fifteen interstate war initiations between allies represent about 20 percent of all the initiations for which I have complete data. Yet allied pairs represent only about 7 percent of all annual regional dyads between 1816 and 1974. In other words, wars between allies are about three times more likely than one would expect from the distribution of bilateral military agreements. The proportion of total dyads involving defense pacts, of course, is much smaller,

4. The remaining case involves the German invasion of Poland in 1939. Poland and Germany had a mutual nonaggression pact at the time of the German attack.

indicating that the propensity for such allies to fight with one another actually is several times larger even than the 3:1 ratio that emerges from the comparison with all allied annual dyads. In fact, if we focus only on Europe—the region with both the most alliance activity and the most war—we find that allies fight with each other almost five times more often than expected by chance.

These results, furthermore, are not limited to interstate wars. Eight of the seventy-three instances of interstate threats for which I have data, or 11 percent of the threats, were between allies, while eleven of the ninety-nine interstate interventions were between allies. As with wars, in these types of conflicts, allies are more likely to fight with each other than with enemies.

One might object that when allies come into conflict with each other, they no longer are really allies. Of course, in the narrowest sense this is true. Still, there is some evidence that suggests that these quarrels, like their domestic counterparts, do not fundamentally alter the relationship between the conflicting parties. For instance, only one of the eight instances of a threat between allies led to the severing of the alliance relationship. A British threat to occupy the Turkish customshouse at Smyrna in 1880 in order to coerce the Turks into succumbing to certain territorial demands of the Montenegrins ended with the capitulation of the Turks and the termination of the Anglo-Turkish defense pact. But defense agreements between Austria-Hungary and Germany, Russia and China, Italy and Albania and the Soviet Union and Poland, survived military threats in 1850, 1898, 1934, and 1956, respectively. Similarly, the Russo-Japanese entente survived their dispute of 1897 and (though only briefly) that of 1900, as the Italo-German entente—later elevated to a defense pact—survived a threat by the Italians in 1934.

Among the cases of military interventions, only the Sino-Russian defense pact failed to survive, with the Boxer Rebellion bringing that alliance to a close. In most of the other instances of interventions between allies, nonaggression pacts were involved, and the defeated adversaries—including Albania, Poland, Latvia, Lithuania, and Estonia—failed to survive as sovereign states, or survived, as in the case of Czechoslovakia in 1968 (and the alliance continued), but under a new government. Only when these disputes involve actual warfare is the alliance unlikely to survive. Even under the extreme conditions of war, however, seven of the fifteen alliances between belligerents did survive. In virtually every case, the circumstances surrounding the conflicts fit precisely with the expectations derived from the theory. The alliances survived because the aggressors were able to impose their will on their allies by placing in power regimes more amenable to their desires than were the old regimes or by persuading the old regimes to maintain the policies desired by the initiators. Deviationist policies were prevented or stifled by persuading the opponents' leaders to be content to preserve their old alliances despite — or perhaps because of — the interference in their countries' domestic affairs. The key factors that make conflicts among allies possible and even probable are (a) the anticipation by the initiator that action can prevent the situation from deteriorating and (b) the expectation that hostile "outsiders" are neutralized. Victory by the initiator presumably reduces the chances that undesired policy changes will take place in the future. Consequently, one way to ascertain whether such conflicts prove useful from the perspective of their initiators is to see how often the initiators win such disputes. Thirteen of the fifteen war initiations, all eleven interventions, and seven of the eight threats ended with the initiator being victorious. More than 90 percent of disputes between allies are won by the initiator. Furthermore, outsiders (that is, those not allied with either initial belligerent) in no instance aided the opponent, although other allies occasionally did (as suggested in proposition 3'). Outsiders or other allies sometimes aid the initiator, apparently sometimes making the difference between victory and defeat (as suggested in proposition 3''). Of the thirty-four conflicts between allies, twenty-nine were initiated by leaders whose nations had positive expected utility, while five (of which three were threats) were initiated despite negative expected utility. In three of those five cases, other nations joined in, leaving the opponent defeated.

Although it is disturbing to realize that allies sometimes fail to aid one another, it is even more disturbing to think that allies may actually represent a serious threat to each other. Yet neither of these results should be surprising. Both are completely consistent with the implications that follow from the expected-utility theory. The likelihood that allies will actually come to one another's aid is dependent on the full array of commitments and interests that each has, as well as on the relative power of each. When an ally is exceptionally weak as compared with its friend and its friend's adversary (even though the utility the allies have for each other may be large), the probability that the ally can influence the outcome of a conflict is small, making its overall expected utility quite small. Similarly, a relatively powerful ally that is distracted will also tend to expect to derive little utility from participating in a conflict on behalf of the ally. Such distractions may arise because the third party perceives little difference between its ally and its ally's opponent or because it has many interests that are different from those of its friend. Allies should be expected to aid one another only when they are powerful enough and care enough to expect to derive substantial utility from joining an ongoing conflict (Altfeld and Bueno de Mesquita 1979). Following the same logic, the expectation of deriving some positive value often exists for relatively strong states that are prepared to engage in a conflict with their own friends. Such situations are usually free from complications arising from the interests of outside parties and are often free even from the interference of other friends who are likely to be neutralized by their joint association with both belligerents. We have now seen that however disturbing this perspective may be, it is consistent with the empirical record.

The fact that allies sometimes engage in conflict with one another should not lead us to reach the mistaken conclusion that alliances, or international friendships, are meaningless. That is not true. While it is true that allies do disproportionately fight with each other, it is also true that in conflicts between states not aligned with each other, states with allies are far more likely to receive substantial support, including fighting aid from allies, than are nonaligned states. Furthermore, as noted earlier, nonaligned nations are generally more likely to be attacked or threatened than are aligned states, with that likelihood being significantly different in the case of interstate interventions short of war. The lesson to be derived from the history of relations between allies is that security can be enhanced by alliances, provided that they are close enough to reflect meaningful shared interests and powerful enough to deter would-be adversaries, and not so close that they isolate either partner from independent friendly relations with other states. Once relations becomes so close that third parties are neutralized in the event of conflict, a weak ally is in real danger of losing control over its future policy options.

NEIGHBORHOOD AND LONG-DISTANCE CONFLICTS

Many observers have noted that states that share common borders or are geographically proximate if not coterminous tend to fight more often than states that are far apart. This is not particularly surprising. Still, there is no reason to believe that a world comprised of geographically isolated states would be free of conflict, nor should we believe that the process by which states choose to have war or peace with their neighbors is any different from the way such choices are made across great distances. In this section I compare neighborhood conflicts to long-distance conflicts from three perspectives. First, do they fit equally well with the notion that positive expected utility is necessary — though not sufficient — for conflict initiators? Second, are the expected-utility calculations equally successful, so that there is not a significant difference in the likelihood of victory or defeat for the initiators of long-distance conflicts as compared with those who start neighborhood disputes? Third, do great powers disproportionately initiate long-distance wars, as suggested by the theory?

Tables 5.30, 5.31, and 5.32 depict the distribution of expected-utility scores among initiators and opponents of long-distance wars, interventions, and threats, with long distance defined as any distance between states that is greater than the range within which I

TABLE 5.30. Expected Utility and the Initiation of
Long-distance Interstate Wars

Expected-utility score	Initiator	Opponent
Greater than or equal to zero	9	0
Less than zero	0	9

Note. Yule's $Q = 1.00$. $\lambda_A = 1.00$.

TABLE 5.31. Expected Utility and the Initiation of
Long-distance Interstate Interventions

Expected-utility score	Initiator	Opponent
Greater than or equal to zero	28	6
Less than zero	16	38

Note. Yule's $Q = .83$. $\lambda_A = .50$.

TABLE 5.32. Expected Utility and the Initiation of
Long-distance Interstate Threats

Expected-utility score	Initiator	Opponent
Greater than or equal to zero	23	2
Less than zero	7	28

Note. Yule's $Q = .96$. $\lambda_A = .70$.

have assumed that they could project their full capabilities. This
range is 680 miles during the period 1816–1918, 1,020 miles during
the interwar years, and 1,360 miles since 1945. As should be readily
apparent, positive expected utility continues to discriminate between initiators and opponents, with the respective Yule's Q values
being 1.00, .83, and .96. The only surprise in these results is that
threats, with their potential to be bluffs, fit the hypothesis so
strongly. Tables 5.33, 5.34, and 5.35 address the perhaps more
central problem of how the initiators fared in long-distance
conflicts as compared with neighborhood conflicts. Estimating the
power loss that a nation suffers in trying to project its capabilities
across great distances is difficult and potentially error prone. Yet as

TABLE 5.33. Is Victory As Likely in Long-distance Wars As
in Neighborhood Wars?

Interstate War	Initiator won	Initiator lost
Long-distance	6	3
Neighborhood	45	21

Note. Yule's $Q = -.03$. $\chi^2(1) = .008$.

TABLE 5.34. Is Victory As Likely in Long-distance Interventions
As in Neighborhood Interventions?

Interstate intervention	Initiator won	Initiator lost
Long-distance	29	9
Neighborhood	49	7

Note. Yule's $Q = -.37$. $\chi^2(1) = 2.002$.

TABLE 5.35. Is Victory As Likely in Long-distance Threats As
in Neighborhood Threats?

Interstate threat	Initiator won	Initiator lost
Long-distance	24	4
Neighborhood	26	10

Note. Yule's $Q = .40$. $\chi^2(1) = 1.678$.

the tables reveal, for all the cases for which I have complete data,
there are no significant differences in the distribution of initiator
victories and defeats when long-distance conflicts are compared to
neighborhood conflicts. The chi-square statistics for these tables are
.008, 2.002, and 1.678, respectively. National decisions regarding
conflicts with opponents that are far away appear to be made in the
same way as such decisions about local adversaries, and they
generally have the same outcome, exactly as the theory leads one to
expect.

The theory leads to the expectation that a principal difference
between long-distance and neighborhood wars is the power of the
initiator. In particular, great powers are expected to initiate a
disproportionate share of long-distance wars. This indeed proves to
be true, with 89 percent of such wars being initiated by major
powers, compared to only 40 percent of neighborhood wars. This
difference would occur by chance fewer than one time in a thousand.
Viewed somewhat differently, 22.9 percent of all wars initiated by
major powers were long-distance wars, while 2.4 percent of the wars
initiated by nonmajor powers were long distance wars. This
difference is large enough so that it would occur fewer than five times
in a thousand by chance alone.

BETTER SWITCH THAN FIGHT

To this point I have shown that states generally initiate conflicts against adversaries from which they believe they can derive positive utility, and generally they win those contests. I have shown that the decision-making pattern appears to be consistent with the theory and consistent across wars, interventions, and threats. The sixth proposition, discussed in chapter 3, suggests a circumstance that makes the decision to initiate a war different from other conflict choices. In particular, that proposition suggests that the targets of an initiator's demands have a strong incentive to negotiate rather than fight if they expect to lose more in a war than they believe the initiator expects to gain. Under those circumstances, the initiator's expectations can be satisfied while also satisfying the opponent's desire to minimize its losses. Only if one of the antagonists has a strong preference for waging war rather than negotiating, independent of the expected outcome, would war occur under such conditions. We can test this deduction by comparing the frequency with which war occurs among conflicting dyads when the opponents expect to lose more than they believe the initiators expect to gain to those cases where this inequality does not exist.

To test this proposition, I compare the expected-utility score of each initiator with that of its opponent for each conflict. If the opponent's expected-utility score is negative, and if its absolute value is larger than the absolute value of the initiator's expected-utility score, then I assume that the opponent believed it would lose more than it believed the initiator thought would be gained. For instance, using my estimates, America's expected utility from a conflict with the Soviet Union during the Cuban missile crisis was .314, while the Soviet's expected utility was −.988. The Russians apparently believed they would lose more by resisting than by giving in to President Kennedy's demand that the missiles be removed. Still, Premier Khruschev claimed that an invasion of Cuba or attack against Soviet ships would mean war. However, once the United States demonstrated its determination by forcing one or more Soviet submarines to surface in front of American warships and boarded a ship carrying Russian cargo bound for Cuba, the Soviets capitulated without firing a shot. The missiles on Cuba were dismantled and shipped backed to the Soviet Union, ending the crisis and averting potentially devastating losses to the Soviet Union associated with missiles that they themselves had said were not needed to protect their security.

Another interesting and less familiar example is Count Leiningen's mission to Constantinople in January 1853. Count Leiningen delivered an Austrian ultimatum declaring that if Turkey failed to end its conflict with Montenegro within ten days, Austria would declare war. Using my estimates, Austria-Hungary's expected utility from such a war was .748, while Turkey's expected loss was a slightly more severe $-.779$. The Austrian threat could be alleviated if Turkey gave up its plans to invade Montenegro, but resistance to Austria's demand could have led to more serious consequences. As Taylor put it: "The Turks saw other, graver troubles approaching; also, they could acknowledge Austrian interest in Montenegro without accepting, as a consequence, any general protectorate over their Christian subjects. Austria did not threaten the independent existence of the Ottoman empire; the Turks could safely give way" (1971, p. 51). By avoiding war with Austria, the Turks reduced the danger that the Crimean War— whose outbreak was only nine months off—would be fought against both Russia and Austria-Hungary, and they did so at a relatively small cost.

Of the 251 dyadic conflicts for which I have expected-utility estimates, 78 involved situations where the initiator's expected gains were smaller than the opponent's expected losses. Of these 78 conflicts, 11—or just over 14 percent—became wars. Of the remaining 173 conflicts in which the opponent did not expect to lose more than the initiator expected to gain, 65, or 38 percent, became wars. Are these differences significant, as the theory suggests they should be? The answer is yes, with chi-square equal to 14.028, indicating that this difference in war frequencies would occur fewer times than once in a thousand by chance alone. Looking at these results somewhat differently, let us compare the frequency with which the relevant inequality in expected-utility scores arises in cases of threats and interventions as compared with cases of war. As already noted, 11 of the 76 dyadic war initiations occurred in the presence of this inequality. Of the threats, 26 of the 73 (or 36 percent) for which I have the necessary data involved opponents that expected to lose more than the initiators expected to gain, while 41 of 102 interventions (or 40 percent) were of this type. The frequency of such situations among the two conflict types that do not involve sustained combat — threats and interventions — as expected, is not significantly different, but each of these types is far more likely to experience the relevant inequality in expected-utility scores than are cases of interstate war (with chi-square for war and threats and war and interventions being 8.916 and 13.934, respectively). These differences are significant, as anticipated by the theory.

What expectations might we have about the eleven instances when the expected-utility inequality failed to prevent a war? Of course, if an initiator is determined to start a war, there is little his opponent can do to stop him under these conditions. Still, we should expect the opponent to extricate himself from the war in a manner consistent with his expectations of a costly defeat if he persists in resisting the initiator's relatively modest demands. Presumably, the next best thing for the opponent, after not getting into the war at all, is to make the fighting of as low an intensity as he possibly can. The less resistance the opponent offers, the more likely the initiator is to realize that he can obtain his objectives without continuing to incur any additional war costs. To test this contention, I have devised a measure of the intensity of combat experienced by the initiator by calculating the number of soldiers per million population per month of war lost by the initiator, based on data in Singer and Small (1972). Comparing the eleven wars that satisfied the expected-utility inequality to the sixty-five warring dyads that did not reveals an enormous difference in the mean intensity of combat. In those cases where the inequality was satisfied, the initiator suffered a loss of 17 soldiers per million population for every month of war. When the inequality was not satisfied, the comparable figure was 457 soldiers lost per million population per month of war. These means are so different that this disparity would not occur by chance even as often as once in a thousand times ($t = -4.541$, $df = 75$).

The results just reported are completely consistent with the expectations raised by proposition 6, discussed earlier. Furthermore, the fact that 85 percent of the threats and interventions possessing the relevant expected-utility inequality were won by the initiators also reinforces the merits of negotiation under these conditions. Only 67 percent of all the dyadic war initiations (but 82 percent of those satisfying the relevant conditions) were won by the initiator, and only 78 percent of the lesser conflicts not involving the inequality were won by their initiators, suggesting that these situations provide a relatively cheap and low-risk means for parties to resolve their differences. Beyond that, these results contain important implications for one of the perennial questions of students of war: why are some disputes resolved without escalating into warfare, while others are not? Although other factors surely impinge on this question — one of which is discussed when I turn to deterrence — the relative magnitude of the expected-utility scores of prospective belligerents certainly appears to be an important condition that often inhibits crises from becoming wars. *When diplomacy can leave both parties better off than they expect to be after fighting a war, neither has an incentive to fight.*

DETERRENCE AND EXPECTED UTILITY

Sometimes when a state initiates a conflict, even while possessing positive expected utility, it loses. Such situations, as we have seen, may be a function of a third-party deterrent effort. As the Neuchâtel affair makes clear, there are circumstances when an initiator with positive expected utility should be expected to back away from any further conflict, even though its demands have not been fulfilled. One such circumstance involves the presence of a deterrent counterthreat. In order for a counterthreat to be credible, the state making it must, as noted in chapter 3, have positive expected utility against the country issuing the original threat. Without positive expected utility, the counterthreatening party would have to behave irrationally to take any concrete action against the original threatener. Such behavior is assumed not to take place by my theory, and indeed, my empirical evidence suggests that such behavior rarely occurs. This means that one way in which states with positive expected utility can lose is for them to be confronted by a third-party nation that can credibly threaten to impose a significant cost on them.

The presence of third-party counterthreats should act as a

deterrent and hence should serve to defuse some serious disputes before they erupt into war. Or, if a deterrent threat is not made until a war is already under way, it should help to terminate the conflict swiftly and relatively cheaply. Thus such threats represent another way, besides the expected-utility inequality discussed in the preceding section, to distinguish serious disputes likely to become wars from those serious disputes that are likely to end without war.

To test whether counterthreats are effective as a deterrent when the third party's expected utility against the initiator of the first threat is positive, I turn to the conflict data set developed by Russett in "The Calculus of Deterrence" (1963) and to an extended version of that data set. Russett identified seventeen situations in which a major power (hereafter MP_1) threatened a pawn state only to find itself the object of a counterthreat from one or more other major powers (hereafter MP_2). In seven of these cases, all of which occurred between 1935 and 1961, the counterthreat successfully deterred MP_1, while in ten cases MP_2's threat failed to deter MP_1 from carrying out its threat. Table 5.36 depicts the number of successful and unsuccessful efforts at deterrence by MP_2 as a function of MP_2's expected utility against MP_1, with a credible threat existing if at least one MP_2 had positive expected utility against MP_1 in a case. Although MP_1's threat against the pawn was credible and rational each time, MP_1 backed down seven times. In six of those seven instances, MP_2's expected utility against MP_1 was positive. The one exception was America's last-minute decision not to back the Bay of Pigs invasion fully. In that instance, Soviet conventional expected utility against the United States was negative, while our expected utility against the Soviet Union was positive. If strategic nuclear deterrence works as it is assumed to do by the American foreign policy community, then Soviet nuclear expected utility

TABLE 5.36. Expected Utility and Deterrence

Expected utility of MP_2 vs. MP_1	Deterrence Effort by MP_2	
	Successful	*Unsuccessful*
Greater than or equal to zero	6	3
Less than zero	1	7

Note. Yule's $Q = .87$. $\lambda_A = .43$.

against the United States might have been the factor leading to this case of successful deterrence without, using my measures, MP_2's having a credible conventional threat against MP_1. Table 5.36, despite this exception, strongly supports the expected-utility theory, with Yule's Q equal to .87, or about the same value as that which it has attained in all of my earlier analyses of expected utility.

Using Russett's coding rules, Gochman's data were examined for deterrence situations involving a pawn, a major-power initiator, and a major-power defender. Thirty-one such cases were identified for the period 1816–1974. Sixteen involved successful deterrence (using Russett's definition), with thirteen of these successes—or more than 80 percent—being situation where MP_2 had positive expected utility against MP_1. Nine of the fifteen cases of unsuccessful deterrence found MP_2 lacking a credible deterrent against MP_1. Yule's Q for this analysis is .73.

The mean incidence of success, given positive expected-utility for MP_2, is .667 and .684 for the Russett and extended data sets, respectively. The mean incidence of success when MP_2 had negative expected utility against MP_1 was only .125 and .333, respectively. The differences in success rates, for both the Russett and the extended data sets, are more significant than the .025 level that I have established as a significance criterion. For the Russett data set, the t statistic is 2.766, while for the extended data set, $t = 1.888$. A credible threat, as reflected by MP_2's positive expected-utility score against MP_1, appears to be necessary (but not always sufficient) for successful deterrence.

Several of the instances of unsuccessful deterrence are sufficiently interesting to merit further examination. Through an inspection of the expected-utility scores we may be able to obtain some insight, for instance, into the outbreak of the Second World War. In the months leading up to the German invasion of Poland in 1939, Hitler's policies had been redrawing the map of Europe. The loss of the Sudetenland, the Anschluss of 1938, and the fall of Czechoslovakia seem, with hindsight, clear harbingers of the coming war and even clearer indications of the folly of appeasement. Yet, Hitler continued to make demands, and until September 1939, Britain and France did nothing other than make ineffective threats. Three questions must be asked: (a) why did Hitler ignore threats from

Britain and France? (b) why did Britain and France fail to carry out their threats for so long? and (c) could a strategy have been devised that would have made Hitler less likely to pursue the war course he had chosen for Germany at least as early as 1937? Of course, we can never know the answers to these questions, but we can make some guesses based on the expected-utility theory and on the consistency of the empirical record with that theory.

When Chamberlain landed in Munich in 1938, he was to play out a drama that seems to have left him forever appearing to have been a blind, naive innocent, beguiled by the evil genius of Adolf Hitler. Yet Britain and France both had allowed themselves to be outmaneuvered diplomatically and economically by Germany long before Chamberlain's plane left for Munich. When the British and French confronted Germany's demand for lebensraum, they were still in the throes of the depression, a depression from which the German economy had largely recovered. Despite British and French objections to Hitler's demands, there was little, at that time, that they could do. Britain's expected utility against Germany in 1938 was, by my reckoning, − .840, while France's expected utility was − .311. Despite their earlier superiority to Germany, neither of these great powers was capable of making a credible threat against German territorial demands in 1938. Yet only a few years before, Hitler had commented that had the French resisted Germany's reoccupation of the Rhineland, "we would have had to withdraw with our tails between our legs, for the military resources at our disposal would have been wholly inadequate for even a moderate resistance" (Manchester 1968, p. 428). Unfortunately, in March 1936 no one thought the time to stop Hitler had come. Indeed, while Hitler's evaluation of the situation in 1936 is completely consistent with the behavior of a rational expected-utility maximizer, the French too behaved in a disastrously rational way. During the year 1936 substantial changes came about in the coalition structure of Europe. French and German decisions in 1936 were, by my measures, made in the face of uncertainty. Germany's expected utility against France was − .066, suggesting that a rational actor would have probably backed down if confronted with a threat from France. The French, however, with an expected-utility score against Germany of − .273, were in no position to make the much-needed threat. And so Hitler, undeterred by any signal from France (or anyone else), began the course that was to carry the world into war.

Could Hitler have been stopped? I believe so. However irrational he may have become by the mid-1940s, at least in the years between 1933 and 1939—the period during which the initiation of war was planned and implemented—Hitler's behavior appears to have been completely consistent with the expected-utility theory. His foreign policy was both guided and constrained (if not restrained) by his calculations about the relative capabilities of his likely adversaries and the credibility of their threats. Speer, for instance, notes that the decision to invade Poland in 1939 rather than waiting, as Hitler was counseled to do by both Goebbels and Goering, was based on careful calculations that were quite similar to those described by my theory. Speer describes the argument of what he calls the "war party" (of which he was a member) as follows:

> Let us assume that because of our rapid rearmament we hold a four to one advantage in strength at the present time [1939]. Since the occupation of Czechoslovakia the other side has been rearming vigorously. They need at least one and a half to two years before their production will reach its maximum yield. Only after 1940 can they begin to catch up with our relatively large headstart. If they produce only as much as we do, however, our proportional superiority will constantly diminish, for in order to maintain it we would have to go on poducing four times as much. We are in no position to do so. Even if they reach only half of our production, the proportion will constantly deteriorate. Right now, on the other hand, we have new weapons in all fields, the other side obsolete types.   (Speer 1971, p. 225)

The precision of these calculations is consistent with developments during the early part of the war (and presages Germany's ultimate inability to keep up with the war-making capabilities of Allied industry), and is consistent with the expectations derived from my theory. According to my estimates of British expected utility, for instance, there was little England could do, given its diplomatic involvements at the time, to stop Hitler in 1939. Britain's expected utility against Germany was $-.682$. In 1940 and 1941, as suggested by the quotation from Speer, English rearmament would be only beginning and therefore would not yet represent a major threat to Hitler's ambitions. The expected-utility scores in those years were $-.608$ and $-.661$, respectively. By 1942 and 1943, however, Britain's superior industrial capabilities, together with those of the United States, began to reverse Germany's successes, again as suggested in the quotation above. In those years, England's expected-utility score, though still negative, moved up sharply, with the actual estimates of expected utility being $-.140$ and $-.145$, respectively. By 1944, Britain's expected utility score against Germany soared to .971, and the defeat of the Nazis was assured.[5]

The evidence from my theory and that of the historical record both support the contention that Hitler's decision to start the war in 1939—neither sooner nor later—was made in a manner consistent with the notion of expected-utility maximization. Furthermore, Germany's foreign policy in the years before 1939 also was made as if by an expected-utility maximizer. From this I infer that Hitler could have been contained if the foreign policies of Britain, France, and perhaps the United States had been more sensitive to their respective expected utilities against Germany. These nations were capable of building diplomatic policies that would have rendered Hitler's ambitions unattainable. They could have rendered their expected utility positive and Germany's negative. Instead, however, they squabbled among themselves; the British, were willing to

5. Several factors allow my estimates of expected utility to reflect the shifting position between the Germans and the British, even though the only capabilities estimates I have for the entire period of the war are the prewar capabilities (in 1938). Those capabilities, coupled with the alliance structure of the time, suggest the likely outcome, even though intermediate setbacks might first arise. For instance, the utility estimates support the expectation that Italy would be defeated, ultimately leaving Germany essentially without important allies in Europe. The data also support the expectation that France would be defeated by Germany (Germany's expected utility against France in 1939 was .167), and that, though it would be very close, Russia would probably prevail over Germany (with Germany's expected utility against Russia in 1941 being $-.063$ and Russia's score against Germany being .009). By the mid-1940s, the British could count on the aid of the Americans, the Russians, and the Free French, as well as the recently defeated Italians, and a number of other countries, in their struggle against the then-isolated Germans. With the array of force tipped in the Allies' favor, Britain's expected utility against Germany swung up sharply.

forgive many of the reparation payments imposed on Germany by Versailles — payments that made it difficult for Germany's industries to afford to purchase British goods — while the French demanded full restitution. The Americans, at the same time, failed to forge closer ties with their erstwhile allies, instead insisting on payment of war debts while supporting the notion of greater charity regarding German reparations. Each of these states formed its own quite distinct international coalitions in the 1930s rather than building a common alliance. Such an alliance might have given them a credible counterthreat against the two principal threats to European (and world) peace in the 1930s — Germany and Russia. Perhaps, had they done so, Hitler would have been true to his word in 1936, abandoning the Rhineland buffer with "our tails between our legs." Had Hitler been defeated at that early date, he might have been defeated politically as well. Of course we will never know, but it is clear that such credible counterthreats are often successful and that Hitler's statements to his inner circle support the proposition that such threats would have deterred him.

EXPECTED UTILITY AND THE SEVERITY OF WAR

Before concluding this chapter we must analyze one final proposition. I have already shown that the behavior of conflict initiators is consistent with the theory and that victory generally rests with the nation having the greater expected utility. Each proposition regarding these issues has found support in a systematic examination of more than one and one-half centuries of history. I have found support even for such perverse notions as that allies are likely to engage in conflict with each other. I have also shown that the expected-utility theory is helpful in distinguishing between conflictual situations that are likely to become wars and those that are not likely to become wars. In particular, I demonstrated that when an opponent believes it will lose more than it thinks its adversary believes can be won, the opponent is much more likely to seek a settlement, yielding to the demands of the initiator without fighting. Furthermore, I showed that states with negative expected utility may be protected from some forms of aggression if they can find a state that is willing and able to threaten their adversary. That is, deterrence seems to work. I would now like to set aside questions about the initiation or outcome of conflicts and focus on the costliness of war.

It will be recalled that I argued that the greater the difference between what the initiator of a war expects to win and what the opponent expects to lose (including the possibility that the opponent believes it can win), the more difficult it is to find a settlement acceptable to both sides, and hence the costlier the war. Two distinct factors impinge on the costliness of war according to this argument. First is the question of whether the opponent believes it can win. If the opponent's expected utility is positive, then it must convince the initiator—which, by the expected-utility-maximization assumption, already presumes it is going to gain from the war—to change from expecting to gain to expecting to lose. Second, whether the two sides agree about which is expected to win or not, if the adversaries disagree on how much must be won or lost, then the opponent must fight to change the mind of the initiator about the actual amount to be gained. In other words, the less convinced each side is about what will constitute an acceptable settlement, the greater the resistance will be to accepting the signals emerging from the battlefield, and hence the costlier the war will be. Conversely, as their utilities increasingly make clear what the likely outcome will be, the costliness of reaching a mutually acceptable settlement diminishes.

Because the two factors I identified both concern reorienting the initiator's expectations, I operationalize the costliness of war from the initiator's perspective. To evaluate the costliness of war, I utilize the index of costliness that I described briefly when I examined the costliness of eleven wars that satisfied the expected-utility inequality in which the initiator's expected gains are smaller than the opponents expected losses. That index can now be explained in greater detail. The costliness index must reflect the intensity of combat. Such intensity presumably reflects both the approximate costs at a given time and an index of the likely costs as the war progresses. The specific index I use is the initiator's battle deaths per million population per month of war. Battle deaths per million population is used because it, more than the battle deaths per se, reflects the impact of the war on the initiator's total population.[6]

Three independent variables are required to test the proposition. First, a dummy variable is constructed to distinguish between those wars in which the initiator and opponent seemed to agree as to which was to be the winner from those where a disagreement is presumed to have existed. The variable (referred to as D_1 in table 5.37) is coded 1.0 whenever the initiator's expected utility is less than or equal to the opponent's expected utility and is coded 0 when the initiator's expected utility is greater than that for the opponent. The second variable is the opponent's perception of the expected stakes of the war, measured as the difference between the initiator's expected utility and the opponent's expected utility from the war (called "stakes" in table 5.37). The third variable is the interaction of the dummy variable with the indicator of the anticipated stakes in the war (called $D_1 \times$ stakes in table 5.37). The second variable, then, reflects the expected change in "resources" likely to be brought on by the war. The larger the value of the second variable, the more likely the opponent is to anticipate heavy losses if it pursues the war vigorously, given that the opponent agrees it is going to lose. The third variable reflects the anticipated change in resources when the initiator and opponent disagree as to which is to be the beneficiary of any such exchange.

The costliness proposition is tested using multiple regression analysis. The expectations derived from the theory are that the dummy variable will be positively associated with the costliness index, while the second variable will be negatively associated with the dependent variable. The interaction term (that is, the third independent variable) should have a positive coefficient. The dummy variable is expected to be positive because the cost to the initiator is presumed to increase when the opponent does not agree that the initiator should win. When there is no disagreement as to which will win — as is the case with the second variable — then the more the opponent expects to lose in a fight, the less it should be

6. Data for the dependent variable are drawn from Singer and Small (1972) except for the October War in the Middle East (1973) and the Bangladesh War of 1971. Data on the dependent variable for those wars are drawn from *Keesing's Contemporary Archive.*

prepared to fight intensely for a lost cause, hence keeping the initiator's costs (and its own costs) low. On the other hand, when the two sides disagree on the outcome, then the greater the magnitude of the war's anticipated stakes, the more they should be willing to try to tip the balance in their favor through intense combat efforts. Hence the third variable should have a positive sign, reflecting the growing costs to the initiator of trying to achieve its expected outcome, when the opponent believes it too has a shot at deriving some gains from the war.

The results of the regression analysis are reported in table 5.37. All the coefficients are in the expected direction. The multiple correlation coefficient for the regression is .601, reflecting the fact that more than 36 percent of the variance in the costliness of war is explained by this test of the proposition. Although a number of other factors must certainly play an important role in determining how costly a war is to be — and costliness might be measured in innumerable ways — these results, along with the earlier analyses, support the notion that warfare (or the threat of warfare) is used in a rational manner as a strategy that affects the likely nature of any compromise solution to a dispute between nations.

This chapter has addressed four central aspects of international conflict, along with several lesser issues. I showed that one respect in which conflict initiators differ from their opponents is in their tendency to have positive expected utility. Opponents tend to have

TABLE 5.37. The Costliness of War

Independent variable	Regression coefficient	t-statistic
Constant	398.98	—
D_1	1286.06	5.086*
Stakes	− 108.75	1.774**
(D_1) (Stakes)	828.34	4.345*

Note. $N = 73$. Multiple $R = .601$. $R = .360$. $F(3, 69) = 12.955$, $p < .001$. Because of missing data, this analysis excludes the Turkish invasion of Cyprus in 1974 and the 1962–67 Egyptian conflict with Yemen and Saudi Arabia.

*$p < .001$. **$P < .05$.

positive expected utility with the frequency that one would expect by chance, while more than 85 percent of war initiators, and almost as many initiators of lesser conflicts, have positive expected utility, a result far different from chance.

The expected-utility estimates proved to be fairly reliable indicators of the subsequent outcome of conflicts, with the side holding positive expected utility winning far more often than the side with negative expected utility. This means that the theory provides a means of projecting not only which is likely to take the first serious step in an international dispute but also which will win. At the same time, the theory identified two important circumstances when an initiator with positive expected utility will step back from waging war. In one such circumstances, the initiator emerges victorious, while under the other circumstance, the opponent, even though it has negative expected utility, emerges as the winner. In the first instance, the opponent believes it has more to lose by fighting than by capitulating to the demands of the initiator, and so the conflict is resolved in favor of the initiator but to the mutual benefit of both parties. The initiator achieves the objective it sought at the outset of the conflict, while the opponent minimizes the risk of losing any more than is absolutely necessary. In the second instance, the initiator's initial objective is thwarted by the unanticipated intervention of a third party that launches a credible, dangerous threat against the initiator. Faced with the prospect of being defeated by the third party, the initiator is deterred from pursuing his initial objective against his original opponent, thus resolving the conflict to the satisfaction of both the third party and the original opponent.

Beyond addressing the conditions under which a dispute will be resolved without its escalating into open warfare, the theory also identifies some factors that encourage nations to pursue a negotiated settlement rather than to continue fighting once a war is under way. In particular, the expected-utility theory identifies a direct link between the costliness of war and the motivation to give up a military settlement in favor of a diplomatic solution to a war, further reinforcing Clausewitz's well-known observation that war is diplomacy by other means.

Although the data used are only rough approximations of the concepts embodied in the theory, the evidence has generally been exceptionally consistent with the expectations derived from the theory. With virtually no exceptions, the evidence has supported the theory, even by the fairly rigorous standards of substantive (and statistical) significance that I set down. Although the .05 level is conventionally used to test for statistical significance, I established the higher threshold of .025. Every significance test applied to the theory surpassed that level when a significant difference was expected to exist, with the exception of one independent variable in the analysis of the costliness hypothesis. Even in that analysis, however, the overall regression results were significant well beyond the .025 level, and it is conceivable that the true significance of the second independent variable is underestimated because of some colinearity among the predictor variables. Even in this one case, that variable was significant at less than the .05 level, although it did not quite attain the .025 level of significance. All analyses involving Yule's Q—the measure of one way association used here—exceeded the .70 threshold I established for substantive significance when the theory suggested that a significant result should emerge, further reinforcing the goodness of fit between the evidence and the theory. Decision makers do appear to behave as if they are expected-utility maximizers, both in their decisions to initiate conflicts and in their decisions to terminate conflicts. The actions of decision makers seem to have been consistent with the theory in the nineteenth and the twentieth centuries, as well as in every part of the globe. Their behavior has been consistent with the theory whether their nations were aligned or nonaligned, powerful or weak, fighting at home or far away. Indeed, it appears that the deductions examined here provide lawlike general statements about the initiation, negotiation, and termination of international conflicts.

6 Speculation about Controlling the War Trap

That decision makers confronting war-and-peace decisions behave as if they are expected-utility maximizers is now well established by the record of about two hundred and fifty conflicts throughout the better part of two centuries. Initiation and negotiation, escalation and capitulation, have all been shown to follow systematically from the expectations of the expected-utility theory. The war trap is sprung by actors willing to plunge into the storm of conflict and combat in search of some treasure of policy or plunder. More often than not, that storm ends as they anticipated, although whether or not the reward ultimately is judged worthy of the price is a question best left for future research. In strictly utilitarian terms, it is the victim, and not the initiator, that is trapped by conflict, trapped by its foreign policy and the expected-utility conditions it creates. In this concluding chapter I would like to focus on escaping from the war trap and, using the information derived from the preceding chapters, to suggest alternative approaches to foreign policy. Before doing so, however, I want to address some limitations that prevent the theory from going beyond necessary conditions to the specification of necessary and sufficient "causes" of international conflict.

TOWARD NECESSARY AND SUFFICIENT CONDITIONS FOR WAR

Almost all initiators of international conflicts appear to have had a reasonable expectation of success in their conflicts, while most opponents did not. Generally, when an opponent could gain more (or more appropriately, lose less) by capitulating rather than pressing his desires, conflicts were resolved without resort to war, with the initiator gaining his objective and the opponent cutting his anticipated losses. When the opponent was able to find a "friend" willing to make a credible threat against the would-be initiator, the opponent achieved success, while the initiator backed down in the face of a superior threat. Although these and many other decisions are consistent with the theory, most situations involving a nation with positive expected utility and its potential foe result in no overt conflict. Two explanations for this fact come to mind. One is a purely utilitarian explanation that I hope to study in the future. The other, alluded to in the first chapter, is strictly nonutilitarian. The nonutilitarian explanation is simply that some leaders under some conditions view violence, including wars of course, as immoral. Alas, such individuals seem rare in the courts of nations. Still, they may exist. These true pacifists will never fight.

Unfortunately, pacifism is a rare strategy that, when used against violent people, often leads to the destruction of the pacifist, even if the aggressor accepts the moral superiority of nonviolence (Shure, Meeker, and Hansford 1965). Violence, however, can be rejected on utilitarian grounds by an actor expecting to gain from its use. Diplomacy is an alternative to violence that I have considered only in passing, but it is almost certainly central to the decision to reject violence in many situations. If one were to compute expected utilities using the decision rules delineated in chapter 3 but relying on indicators of the probability and utility of success (or failure) based on diplomacy rather than on military capabilities, one would have added an important additional component to the calculus. Thus leaders expecting a larger net gain through diplomacy than through war (or lesser acts of violence) should rationally elect to pursue their goals through diplomatic bargaining and negotiating. This is true even if the expected gross gain from war is larger than the gross gain from diplomacy, provided that the cost differential is large enough (as it frequently is) to make the net effect of diplomacy preferable to war. Once the option of using diplomacy to settle disputes is added to the theory, one must also calculate the expected strategic utility attached to diplomacy or to a show of force, independent of the effect those strategies have on the outcome. This is important because some individuals prefer fighting to bargaining, even if they think they can do better materially by bargaining.[1] Frederick the Great of Prussia, for instance, attached great value to waging war as an end in itself. He once observed, for instance: "The ox must plow the furrow, the nightingale must sing, the dolphin must swim, and I — I must make war." Even those cherishing peace and preferring diplomatic solutions over violent solutions to international disputes, however, must at least act as if they are prepared to fight. The expected value of diplomacy is almost certainly linked in the minds of both the aggressor and his opponent to the expected value of war. In this vein even those most strongly opposed to violence but interested in protecting the sovereignty of their nation and promoting what they believe to be the national interest must heed Frederick the Great's dictum "Diplomacy without armaments is like music without instruments" or Carl von Clausewitz's well-known observation that war is "only diplomacy somewhat intensified."

Beyond the evaluation of expected utility from diplomacy, other areas need investigation to refine the theory. The theory is currently limited to the analysis of a particular type of rational actor — an expected-utility maximizer. Although the historical record fits this perspective rather well, it is possible for rational actors to follow decision rules different from those set out here. Such actors may be satisficers, minimax or maximin strategists, minimax regret strategists, and so on. Each of these types of rationality *can* be accommodated by an expected-utility theory, but the specific decision rules imposed would have to be modified to fit the strategy that the analyst believes the relevant decision maker employs. Similarly, and as noted earlier, the risk-related and uncertainty-related decision rules used here are reasonable, but they do not exhaust the array of reasonable rules. Much more development is needed in the identification and evaluation of decision maker's responses to risk and uncertainty. Rather than treating all actors as if they are merely risk

1. Of course, decision makers must expect to gain utility from a war's outcome in order to wage war rationally, even if they have a strategic preference for fighting rather than bargaining. That is, I assume that the utility from fighting (as a strategy) cannot overwhelm a negative expected-utility outcome from waging war. See chapter 3 for a more extended discussion of this point.

acceptant or risk avoidant, future research should strive to extend the analysis of these characteristics along the continuum on which they must surely fall in reality.

Having recognized such limitations of the expected-utility theory developed in this study, I turn now to an examination of potential uses of the theory and evidence presented here. In doing so I hope to suggest how the expected-utility calculus, coupled with the wisdom and intuition of experienced policymakers, can help reveal nuances and unanticipated consequences of different foreign policy options. In doing so, I do not mean to imply that the expected-utility approach represents an alternative to currently used means of evaluating and analyzing foreign policies. Rather, I would like to suggest that the theory provides a useful addendum, a supplement capable of providing information that more conventional approaches do not offer. Of course, most of the time, expert foreign policy makers are wise enough and knowledgeable enough that the theory will not reveal much that is new to them. But sometimes it can. Those who are doubtful should study closely the literature of diplomatic history or the memoirs of renowned diplomats to see how many of the deductions I have discussed—such as those relating to conflicts among allies—are not widely known or understood. Examination of some of the applications discussed below will also reveal that the expected-utility framework has been used to predict successfully events that were not widely anticipated among the relevant portions of the foreign-policy-making community. The potential value of the theory as a policy tool, it seems to me, is the degree to which it focuses attention on a relatively small set of seemingly critical questions—questions of utility and capabilities—that allow detailed analyses of situations of which the analyst may have little personal knowledge. Thus the theory helps to direct and focus further inquiry into a situation, providing the analyst with one more check against the wisdom he has acquired in a lifetime of diplomacy.

FUTURE PEACE, FUTURE WAR: A UTILITARIAN VIEW OF THE MIDDLE EAST

Although one may find objectionable the notion that decision makers act in accordance with the mathematical description of rational behavior set out earlier in this study, the evidence does not support such skepticism. Despite the use of crude, error-prone indicators that are likely to produce weakened statistical associations, I have exposed consistently strong relationships between the logically derived expectations of the theory and the historical record. Much of foreign policy may sometimes appear irrational, but when decisions about serious international conflicts are taken, leaders act like expected-utility maximizers. Those willing to accept this conclusion and equipped with far better information than mine about any particular present or future dispute have the potential to influence the course of events. Conflicts are rarely initiated by actors with negative expected utility and, as the evidence has shown, are rarely initiated against opponents with positive expected utility. Expected-utility values can be, and often are, heavily influenced by the policies of third parties. Indeed, third parties interested in preventing overt aggression can, by altering their own policies and projecting appropriate interests, deprive a potential aggressor of the positive expected-utility score required to contemplate initiating a conflict.

Convincing an actor that he cannot succeed may be a difficult and sometimes impossible task. It makes little sense to bluff about one's true interests in a potential dispute if one favors the would-be initiator. Efforts to dissuade him from aggression by "sophisticated voting," in which one signals a preference for the opponent when one's true preference is for the initiator, work contrary to one's own interests. Such acts may lead to the loss of a friend (the would-be initiator) or even incite the potential victim to become an aggressor. But sincere shifts in policy, used to signal all parties in a potential dispute that one's preferences lie with peace rather than with either of them, may be a crucial element dissuading all parties from believing that they can succeed through warfare. American efforts in the late 1970s to create peace in the Middle East are an example of such a situation. The combination of the United States' longstanding interest in and sympathy for the Israelis, coupled with American dependence on Arab oil, created a situation in which American interests were best served by peace in the region. As a pivotal actor, capable of depriving any potential antagonist of positive expected utility, the government of the United States was in a position to

enforce peace, provided it followed the most appropriate policy.
Were the outcomes that emerged from the Camp David summit
between President Carter, President Sadat, and Prime Minister
Begin, and the subsequent treaties signed by Israel and Egypt, truly
instruments of peace? Did they diminish the risk of war in the Middle
East? Did they leave unchanged or even increase the jeopardy faced
by either Israel or Egypt? These are questions that can be partially
answered by an expected-utility analysis. The theory identifies
conditions under which adversaries might come to blows, might
reach negotiated solutions to their problems, or might avoid war-
threatening conflicts altogether.

In attempting to respond to the questions just posed, I move now
from the rigorous but overly rigid operational procedures I have
used in the analytic portions of this study to broader, more intuitive,
and (I hope) more informed, operationalizations of utility. Rather
than confining my perspective solely to the formal alliances existing
among nations in the Middle East, I now extend my classificatory
scheme to reflect the preference ordering of each state for each other
state in the area. My own knowledge of the Middle East is limited, so
that I must still make crude estimates and find myself being
restricted to five broad categories of relationship, ranging from the
close ties implied by a defense pact to nonallied but not openly
hostile states to nonallied but hostile states. Syria and Egypt, for
instance, are now treated as if they are no longer allied with each
other in the Arab League; Israel and Iran are treated as being
nonallied and openly hostile (as are Israel and Syria, Libya, Iraq,
and the Yemeni People's Republic). Iraq, Libya, and the People's
Republic of Yemen are also assumed to be no longer allied with
Egypt, while all other members of the Arab League (except Oman,
Sudan, and Morocco) are viewed as having diminished common
interests with Egypt, reflected by the fact that they are now being
treated as if their defense pacts with Egypt had been reduced to
nonaggression pacts. This recoding was prompted by the severing of
diplomatic relations between Egypt and many Arab states, the
support that some Arab states gave economic sanctions against
Egypt, and the refusal of these states to endorse more severe
actions, including Egypt's expulsion from the Arab League. Some
Arab states seem to be treading a middle ground, still hoping to

reach an amicable solution to their differences with Egypt but no longer endowing Egypt with the trust and commitment implied by their earlier relations. Morocco, Sudan, and Oman have endorsed the Camp David accords and so are still assumed to view Egypt as the closest of allies. The relationship between the United States and Iran in 1979 is assumed to have deteriorated to the point where they are nonallied and openly hostile toward each other.

With these still simplistic—though somewhat less simplistic than earlier—approximations of the relations between states in the Middle East region, the expected-utility theory reveals several interesting and dramatic changes. The once reasonably cohesive Arab League, united at least in opposition to Israel, is now sharply divided. A hard-line coalition, including Syria, Libya, Iraq, the People's Republic of Yemen, and non-Arab Iran, vies for domination of the Arab League with an alternative coalition that includes such critical states as Saudi Arabia, Jordan, and Lebanon. Israel now finds itself fairly friendly with Egypt, while Egypt still counts Morocco, Sudan, and Oman among its Arab friends. These states are still hostile toward Israel, but less so than they were before. What is more, they continue to maintain reasonable relations with the rest of the Arab League, representing a potential "detente-like" bridge between Israel and the Arab world.

The new coalition structure represents a sharp decline in the clarity of international commitments in the Middle East, with the region's overall "tightness" score having declined from .937 to .804 in just one year. Given the prevailing uncertainties, especially as to which Arabs would support which other Arabs and how much, in the event of a war between, say, Israel and Syria, or between Libya and Egypt or Egypt and Israel, we must assume that expected utility is calculated under uncertainty. Those calculations reveal that no hard-line state in 1980 could expect to gain from attacking Israel, a condition which did not exist before the Egyptian-Israeli rapprochement of 1979. Israel, too, does not expect to gain from attacking any of the hard-line or moderate Arab states, although Israel in 1979 and 1980, ironically, possessed positive expected utility against Egypt—a score it did not have in 1978. With the prevailing uncertainty, Egypt too is secure against the hard-liners (and the moderates), while they too are secure against an Egyptian threat. Thus so long as uncertainties remain, peace, or at least the absence of overt combat, has come to the most troubled part of the Middle East.

What is likely to happen to the uneasy peace achieved by Presidents Carter and Sadat and Prime Minister Begin as the commitments of the late 1970s are permitted to solidify? With time and the stabilization of Arab-Israeli relations, national leaders will form clearer expectations about the likely behavior of other states. As expectations become clearer, uncertainty will play a diminishing role in their expected-utility calculations. In the relative absence of uncertainty, Egypt is likely to become increasingly vulnerable to pressure from some of the moderate Arab states, especially Jordan. Israel will probably continue to represent a potential threat to Egyptian interests, suggesting that Israel is in a strong position to drive a hard bargain in bilateral negotiations with Egypt. On the other hand, Israel too will probably become more vulnerable. As uncertainty diminishes, Saudi Arabia, Iraq, and Iran will probably move from having negative expected utility to having positive expected utility against Israel. What is more, Israel's expected utility against Iran, estimated to be −.468, will likely place Israel in an extremely weak bargaining position if the Iranian regime of Ayatollah Khomeini directly—or through proxies—chooses to threaten Israel. Iran's expected utility without uncertainty is estimated to be .339, so that the Israelis are likely to believe that they have even more to lose in a dispute with Iran than Iran expects to gain. We have seen that this type of situation ends successfully for the actor with positive expected utility about 90 percent of the time.

By applying the expected-utility theory to the current situation in the Middle East we can see, within the limits of the data that have been used, that the peace initiatives of 1977–1979 have bought time. They have reduced the threat of violent conflict between the Arabs and Israel. Even during the next few years, and despite the realignment of Iran, fewer states are likely to be in a position to menace Israel than might have been before the Egyptian-Israeli rapprochement. Though Egypt's position has somewhat deteriorated, it has not changed markedly, suggesting that the external costs of the rapprochement are probably small as compared with the territorial and internal political gains achieved by President Sadat.

Where the Arab-Israeli dispute is concerned, then, genuine steps toward reducing conflict or the threat of war have been taken. Yet these steps are not without dangerous and perhaps unanticipated risks. One consequence anticipated by the expected-utility calculus and already revealing itself in the Middle East is a sharp increase in the capacity of the Iraqi and Iranian governments to disrupt politics in the oil-rich Arabian peninsula. As recently as 1978, the expected-utility values for Iraq vis-à-vis Saudi Arabia, the Yemen Arab Republic, Kuwait, Bahrein, Qatar, Oman, the United Arab Emirates, Iran, and Jordan and Lebanon were all negative. Now all these expected-utility scores are positive, suggesting that Iraq has become a critical force in that part of the world. This is an unhappy development for the United States, both because historically we have had little leverage in Baghdad and because, with the fall of the shah of Iran, oil from Saudi Arabia—and the Persian Gulf—has become absolutely critical to the preservation of our interests and those of our closest allies. The emergence of Iraqi influence, long diminished by Iraq's rivalry with Syria, must surely draw the careful attention of Middle East watchers. Whether there exist policy options that are feasible and that will simultaneously preserve the gains achieved for Israeli security while diminishing Iraq's enhanced position is an issue that can be resolved by the joint efforts of the expected-utility theory and knowledgeable policymakers. Would more explicit guarantees of Saudi Arabian security, for instance, eliminate any possible Iraqi threat and still insure Israel's security against Arab aggression—or Arab security against Israeli aggression? Do other options produce the desired results without adding still other unanticipated consequences? The answer, at least in the case of an American-Saudi agreement, say, at the level of a mutual defense pact, is no! Such an agreement would weaken the cohesion of the moderate Arab bloc (presuming that a regionwide pact was not formed among those states and the United States), extending the period of uncertainty for at least another year or two. However, with the diminished cohesion of that bloc would come several important and presumably undesirable changes in expected-utility scores. While Iraq's ability to menace Saudi Arabia would be virtually eliminated, as indeed would Iraq's leverage with the peninsula states, Iraq would be able, even under conditions of uncertainty, to threaten Israeli interests, as would Libya. Once the uncertainty ended, Iraq would again be likely to find itself in a good position to influence greatly the policies of the moderate states located in the Arabian peninsula. Thus a mutual defense pact between the United States and Saudi Arabia would yield a credible guarantee to one friend at the expense of another. On the other hand, a larger security system incorporating many of the Persian Gulf states in an alliance with the United States—though still unlikely—would diminish both Iraq's and Iran's positions as potentially dominant regional powers. If many of the peninsula states could be convinced that such an alliance—including Israel as a member—would serve their security interests against the rising but opposed positions of Iran and Iraq, then stability might be brought to the Middle East. Although the Soviets would surely oppose such an agreement and would probably forge an alternative alliance with such states as Syria or Libya, the expected-utility theory suggests that they do not currently pose a credible threat against the United States, provided we are prepared to commit ourselves seriously to protecting our interests and those of our allies.

Whether or not the American government enters into a formal agreement with the Saudi Arabian government, our expected utility against all states in the Middle East is large enough to make us potentially capable of deterring actions contrary to our interests, provided we are willing to use our resources to make credible threats. As we saw in the preceding chapter, when a would-be aggressor has negative expected utility against a state that declares its intention to defend the threatened state, deterrence is usually successful. Such credible counterthreats, however, must be made sincerely enough for the potential aggressor to believe that force will be used. The increased tensions in the Middle East, arising from the internal instability in Iran and the Soviet invasion of Afghanistan, are likely to lead to a reassessment of American priorities. These and other events will probably facilitate the development of the motivation needed to render America's deterrent posture in the Middle East as credible as it must be to preserve some semblance of peace and stability in vital parts of that area.

Whether a workable solution to the Middle Eastern dilemma— the desire to protect both Israel and our vital oil links throughout the Arabian peninsula — is possible is beyond the scope of this essay. I merely wish to demonstrate how one might use the expected-utility calculus to estimate the likely direct and indirect consequences of policy shifts in the Middle East or elsewhere. In a later section I return to a discussion of the Middle East to analyze internal sources of political instability.

FUTURE PEACE, FUTURE WAR: A UTILITARIAN VIEW OF ASIA

The last few years of the 1970s brought great changes to the political map not only of the Middle East but also of Asia. The United States' recognition of the People's Republic of China brought with it the demise of the American defense arrangement with the Republic of China. Also lost among the anti-Communist alliances forged during the Cold War was the South East Asia Treaty Organization. Japan, long a most cautious and quiet participant in Asian foreign policy, emerged from its period of political — but not economic — "isolation" with the signing of a mutual treaty with the People's Republic of China. The Russians too took new action in Asia, forging a defense agreement with the Vietnamese. On the other side of Asia, Afghanistan came under the domination of one after another pro-Soviet government that found itself bedeviled by a number of anti-Marxist resistance movements. By Christmas 1979, anti-Marxist resistance had become serious enough to lead to a Soviet invasion and to the establishment of a Russian-installed regime in Kabul. I examine this regime more closely in the next section.

Pakistan, too, experienced upheaval during the closing years of the 1970s, especially after the government of General Zia hanged the one-time head of state, Zulfikar Ali Bhutto. India ushered in 1977 by returning to the slim ranks of Asian democracies, only to find the nation plunged into the destabilizing upheavals of the most opportunistic brand of coalition politics, followed by the return to power of Indira Gandhi's Congress Party in January 1980. These and other events have made Asia probably the most volatile and changing region of the world. How, if at all, have these changes affected the danger of international conflict in that area? Again I turn to the expected-utility calculus in an attempt to address this question tentatively.

The Vietnamese invasion of Cambodia in late 1978 and the Chinese attack of Vietnam a few weeks later were in some respects not particularly surprising events. Vietnamese-Cambodian animosities stretch back to antiquity, as does the ethnic conflict between the Chinese and the Vietnamese. Perhaps what is surprising is that these events happened in 1978–1979 and not in 1975 or 1976 or 1977. The motive for conflict was present then, as it is now and indeed has been for centuries. Yet the opportunity may not have been present in those earlier years. Possibly the Vietnamese invasion of Cambodia occurred in 1978 merely by chance. Although there is no way to choose among the many plausible alternative explanations for the timing of the Vietnamese attack against the Pol Pot regime, that invasion is consistent with the expected-utility theory both in a superficial way (Vietnam had positive expected utility against Cambodia) and in more subtle ways. The year 1978 marked the signing of the Russo-Vietnamese defense agreement, which followed shortly after the Vietnamese and Laotians signed a mutual entente. That entente expresses concern for the fraternal relations of the Vietnamese and Laotians with the Cambodians, yet the Cambodians were not included in the pact. This alliance is one signal suggesting which side Laos—a country bordering on both Cambodia and Vietnam—would be likely to favor. The neutralization of any Laotian support for Cambodia against which Vietnam possessed positive expected utility—reduces the number of local opponents the Vietnamese might have to face. More importantly, because it was a more credible threat, the Laotian and Russian alliances neutralized the only other nation bordering on Cambodia and therefore capable of aiding the Cambodians in combat without actually attacking Vietnam. That country, of course, is Thailand. As recently as 1977, Vietnamese expected utility against Thailand was negative, suggesting that they dared not risk a conflict with the Thais. By 1978, however, Vietnam had, by my calculations, positive expected utility against both Thailand and Cambodia and was thus in a position to threaten the Thais into acquiescence during the invasion of Cambodia. Indeed, the Vietnamese did threaten (and continue to threaten) reprisals against Thailand if the Thais offered significant aid to Vietnam's Cambodian foes.

One additional element that may have figured into the Vietnamese calculus in 1978 that was not present earlier was the belief that Chinese intervention would be deterred by the Soviet commitment to Vietnam. This seems to be a reasonable expectation, since China, despite positive expected utility against Vietnam, should have expected to lose more than it could gain if the Russians intervened. In one respect, this calculation seems correct. Although China attacked Vietnam, it did not do so until after the Vietnamese had succeeded in overthrowing the Cambodian regime. In other words, the Chinese invasion of Vietnam, though partially motivated by the Vietnamese attack of Cambodia (and partially motivated by Vietnam's treatment of its large ethnic Chinese population), constitutes a separate and distinct military operation. The Chinese did not enter an ongoing war to save the Cambodian government but rather fought a distinct action against Vietnam. Even in victory, the Chinese were not able to impose a change in Cambodian governments more favorable to them, nor were they able to compel the Vietnamese to withdraw their occupation force from Cambodia. In that sense, the Chinese obviously did not exert as much force against Vietnam as they were capable of doing, a fact suggesting that they did act with some restraint. That restraint may have been the result of Soviet statements urging the Chinese not to go too far, lest they incur "serious consequences." At the same time, the Chinese were not completely deterred by the cautiously threatening statements emanating from Moscow. They did invade Vietnam, thereby testing the sincerity of the Russian commitment to the Vietnamese, a commitment that turned out to be too weak to foster a direct Soviet combat role in the Sino-Vietnamese war. This is an outcome that is not particularly surprising, in light of the fact that (at least, using my indicators) there was not a very large difference in shared interest between the Russians and the Vietnamese as compared with the Russians and the Chinese in Asia. To be sure, the Soviet Union did favor Vietnam, with a utility score of .39, up sharply from its value earlier in the 1970s, while the Sino-Soviet score was dropping dramatically during the same period. Still, the Sino-Soviet utility score, using my crude indicator of alliance, was still weakly positive.

During the same period, American-Soviet shared interests were deteriorating in Asia, while the Americans were plainly moving closer to the Chinese. This fact, together with the relatively weak preference of the Russians for the Vietnamese, may have been enough to convince the Soviet leadership that direct intervention in the Sino-Vietnamese war carried greater risks than the potential gains were worth.

The expected-utility theory seems to provide some useful insights into recent events in Asia. As with the Middle Eastern example, this discussion is intended to show how the theory might be used to interpret or anticipate foreign policy shifts that may bear directly on the risk that international disputes will erupt into violent conflict. By introducing various American policy positions in such situations, one can gain some indication of the potential unanticipated consequences of such policy shifts. One can, for instance, observe which nations become more (or less) capable of deriving benefits from aggressive acts, and which countries are their prospective targets. Policymakers might also derive useful information about the credibility and likelihood of deterrent threats arising in response to new sources of conflict. Or they might identify policy options that would facilitate the development of such deterrent counterthreats. With the information provided by the expected-utility theory used as a supplement to other sources of information, diplomats may find themselves better able to evaluate changing patterns of authority and interaction in such troubled areas as the Middle East, Asia, and Africa.

INTERNAL CONFLICT AND EXPECTED UTILITY

Throughout this book I have focused on the applications of my expected-utility theory to the analysis of international conflict. Yet there is no reason why the theory should not also be able to account for intranational conflict, provided that the necessary data can be obtained. I would like to pause now to examine the potential explanatory or predictive power of the theory in the context of two recent examples of serious internal conflict.

As noted earlier, the latter part of the 1970s saw the Middle East facing significant political changes and instability. One important source of such instability was the Islamic revolution in Iran, a revolution that brought the downfall of the Pahlavi dynasty. Shortly after the fall of the shah, the virtual unanimity of the masses in opposition to the monarchy began to crumble as new issues surfaced, revealing old and new divisions in the body politic. By the autumn 1979, at least ten significant, organized political groups could be identified in Iran. These included the Islamic Republic party of Ayatollah Khomeini, the People's Moslem Republic party, led by Ayatollah Shariatmadari, the Freedom Front, led by then prime minister Mehdi Bazargan, the Unity party of Ayatollah Khalkhali, the supporters of Shahpur Bakhtiar, the first Iranian prime minister after the shah, the National Front, the anti-Soviet marxists, dominated by the Fedayan, the pro-Soviet Tudeh Party, and the leftist Mujahaddin.

The utility that each group has for each other group (and also for other countries in the region) was ascertained by the following method. First, an estimate of each group's preference ordering across all the other groups was obtained from leading specialists in Iranian politics. These preference orderings were then correlated using tau B, as described in chapter 4, to learn how similar the policy outlook of each group was to that of each other group. These correlations were used as indicators of utility. Applying the clustering technique described in chapter 4, I then identified the underlying "coalition" structure of the competing political interests in Iran. That clustering, performed in October 1979, before the seizure of the American embassy in Teheran, revealed that the most powerful group—the Islamic Republic party—was part of a very large but loosely knit coalition consisting of the Islamic Republic party, the People's Moslem Republic party, the Freedom Front, and the Unity party. The Royalist, National Front, and Bakhtiar supporters formed a separate coalition, while the leftist groups seemed to form a third—and the most cohesive—coalition. The central question I hoped to answer through the expected-utility analysis was whether any of these groups were capable of mounting a credible challenge to the Khomeini regime.[2] Interestingly, the

2. It should be noted that the information provided to me did not lend itself to an analysis along ethnic lines, except that the supporters of the People's Moslem

analysis revealed that only one political group possessed positive expected utility against the Islamic Republic party. That group was the People's Moslem Republic party, led by Ayatollah Shariatmadari. The expected-utility analysis suggested that this group was a rather cautious, risk-averse group, possessing a small positive score of .035 vis-à-vis Khomeini and his supporters. On December 7, 1979 one group burst into open rebellion against the newly promulgated Iranian constitution. That group was the People's Moslem Republic party—the one group able to launch such a challenge, according to the analysis.

As I noted earlier, while Iran was still enmeshed in a political crisis, Afghanistan experienced a Soviet invasion and coup. Using data on internal and external preference orderings for Afghanistan, I undertook three analyses. First, I examined Soviet expected utility vis-à-vis the regime of Hafizullah Amin to ascertain whether a Soviet invasion should have come as a surprise to members of the American foreign policy establishment. As expected, the Soviets possessed positive expected utility against Afghanistan, with their utility for each other being high enough so that all relevant prospective third parties were neutralized. The Russians were in a position to act with impunity. They had few reasons to fear that they would incur any serious external costs for invading their Afghani ally.

Two additional analyses were undertaken to see whether any of the significant, politically organized groups in Afghanistan were capable of challenging the new government, either if the Soviet military presence remained or if it was assumed that the Soviets would withdraw. The latter analysis was undertaken in part to provide a basis for judging whether a Soviet withdrawal should be expected. The analysis reveals that from the Soviet perspective, the ouster of the Amin regime was warranted by the fact that Amin's government was vulnerable to the Pakistan-based Muslim rebels, while the new ruling group was not. The analysis showed that the security of the new government, however, depended on the Soviet

---

Republic party were drawn primarily from the Azerbaijani portions of Iran. My informants did not include the military, the Kurds, or the Baluchis in their ordering of organized political interests.

presence. If the Russians had withdrawn quickly, the new government would have become vulnerable to a number of opposition groups, including the Muslim rebels.

Given a Soviet presence, only two groups appear capable of mounting a challenge to the Russian-installed regime. One, of course, is the Russians themselves. So long as they maintain an active interest in keeping Afghanistan within their sphere of influence, the Russians will be able to insure that the leadership in Kabul complies with their desires. Surprisingly, the government bureaucracy emerges from the analyses with positive expected utility against the ruling Babrak Karmal regime, although they also emerge as probably too risk averse to carry their capability to a full conclusion. Nevertheless, they do potentially represent a thorn in the side of the government. The bureaucracy has managed to maintain good relations with both the leadership of the ousted political group and the Russian-backed group, while also having good relations with the Russians, the military, and even some of the opposition groups. The middle-class bureaucrats seen to have particularly close relations with the Pushtuns, Afghanistan's largest ethnic group. Whether they will take advantage of their position remains unknown at this writing.[3]

The analyses of Iranian and Afghani internal affairs, though crude and simplistic, particularly in their failure to distinguish among specific policy areas, are nevertheless suggestive of ways in which the expected-utility theory might be used to investigate potential sources of internal instability and conflict. All the deductions about national behavior can readily be extended and applied to political conflict in other arenas and, as the Iranian analysis shows, with the prospect of predictive as well as explanatory power.

I have talked at great length about the relationship between

---

3. On February 25, 1980, a front page story in the *New York Times* reported that a strike by Afghani civil servants had so paralyzed the government of Babrak Karmal that the Soviet military commander had to take temporary charge of the government. At this writing, in July 1980, a second strike by civil servants has again brought the Afghan government to the brink of collapse, with recent reports even indicating that President Karmal has attempted to take his own life.

expected utility and the initiation, termination, escalation, and cost of international conflict. At the outset I suggested that several lawlike generalizations would be derived from the expected-utility framework. Whether that objective has been achieved must be judged by the reader. I can only note that all the criteria I set down for judging the theory's usefulness in the light of the evidence have been satisfied. None of the propositions deduced from the theory — whether intuitively pleasing or seemingly perverse — failed to meet the test of a rather extensive set of empirical analyses. The apparent success of the theory encourages me to believe that the expected-utility framework provides a useful perspective from which to study necessary, if not sufficient, conditions for conflict. I am also encouraged by the realization that there is nothing inherent in the formulation of the theory that necessarily restricts its potential value to international conflict. Indeed, the illustrative analyses of preference orderings among political groups, both in Iran and Afghanistan (and indeed elsewhere as well), suggest that the theory can be used to forecast probable coalition structures and strategies as well as likely sources of internal political instability — and their attendant outcomes — in a number of critical political settings. While the value of the expected-utility framework in these other contexts remains a subject for future study, nothing in the theory's logic suggests that it will fail.

The course I set at the beginning was an ambitious one. Whatever the merits or failings of my endeavor, it has taken me to many unexpected questions and has suggested many unexpected answers. Whether or not the goal of peace remains as elusive as before, it remains the obligation of each of us to continue the journey. In doing so, we should bear in mind Saint Augustine's observation about scientific inquiry, even when we are led to unpleasant or unexpected results:

> We should not hold rashly an opinion in a Scientific matter, so that we may not come to hate later whatever truth may reveal to us, out of love for our own error.

Appendix

LIST OF ABBREVIATIONS USED IN TABLES A-C

ALB	Albania	FRN	France
ARG	Argentina	GDR	German Democratic
AUH	Austria-Hungary		Republic
AUL	Australia	GMY	Prussia before 1870;
AUS	Austria		Germany, 1870–1945
BAD	Baden	GRC	Greece
BAV	Bavaria	GUA	Guatemala
BEL	Belgium	HAN	Hanover
BOL	Bolivia	HOL	Holland
BRA	Brazil	HON	Honduras
BUL	Bulgaria	HSE	Hesse Electoral
BUR	Burma	HSG	Hesse Gran Ducal
CHL	Chile	HUN	Hungary
CHN	China before 1949;	IND	India
	People's Republic of	INS	Indonesia
	China	IRN	Iran
COL	Colombia	IRQ	Iraq
CUB	Cuba	ISR	Israel
CYP	Cyprus	ITA	Italy after 1860;
CZE	Czechoslovakia		Sardinia before 1860
DEN	Denmark	JOR	Jordan
DOM	Dominican Republic	JPN	Japan
DRV	Democratic Republic of	KOR	Korea before 1948
	Vietnam	LAT	Latvia
ECU	Ecuador	LEB	Lebanon
EGY	Egypt	LIT	Lithuania
EST	Estonia	MAL	Malaysia
ETH	Ethiopia	MEX	Mexico
FIN	Finland	MON	Mongolia

(continued)

MOR	Morocco	SAL	El Salvador
NIC	Nicaragua	SAU	Saudi Arabia
NOR	Norway	SAX	Saxony
NEW	New Zealand	SIC	The Two Sicilies
PAK	Pakistan	SPN	Spain
PAN	Panama	SWZ	Switzerland
PAP	Papal States	SYR	Syria
PAR	Paraguay	TAI	Taiwan
POL	Poland	TUN	Tunisia
POR	Portugal	TUR	Turkey
PRK	People's Republic of Korea (North Korea)	UK	United Kingdom
		USA	United States of America
ROK	Republic of Korea (South Korea)	USR	Soviet Union, 1917-present
RUM	Rumania	VEN	Venezuela
RUS	Russia before 1917	WRT	Wuerttemberg
RVN	Republic of Vietnam (South Vietnam)	YEM	Yemen
		YUG	Yugoslavia

TABLE A. Interstate Threats

Year	Initiator	Opponent	$E(U_i)$	$E(U_j)$	Winner
1821	RUS	TUR	3.100	− 3.100	TUR
1826	RUS	TUR	.527	− .527	RUS
1840	FRN	UK	− .600	.089	UK
1840	FRN	GMY	− .300	− .841	GMY
1850	AUH	GMY	− .051	.051	AUH
1853	AUH	TUR	.748	− .779	AUH
1854	AUH	RUS	− .199	.137	AUH
1856	GMY	SWZ	1.495	− 1.495	SWZ
1860	FRN	ITA	.473	− .473	FRN
1861	UK	USA	.787	− 1.086	UK
1865	USA	FRN	.663	− .552	USA
1876	RUS	TUR	1.076	− 1.076	RUS
1878	UK	RUS	.549	− .708	RUS
1880	UK	TUR	.000	− .000	UK
1880	FRN	TUR	− .014	− .148	FRN
1880	RUS	TUR	.091	− .091	RUS
1880	GMY	TUR	.306	− .329	GMY
1880	AUH	TUR	.174	− .215	AUH
1880	ITA	TUR	− .487	.405[a]	ITA
1881	TUR	FRN	− .736	.554	FRN
1885	UK	RUS	− .083	− .526	RUS
1890	UK	POR	1.581	− 1.575	UK
1895	RUS	JPN	.716	− .716	RUS
1895	GMY	JPN	.229	− 1.024	GMY
1895	FRN	JPN	.524	1.413	FRN
1897	UK	RUS	− .262	− .476	UK
1897	UK	KOR	1.085	− 1.100	UK
1897	JPN	RUS	− .451	− .002	JPN
1897	JPN	KOR	2.011	− 2.005	JPN
1898	RUS	CHN	.027	− .027	RUS
1898	UK	CHN	− .432	− .501	UK
1898	UK	TUR	.698	− .864	UK
1898	FRN	TUR	.914	− 1.090	FRN
1898	RUS	TUR	1.172	− 1.172	RUS
1898	ITA	TUR	− .059	− 1.580	ITA
1898	UK	FRN	.074	− .074	UK
1899	RUS	KOR	2.188	− 2.188	RUS
1900	JPN	RUS	− .402	− .073	RUS

TABLE A (continued)

Year	Initiator	Opponent	$E(U_i)$	$E(U_j)$	Winner
1900	FRN	DOM	1.159	− 1.188	FRN
1903	GMY	DOM	1.179	− 1.209	GMY
1906	UK	TUR	1.120	− 1.250	UK
1908	YUG	AUH	− 2.603	1.755	AUH
1911	GMY	FRN	− .151	.152	GMY
1911	UK	GMY	.016	− .016	GMY
1912	RUS	BUL	2.280	− 2.216	RUS
1912	AUH	YUG	1.981	− 1.981	AUH
1913	RUS	TUR	1.606	− 1.606	RUS
1913	AUH	YUG	2.131	− 2.131	AUH
1921	USA	PAN	1.196	− 1.198	USA
1921	FRN	GMY	.077	− .077	FRN
1921	UK	GMY	.290	− .290	UK
1921	BEL	GMY	− .270	.270	BEL
1921	ITA	GMY	− .450	.450	ITA
1922	UK	GRC	.880	− .950	UK
1922	FRN	GRC	1.070	− 1.140	FRN
1922	ITA	GRC	.590	− .590	ITA
1934	ITA	GMY	− .604	.604	ITA
1934	ITA	ALB	1.490	− 1.490	ITA
1940	FRN	USR	− .889	.741	USR
1940	UK	USR	− .783	.577	USR
1940	JPN	UK	.132	− 1.383	JPN
1956	USR	UK	− .005	− .173	USR
1956	USR	FRN	− .136	.003	USR
1956	USR	POL	.014	− .014	USR
1957	USR	TUR	.171	− .171	USR
1957	USA	USR	.273	− .677	?[b]
1958	USA	CHN	.437	− .885	USA
1960	USR	TUR	.235	− .235	?[b]
1960	USR	PAK	.614	− .614	?[b]
1960	USR	NOR	.248	− .195	?[b]
1962	USR	USA	− .988	.314	USA
1962	USA	CUB	1.263	− 1.263	USA
1965	CHN	IND	.448	− .448	CHN

[a]A risk-averse nation that failed to satisfy all of the decision rules for a risk-averse actor.

[b]I was unable to designate one side or the other as the winner.

TABLE B. Interstate Interventions

Year	Initiator	Opponent	$E(U_i)$	$E(U_j)$	Winner
1828	FRN	TUR	1.515	−1.666	FRN
1832	FRN	HOL	.893	−.893	FRN
1832	UK	HOL	.948	−.948	UK
1838	FRN	MEX	1.594	−2.000	FRN
1838	FRN	ARG	1.179	−1.200	FRN
1845	FRN	ARG	1.316	−1.339	FRN
1845	UK	ARG	1.553	−1.581	UK
1847	AUH	PAP	1.601	−1.601	AUH
1850	UK	GRC	1.013	−1.027	UK
1854	UK	GRC	1.011	−1.026	UK
1854	FRN	GRC	.988	−1.014	FRN
1860	FRN	ITA	.473	−.473	ITA
1861	FRN	MEX	1.609	−1.638	FRN
1861	UK	MEX	1.342	−1.366	UK
1861	SPN	MEX	1.598	−1.626	SPN
1886	UK	GRC	1.006	−1.037	UK
1886	AUH	GRC	2.901	−2.390	AUH
1886	GMY	GRC	1.895	−1.882	GMY
1886	RUS	GRC	1.875	−1.818	RUS
1886	ITA	GRC	2.384	−2.384	ITA
1894	UK	NIC	1.184	−1.200	UK
1897	RUS	GRC	1.663	−1.616	RUS
1897	AUH	GRC	2.460	−2.443	AUH
1897	GMY	GRC	1.618	−1.608	GMY
1897	ITA	GRC	2.348	−2.348	ITA
1897	FRN	GRC	1.471	−1.454	FRN
1897	UK	GRC	1.014	−1.040	UK
1897	GMY	CHN	−.657	−.275	GMY
1898	FRN	CHN	−.272	−.438	FRN
1900	RUS	CHN	−.160	−.099	RUS
1900	GMY	CHN	−.697	−.984	GMY
1900	JPN	CHN	−.306	.219	JPN
1900	FRN	CHN	−.323	−.427	FRN
1900	UK	CHN	−.443	−1.050	UK
1900	USA	CHN	−.112	−.949	USA
1902	GMY	VEN	1.156	−1.199	?[b]
1902	UK	VEN	1.169	−1.199	?[b]
1902	ITA	VEN	.884	−1.198	?[b]

TABLE B (*continued*)

Year	Initiator	Opponent	$E(U_i)$	$E(U_j)$	Winner
1905	AUH	TUR	1.549	− 1.586	AUH
1905	RUS	TUR	.631	− 1.449	RUS
1905	UK	TUR	1.120	.060[a]	UK
1905	FRN	TUR	.391	− 1.663	FRN
1905	ITA	TUR	1.786	− 1.858	ITA
1907	FRN	MOR	2.505	− 2.444	FRN
1908	RUS	IRN	1.937	− 1.937	RUS
1911	RUS	IRN	2.005	− 2.005	RUS
1914	USA	MEX	.972	− .972	USA
1916	USA	MEX	.972	− .972	MEX
1916	USA	DOM	1.090	− 1.090	USA
1918	USR	EST	1.002	− 1.002	USR
1918	USR	UK	− .691	.453	UK
1920	UK	TUR	1.010	− 1.080	UK
1920	FRN	TUR	.890	− 1.010	FRN
1920	ITA	TUR	.680	− .680	ITA
1921	FRN	GMY	.077	− .077	FRN
1921	UK	GMY	.290	− .290	UK
1921	BEL	GMY	− .270	.270	BEL
1923	FRN	GMY	.085	− .085	?[b]
1923	BEL	GMY	− .270	.270	?[b]
1923	ITA	GRC	.590	− .590	GRC
1929	USR	CHN	.180	− .180	USR
1934	JPN	CHN	.010	− .010	JPN
1934	ETH	ITA	− .305	.369	ITA
1938	JPN	UK	.285	− 1.529	UK
1938	JPN	FRN	− .705	− .042	FRN
1938	JPN	USR	.025	− .087	USR
1938	GMY	AUS	1.587	− 1.587	GMY
1938	GMY	CZE	.739	− .739	GMY
1939	GMY	CZE	.691	− .691	GMY
1939	GMY	LIT	.849	− .849	GMY
1939	ITA	ALB	.830	− 830	ITA
1939	USR	POL	.410	− .414	USR
1939	USR	EST	.654	− .654	USR
1939	USR	LAT	.652	− .652	USR
1939	USR	LIT	.692	− .692	USR
1940	JPN	FRN	.275	− 1.484	JPN

Year	Initiator	Opponent	$E(U_i)$	$E(U_j)$	Winner
1940	USR	RUM	1.154	− 1.165	USR
1948	USR	USA	− .674	.241	USA
1948	USR	UK	.091	− .348	UK
1948	USR	FRN	.417	− .552	FRN
1950	CHN	TAI	1.339	− 1.351	CHN
1951	EGY	UK	− 2.338	2.399	UK
1954	CHN	TAI	.971	.982	TAI
1956	CHN	BUR	1.373	− 1.373	CHN
1957	YEM	UK	− 2.847	1.100	UK
1958	FRN	TUN	3.967	− 3.967	?[b]
1958	CHN	TAI	.890	− .907	TAI
1959	CHN	IND	.334	− .844	CHN
1961	TUN	FRN	− 3.894	3.894	?[b]
1962	CHN	TAI	.747	− .766	?[b]
1962	USA	USR	.314	− .988	USA
1963	INS	MAL	− .495	.456	MAL
1964	INS	UK	− 2.177	2.656	UK
1964	INS	AUL	− 2.493	2.123[a]	AUL
1964	INS	NEW	− 2.624	2.123[a]	NEW
1964	UK	YEM	4.075	− 3.333	?[b]
1967	CHN	IND	.448	− .448	IND
1968	USR	CZE	− .008	.006	USR
1968	POL	CZE	.000	− .000	POL
1968	HUN	CZE	− .000	.000	HUN
1968	BUL	CZE	− .000	.000	BUL
1968	GDR	CZE	.000	− .000	GDR

[a] A risk-averse nation that failed to satisfy all of the decision rules for a risk-averse actor.

[b] I was unable to designate one side or the other as the winner.

TABLE C. Interstate Wars

Year	Initiator	Opponent	$E(U_i)$	$E(U_j)$	Winner
1823	FRN	SPN	1.951	− 1.951	FRN
1827	UK	TUR	1.295	− 1.385	UK
1827	FRN	TUR	1.382	− 1.508	FRN
1827	RUS	TUR	1.323	− 1.323	RUS
1828	RUS	TUR	.379	− 1.430	RUS
1846	USA	MEX	.483	− .754	USA
1848	ITA	AUH	− 1.496	1.496	AUH
1848	GMY	DEN	1.883	− 1.883	GMY
1849	FRN	PAP	.958	− .958	FRN
1851	BRA	ARG	.492	− .492	BRA
1853	TUR	RUS	− .756	1.347	TUR
1856	UK	IRN	1.038	− 1.093	UK
1859	AUH	ITA	.583	− .583	ITA
1859	SPN	MOR	1.053	− 1.053	SPN
1860	ITA	PAP	.826	− .826	ITA
1860	ITA	SIC	.337	− .337	ITA
1862	FRN	MEX	1.529	− 1.989	MEX
1863	COL	ECU	.016	− .016	COL
1864	GMY	DEN	.403	− 2.391	GMY
1865	SPN	CHL	.484	− 1.055	CHL
1866	GMY	AUH	.000	.000	GMY
1866	GMY	BAD	.000	− .000	GMY
1866	GMY	BAV	.000	− .000	GMY
1866	GMY	SAX	.000	− .000	GMY
1866	GMY	HSE	.000	− .000	GMY
1866	GMY	HSG	.000	− .000	GMY
1866	GMY	WRT	.000	− .000	GMY
1866	GMY	HAN	.000	− .000	GMY
1870	FRN	GMY	.108	− .108	GMY
1877	RUS	TUR	1.076	− 1.076	RUS
1885	GUA	SAL	.236	− .236	SAL
1897	GRC	TUR	− .866	.866	TUR
1898	USA	SPN	.620	− .964	USA
1904	JPN	RUS	.102	− .102	JPN
1906	GUA	HON	.501	− .501	GUA
1906	GUA	SAL	.424	− .424	GUA
1907	NIC	HON	− .396	.396	NIC
1907	NIC	SAL	− .510	.510	NIC

Year	Initiator	Opponent	$E(U_i)$	$E(U_j)$	Winner
1909	SPN	MOR	2.551	-2.551	SPN
1911	ITA	TUR	1.787	-1.861	ITA
1912	YUG	TUR	$-.384$	.384	YUG
1913	BUL	YUG	.000	.000	YUG
1913	BUL	GRC	.000	.000	GRC
1914	AUH	YUG	2.010	-2.010	YUG
1919	RUM	HUN	.427	$-.427$	RUM
1919	GRC	TUR	.080	$-.080$	TUR
1931	JPN	CHN	.010	$-.010$	JPN
1932	PAR	BOL	$-.318$	.318	PAR
1935	ITA	ETH	.305	$-.369$	ITA
1937	JPN	CHN	.042	$-.042$	JPN
1939	JPN	USR	.029	$-.029$	USR
1939	JPN	MON	.998	$-.953$	MON
1939	GMY	POL	.306	$-.306$	POL
1939	USR	FIN	.842	$-.842$	USR
1948	EGY	ISR	1.116	-1.116	ISR
1948	IRQ	ISR	$.933^a$	$-.933$	ISR
1948	SYR	ISR	.303	$-.303$	ISR
1948	LEB	ISR	.252	$-.252$	ISR
1948	JOR	ISR	.909	$-.909$	ISR
1950	PRK	ROK	$-.209$	.209	$?^b$
1956	USR	HUN	.018	$-.017$	USR
1956	ISR	EGY	.013	$-.013$	ISR
1962	CHN	IND	.611	$-.611$	CHN
1962	EGY	YEM	.000	$-.000$	EGY
1962	EGY	SAU	.000	$-.000$	EGY
1965	IND	PAK	$-.005$	$.005^a$	PAK
1965	RVN	DRV	.846	$-.846$	DRV
1965	USA	DRV	1.299	-1.153	DRV
1967	ISR	EGY	.312	$-.312$	ISR
1967	ISR	SYR	.316	$-.316$	ISR
1967	ISR	JOR	.366	$-.366$	ISR
1969	SAL	HON	.000	$-.000$	SAL
1971	IND	PAK	.673	$-.673$	IND
1973	EGY	ISR	.343	$-.343$	ISR
1973	SYR	ISR	$.722^a$	$-.722$	ISR
1974	TUR	CYP	1.968	-1.968	TUR

[a] A risk-averse nation that failed to satisfy all of the decision rules for a risk-averse actor.

[b] I was unable to designate one side or the other as the winner.

References

H. Alker (1964). "Dimensions of Conflict in the General Assembly," *American Political Science Review* 58:642–57.

H. Alker and D. Puchalu (1968). "Trends in Economic Partnership: The North Atlantic Area, 1928–1963," in J. D. Singer, ed., *Quantitative International Politics: Insights and Evidence*. Free Press: New York.

H. Alker and B. Russett (1965). *World Politics in the General Assembly*. New Haven: Yale University Press.

G. Allison and M. Halperin (1972). "Bureaucratic Politics: A Paradigm and Some Policy Implications," in R. Tanter and R. Ullman, eds., *Theory and Policy in International Relations*. Princeton, N.J.: Princeton University Press.

M. Altfeld (1979). "The Reaction of Third States toward Wars." Ph.D. dissertation, University of Rochester.

M. Altfeld and B. Bueno de Mesquita (1979). "Choosing Sides in Wars," *International Studies Quarterly* 23:87–112.

K. Arrow (1951). *Social Choice and Individual Values*. New York: John Wiley.

G. Blainey (1973). *The Causes of War*. New York: Free Press.

E. Bonjour, H. Offler, and G. Potter (1952). *A Short History of Switzerland*. Oxford: Clarendon Press.

K. Boulding (1963). *Conflict and Defense: a General Theory*. New York: Harper and Row.

H. Buckle (1873). *History of Civilization in England*. London: Longmans, Green.

B. Bueno de Mesquita (1975). "Measuring Systemic Polarity," *Journal of Conflict Resolution* 19:187–216.

212   REFERENCES

B. Bueno de Mesquita (1978). "Systemic Polarization and the Occurrence and Duration of War," *Journal of Conflict Resolution* 22:241–67.

B. Bueno de Mesquita (1980). "Theories of International Conflict: An Analysis and an Appraisal," in T. R. Gurr, ed. *Handbook of Political Conflict*. New York: Free Press.

K. Dändliker (1899). *A Short History of Switzerland*, trans. E. Salisbury. London: Swan Sonnenschein.

W. Fucks (1965). *Formeln zur Macht*. Stuttgart: Deutsche Verlaganstalt.

A. George, D. Hall, and W. Simons (1971). *The Limits of Coercive Diplomacy: Laos, Cuba, Vietnam*. Boston: Little, Brown.

C. Gochman (1975). "Status, Conflict, and War: The Major Powers, 1820–1970." Ph.D. dissertation, University of Michigan.

E. Gulick (1955). *Europe's Classical Balance of Power*. Ithaca, N.Y.: Cornell University Press.

M. Haas (1970). "International Subsystems: Stability and Polarity," *American Political Science Review* 64:98–113.

O. Holsti (1972). *Crisis, Escalation, War*. Montreal: McGill-Queens University Press.

O. Holsti, R. North, and R. Brody (1968). "Perception and Action in the 1914 Crisis," in J. D. Singer, ed., *Quantitative International Politics: Insights and Evidence*. New York: Free Press.

C. H. Huang (1979). "Risk Taking Propensities and Waging War," mimeographed. Rochester, N.Y.: University of Rochester.

L. Hug and R. Stead (1902). *Switzerland*. New York: G. P. Putnam.

I. Kant (1950). *Prolegomena to Any Future Metaphysics That Will Be Able to Present Itself as a Science*. L. W. Beck, trans. New York: Library of Liberal Arts.

R. Kennedy (1969). *Thirteen Days: A Memoir of the Cuban Missile Crisis*. New York: W. W. Norton.

H. A. Kissinger (1979). *White House Years*. Boston: Little, Brown

P. Lankford (1974). "Comparative Analysis of Clique Identification Methods," *Sociometry* 37:287–305.

V. I. Lenin (1933). *Imperialism: The Highest Stage of Capitalism*. New York: International Publishers.

W. Manchester (1968). *The Arms of Krupp: 1587–1968*. Boston: Little, Brown.

L. McQuitty (1957). "Elementary Linkage Analysis for Isolating

Both Orthogonal Types and Typal Relevancies," *Educational and Psychological Measurement* 17:202–29.

D. Middleton (1978). "The Strategy of the Unspeakable," *New York Times*. April 9.

M. Midlarsky (1975). *On War: Political Violence in the International System*. New York: Free Press.

M. Midlarsky (1979). "Equilibria in the Nineteenth Century Balance of Power System." Paper delivered at the Thirty-Seventh Annual Meeting of the Midwest Political Science Association, Chicago, April 20, 1979.

W. Oechsli (1922). *History of Switzerland*: 1499–1914, trans. E. Paul and C. Paul. Cambridge: Cambridge University Press.

Official Airline Guide (1978) Oak Brook, Ill.: Reuben H. Donnelley.

A. F. K. Organski (1968). *World Politics*, 2nd ed. New York: Alfred Knopf.

A. F. K. Organski and J. Kugler (1980). *The War Ledger*. Chicago: University of Chicago Press.

A. F. K. Organski, A. Lamborn, and B. Bueno de Mesquita (1973). "The Effective Population in International Politics," in R. Clinton, et al, eds., *Political Science in Population Studies*. Lexington, Mass.: D. C. Heath.

J. Ray (1979). *Global Politics*. Boston: Houghton Mifflin.

S. Rosen (1972). "War Power and the Willingness to Suffer," in B. Russett, ed., *Peace, War, and Numbers*. Beverly Hills; Sage.

B. Russett (1963). "The Calculus of Deterrence," *Journal of Conflict Resolution* 7:97–109.

B. Russett (1968). "Delineating International Regions," in J. D. Singer, ed. *Quantitative International Politics: Insights and Evidence*. New York: Free Press.

B. Russett (1971). "An Empirical Typology of International Military Alliances," *Midwest Journal of Political Science* 15:262–89.

B. Russett (1972). *No Clear and Present Danger: A Skeptical View of the United States' Entry into World War II*. New York: Harper and Row.

I. R. Savage and K. Deutsch (1960). "A Statistical Model of the Gross Analysis of Transaction Flows," *Econometrica* 28:551–72.

A. Sen (1970). *Collective Choice and Social Welfare*. San Francisco: Holden-Day.

G. Shure, R. Meeker, and E. Hansford (1965). "The Effectiveness of

Pacifist Strategies in Bargaining Games," *Journal of Conflict Resolution* 9:106–17.

J. D. Singer, S. Bremer, and J. Stuckey (1972). "Capability Distribution, Uncertainty, and Major Power War, 1820–1965," in B. Russett, ed., *Peace, War, and Numbers*. Beverly Hills: Sage.

J. D. Singer and M. Small (1966). "The Composition and Status Ordering of the International System: 1815–1940," *World Politics* 18:236–82.

J. D. Singer and M. Small (1968). "Alliance Aggregation and the Onset of War, 1815–1945," in J. D. Singer, ed., *Quantitative International Politics: Insights and Evidence*. New York: Free Press.

J. D. Singer and M. Small (1972). *The Wages of War, 1816–1965: A Statistical Handbook*. New York: John Wiley.

P. Smoker (1968). "Analyses of Conflict Behaviors in an International Processes Simulation and an International System, 1955–1960," mimeographed. Lancaster, U.K.: University of Lancaster.

A. Speer (1971). *Inside the Third Reich: Memoirs*. New York: Avon.

H. Starr (1972). *The War Coalitions*. Lexington, Mass.: D. C. Heath.

J. Stoessinger (1973). *The Might of Nations: World Polities in Our Time*. New York: St. Martins.

A. J. P. Taylor (1971). *The Struggle for Mastery in Europe*, 1848–1918. Oxford: Clarendon Press.

Thucydides [1959]. *History of the Peloponnesian War*, trans. T. Hobbes. Ann Arbor, Mich.: University of Michigan Press.

U.S. Navy, Oceanographic Office (1965). *Distance between Ports*. Washington, D.C.: U.S. Government Printing Office.

M. Wallace (1972). "Status, Formal Organization, and Arms Levels as Factors Leading to the Onset of War, 1820–1964," in B. Russett, ed., *Peace, War, and Numbers*. Beverly Hills: Sage.

M. Wallace (1973). "Alliance Polarization, Cross-Cutting, and International War, 1815–1964: Measurement Procedure and Some Preliminary Evidence," *Journal of Conflict Resolution* 17:575–604.

M. Wallace and J. D. Singer (1970). "Intergovernmental Organization in the Global System, 1815–1964. A Quantitative Description," *International Organization* 24:239–87.

K. Waltz (1975). "Theory of International Relations," in F. Greenstein and N. Polsby, eds., *Handbook of Political Science*, vol. 8, *International Politics*. Reading, Mass.: Addison-Wesley.

R. Wohlstetter (1962). *Pearl Harbor: Warning and Decision*, Stanford, Calif.: Stanford University Press.

Index

Afghanistan: invasion of, 81–82, 191, 192; conflict in, 197–98
Africa: as geopolitical region, 95, 96–97; expected utility in, 139n
Agenda manipulation, 14–15
Albania, 161
Algeria, 42
Aligned states, 69, 72–73, 144
Alignment: defined, 67. See also Nonaligned states
Alliances: limitations of, 6, 112–14; changes in, 37–38; in World War I, 38; and utility, 109, 111–12; honoring of, 113, 163; coding criteria, 114, 115; types, 114, 128, 145; and security, 123–24, 150, 151, 152, 163–64; in contending theories, 141; effects on conflict, 151–54
Allies: conflict among, x, 74, 76–78, 81–83, 159–64; as combat partners, 113, 163; and third parties, 160
Allison, Graham, 16
Altfeld, Michael, 99n
Americas: as geopolitical region, 95–96; capabilities for, 103n; expected utility in, 138, 139
Amin, Hafizullah, 81, 82, 197. See also Afghanistan
Anschluss, 172
Appeasement, 6, 172
Arab League, 187, 188, 190
Arab states: relations with Israel, 187,

188, 189; relations with Egypt, 187–88, 189. See also individual countries
Arms race, 2, 5
Arrow, Kenneth, 13
Arrow's paradox, 15, 16n, 17, 23
Asia: as geopolitical region, 95, 96; expected utility in, 138, 139
"As if" principle, 28, 29, 32, 138, 175
Assumptions: reality of, 9, 10, 16, 67; usefulness of, 10; list of, 20
Austria-Hungary: in World War I, 38, 100n, 132; relations with Turkey, 38, 168; in Crimean War, 71, 168; relations with Germany, 82–83, 114, 147, 149, 160, 161; relations with German states, 83, 124; as major power, 98n; relations with Italy, 99n; in Neuchâtel Affair, 147, 149

Balance of power, 2, 3, 96, 132; alliances in, 5, 141, 150; in Crimean War, 71; and peace, 72, 132; compared to expected utility, 140–45
Balkans, 71. See also individual countries
Balkan Wars: First, 38, 160; Second, 160
Bangladesh War, 100n
Bay of Pigs, 171
Begin, Menachem, 187, 189
Belgium, invasion of, 100n
Bhutto, Zulfikar Ali, 192

217